Writers by

Contributions to Southern Appalachian Studies

Writers by the River

Reflections on 40+ Years
of the Highland Summer Conference

Edited by DONIA S. ELEY *and*
GRACE TONEY EDWARDS

CONTRIBUTIONS TO
SOUTHERN APPALACHIAN STUDIES, 51

McFarland & Company, Inc., Publishers
Jefferson, North Carolina

LIBRARY OF CONGRESS CATALOGUING-IN-PUBLICATION DATA

Names: Eley, Donia S., editor. | Edwards, Grace Toney, editor.
Title: Writers by the river : reflections on 40+ years of the Highland
Summer Conference / edited by Donia S. Eley and Grace Toney Edwards.
Description: Jefferson, North Carolina : McFarland & Company, Inc.,
Publishers, 2021. | Series: Contributions to Southern Appalachian
studies ; 51 | Includes index.
Identifiers: LCCN 2021011539 | ISBN 9781476684062 (paperback : acid free paper) ∞
ISBN 9781476641973 (ebook)
Subjects: LCSH: American literature—Appalachian Region. | Appalachian
Region—Literary collections. | Appalachian Region—In literature. |
BISAC: LITERARY COLLECTIONS / American / General
Classification: LCC PS537 .W7 2021 | DDC 810.8/097569—dc23
LC record available at https://lccn.loc.gov/2021011539

BRITISH LIBRARY CATALOGUING DATA ARE AVAILABLE

ISBN (print) 978-1-4766-8406-2
ISBN (ebook) 978-1-4766-4197-3

Front cover image by Grace Toney Edwards

Printed in the United States of America

*McFarland & Company, Inc., Publishers
Box 611, Jefferson, North Carolina 28640
www.mcfarlandpub.com*

Dedication

Ricky Cox has long been involved in every aspect of the Highland Summer Conference (HSC) beginning as a student in the 1980s. Often in the background or on the sidelines, Ricky has been an essential part of planning and seeing to the smoothly run machine of the HSC. He has introduced visiting authors to parts of the New River Valley he knew they would find interesting, captured hours of audio, video, and still shots of authors and performers, delighted audiences with music and storytelling, chauffeured vans of conference participants to the Floyd Country Store, to the Carter Fold in Hiltons, Virginia, and to RU's Selu Retreat Center, the current home of the HSC. And he's carried carts of George Brosi's Appalachian Mountain books up and down steps year after year. George wrote, "Nobody in the world is more helpful than Ricky Cox!" We agree, and dedicate this anthology to Ricky Cox.

Acknowledgments

We acknowledge every author featured in our anthology and thank them for their enthusiastic response and participation in our book. We also thank the scores of individuals who have worked in many dimensions for over forty years to make the annual Highland Summer Conference (HSC) at Radford University (RU) a success. From the inauguration of the HSC in the '70s until present day, faculty and staff have worked diligently each year to plan a time of inspiration for aspiring writers through engaging legendary authors in Appalachian literature and culture to come to RU and share their passions. While writing has been the primary focus of the HSC, students and community members have enjoyed a retreat filled with readings, social gatherings, music, and field trips around the region. To all participating authors and staff, we thank you.

We are also grateful to the publications who have granted us permission to reprint some of the creative works in this anthology. Each publication is acknowledged individually at the appropriate spot in the text.

Family and friends have provided immeasurable support and encouragement during the three-year effort to bring this book to fruition. In large ways and small gestures, their contributions made a difference. To John Nemeth, Jeff Mann and John Ross, Gary Hancock, the BBs, Paul Haaf, Ricky Cox, the Eleys, Margaret Cox, and Jennifer White, you are appreciated.

Table of Contents

Preface

GRACE TONEY EDWARDS

The Highland Summer Conference (HSC) at Radford University in Radford, Virginia, is in its forty-third year of nurturing creative writing among students, community residents, and published writers themselves. It is a one- or two-week workshop conducted by visiting authors with connections to the Appalachian region. When I first arrived as a new faculty member at RU in 1980, the HSC, still a fledgling entity, immediately became part of my work assignment. After some time and experience to learn my way, I was invited to become the director of the conference in 1983. I served in that capacity until my retirement in 2010. Not only did that job entail planning, organizing, and implementing the two-week event, but it also afforded me the opportunity to sit in the classes of the visiting authors/teachers and to participate as fully as I wished. From that array of talented writers who came to campus every summer, I gleaned many valuable teaching tips for my own classes, valuable life lessons, and occasionally seeds of my own writing that have sprouted here and there. Since my retirement, I have continued to support and attend Highland Summer Conference events each year.

With more than forty years' immersion in HSC activities, another phase was bound to come. Hence, the idea for this book. It grew out of conversations that colleague Donia S. Eley and I began having around 2017. She has been a student at HSC several times over the years and has followed its successes with the same wonder and admiration that I have. Part of that wonder is based on the skill and generosity of the many prestigious Appalachian authors who have given of their time and energy to travel to Radford to teach in the one- or two-week workshops. Another part of the wonder derives from the successes of the ever-increasing number of students who have studied with the visiting authors and who, in turn, have become publishing authors in their own right. We believed that these efforts needed to be recognized, documented, and praised. For, in its own microcosmic way, this conference depicts the history and growth of Appalachian literature as a co-equal genre with all traditions of creative writing.

Over time we decided to invite authors and student-authors to submit reflective essays on what the Highland Summer Conference experience has been like for them. We wanted to know whether it has shaped their writing, maybe even their lives, in ways they could specifically articulate. The response has been overwhelmingly informative and gratifying. We also invited all authors to submit pieces of their own writing, preferably not previously published. Again, the returns have shown us what a wealth of talent the HSC has tapped into.

This book, then, is a collection of reflective essays and creative pieces of poetry, fiction, and nonfiction that forty-one contributors have submitted. In the "Introduction" by Donia S. Eley and the essay called "Highland Summer Conference: The Beginning" by Parks Lanier, Jr., the reader will learn more about the authors represented here, as well as anecdotes about the whole enterprise. My essay entitled "In Memoriam: They Came, Left Gifts, and Now Are Gone" describes the eleven beloved authors who are no longer with us but who made huge impacts on the Highland Summer Conference and its participants. Each writer here has a unique story to tell, and we are grateful for the opportunity to share it.

Contributors to this collection were not able to identify their photographers in every instance. Anyone who took one of these photographs is welcome to contact the editors, so that their name can be included in a later printing.

Some works in this collection appeared in previous publications as explained in the footnotes below the work. If the author retained copyright, then information about previous publication may not be included. Information about any individual piece and possible previous publication may be obtained by contacting the editors, Donia Eley at doniaeley@com cast.com and Grace Toney Edwards at gracetoneyedwards@gmail.com.

We thank the following publishers for permission to reprint these pieces:

Draft Horse: The Literary Journal of Work and No Work, "Where Are You Now, Marlos Perkos?"

Lethe Press, "Country Kitchen—Christiansburg, Virginia," "Gay Redneck, With Baby Stroller," "Redneck Food" (For Dorothy Allison and Erica Abrams Locklear).

LSU Press, *My Surly Heart*, "Where Do You Come From?" "What Can You Tell Me About Your Father?" "What About Your Mother?" "Art for Money," "What Are You Up To?" "Elrica," "Some Kitchens," "Inez."

The Magazine of Radford University, "A Journey into the Heart."

Sow's Ear Press, *Looking for a Landing*, "The Part Gone."

Texas Review Press, *The Mad Farmer's Wife*, "A Woman Born to Farming" (After Wendell Berry's "A Man Born to Farming)."

Texas Review Press, *One Light*, "One Light," "Emergency Room," "Pitched Past Grief," "Elegy."

Introduction

Donia S. Eley

This anthology is a celebration, as it seems are most anthologies. What binds this book together are memories, storytelling, and reflections from multiple voices on a time and place, the annual long-running Highland Summer Writing Conference (HSC) held each June or July for over forty years along the banks of the ancient New River at Radford University. The time and place, the HSC, is the commonality among the voices sharing diverse experiences and writing in this celebratory anthology.

Since its inception in 1978 and continuing today, the respected HSC plays a big part in perpetuating Appalachian literature and

Donia S. Eley.

supporting and encouraging Appalachian authors. Most of the major Appalachian publishing writers have journeyed to the HSC at Radford over the course of forty-plus years. Some were at the height of their careers; some were at the beginning. Dr. Grace Toney Edwards said, "We asked and they came." That they did, with gracious and generous offerings.

Some came once, some came several times, some to teach for a full week or two, others to read their works, to perform; and even more came to learn. George Ella Lyon and Bill Brown have led the HSC six times each. Jeff Daniel Marion and David Huddle, five times. Jim Wayne Miller, Jack Higgs,

Wilma Dykeman, and Rita Sims Quillen, four times. The presence of some authors looms so large it seems as if they have been there every year or so. One of those, Cherokee poet Marilou Awiakta, was a teacher in the classroom, a reader for evening performances, and an interviewee on videotape for the archives. Her sessions were always interactive, encouraging listener and reader participation, as does her essay in this collection. She was also at Selu Conservancy, Radford's current HSC retreat location, when it was being built and which she named for the Cherokee Mother of Corn.

You will read the colorful history of the beginnings of HSC by Parks Lanier, Jr., who has been there since its inception in 1978. Parks conducted video interviews with every visiting author until 2008 when Dr. Theresa L. Burriss took over the interviewer's role. In 2010 Dr. Burriss became Director of the HSC and Director of the Appalachian Regional and Rural Studies Center following the retirement of Dr. Edwards.

Grace Toney Edwards, who directed the HSC from 1983 through 2010, shares memories of legends of Appalachian literature who answered the call to teach in the creative writing workshops but now are no longer with us. She begins with her mentor, Dr. Cratis Williams, who led one of the classes at the very first gathering and again a few years later. She moves forward through losses of leaders and friends such as Wilma Dykeman, Jim Wayne Miller, Jack Higgs, and most recently, Kathryn Stripling Byer. She writes also of the loss of another constant at the HSC, her longtime colleague and friend, the late JoAnn Aust Asbury.

Ricky Cox, who started out as a student in the Conference and then became an assistant when he joined the ranks of RU faculty, recounts experiences from the sidelines and adventures outside the classroom. Ruth B. Derrick, who followed JoAnn Asbury as Assistant Director, provides her own stories, as student and as staff member. Since both Ricky and Ruth were initially students, they have contributed their own HSC-influenced creative essays and poems as part of this rich treasury.

A more recent HSC student weaves a fascinating true tale of how she left the shampoo bowl after thirty-five years for a complete makeover, transforming herself into a teacher and writer, attributing part of her success to sitting at the feet of Appalachian authors at the HSC. Other students, once budding authors who are now successful writers, and a beloved bookseller/editor/legend enthusiastically tell how their writing, indeed their lives, have been impacted by the HSC experience. Some have moved on to become tenure-track professors, directors of creative writing programs, even productive retirees, and most importantly, publishing authors.

Among the workshop leaders, one of the most prolific authors and a highly respected teacher, David Huddle, writes of the epiphany he experienced at Radford, both personally and professionally. After years of believing otherwise, he learned that he is indeed an Appalachian author and can appreciate the region from which he comes. Other leaders indicate impacts on their writing that have enhanced their careers for decades, such as George Ella Lyon's story of the genesis of her internationally known poem "Where I'm From." Some who have graced our halls, classrooms, dining excursions, and extracurricular road trips have not been able to write for this collection, but we remember them too with great fondness. Among these are Darnell Arnoult, Anndrena Belcher, Cathy Smith Bowers, Denise Giardina, Silas House, Sharyn McCrumb and more. To include words from every Appalachian author or performer who has been part of our community would require a second volume! However, the appendix at the end of this book shows all the people who have led workshops or given readings/performances at the Conference.

A look at the Table of Contents of this anthology shows a litany of notable contributors to Appalachian literature over the past four decades. All these have participated in the HSC and here they reflect on their experiences. Adding to their reflections, they have generously submitted additional pieces of writing, much of it new and not previously published.

As I ponder this gathering of talent, skill, generosity, and love, I wonder…. Is it possible to write about Appalachia, its people, culture, literature, music, language, and not be reminded of Loyal Jones's "Appalachian Values?" I think not. Loyal himself is here in this book as a generous example of the response to our current call: "We asked and they came." Loyal has contributed a memory and a poem.

The values are all present in this volume and in the Highland Summer Conference itself. "Love of Place; Independence, Self-Reliance and Pride; Neighborliness; Familism; Humility and Modesty; Sense of Beauty; Patriotism; Religion; Personalism; and Sense of Humor." They've flourished for four decades and more in the Highland Summer Conference; may they live in this venue for another forty years!

PART I

Inspiration

Grace Toney Edwards

In Memoriam: They Came, Left Gifts, and Now Are Gone

So many faces, so many voices, so many beautiful words flowing from the page—these are the images flashing through my memory as I look back over forty years and more of the Highland Summer Conference at Radford University. Those faces, voices, and words mingle with infectious laughter, barbeque and baked beans, rich dark brownies, cups and cups of coffee—they keep coming, those sights, sounds, smells, tastes, and touches.

Of course, in the span of forty years, chances are that some of the wonderfully talented writers who graced our classrooms will have gone on to greater rewards and are therefore unable to accept our invitation today to write of their experiences. My job then is to describe them as I recall their presence among us.

I start with my friend and mentor, **Dr. Cratis Williams** (1911–1985), known to many as Mr. Appalachia. He came at the beginning of HSC in 1978 and again a few years later in 1982. His job was to introduce the discipline of Appalachian Studies with a focus particularly on Appalachian

Grace Toney Edwards (photograph by John C. Nemeth).

8

Cratis Williams.

literature and folklore. In those early days not many people knew whether such a genre as Appalachian literature truly existed. Dr. Williams had spent years reading, studying, and writing more than 1600 pages in his doctoral dissertation at New York University. Entitled *The Southern Mountaineer in Fact and Fiction,* this massive work verified that the genre did indeed exist and was a legitimate field of scholarship. With his delightful stories about his own growing-up days in the Big Sandy Valley in eastern Kentucky and his rendition of old English and Scottish ballads from early family memories, he enthralled students and faculty alike. He introduced us to writers we had never heard of and urged us to read them. To our delight, we discovered people like James Still, Harriette Arnow, and Wilma Dykeman who have now become staples in the Appalachian literary canon. He entertained us with stories, songs, and sermons in his native dialect. He explained to us the roots of Appalachian language and helped us to see that our speech patterns had a syntax and grammar just as legitimate as any other American dialect. He gave those of us from the region reason to feel proud of our heritage, our speech, our culture. And he gave those from outside the region a new perspective on how to value what they were seeing and hearing in this unique place called Appalachia. In addition to his dissertation mentioned above, books written by Dr. Williams but published posthumously include *Southern Mountain Speech, I Become a Teacher, Tales from Sacred Wind,* and *The Cratis Williams Chronicles.*

One of Dr. Williams's disciples was a young poet, novelist, and German literature scholar named **Dr. Jim Wayne Miller** (1936–1996). Coming from western North Carolina (Leicester in Buncombe County) in an area similar to that in which Dr. Williams had spent the bulk of his adult career (Boone in Watauga County), Jim Wayne shared many commonalities with the master. He too was blessed with stories and songs from his own childhood, and he spoke with a poet's eye and ear. His glittering eyes mesmerized his audience when he began to read about the "Brier," in many views a pejorative name comparable to "hillbilly" or "redneck," but one that Jim Wayne preferred to use because it suited his narrator's voice. His long poem "Brier Sermon" calls on the reader/listener to remember her roots, to go "back to what you were before without losing what you've since become" ("Brier Sermon," *The Mountains Have Come Closer*, 1980).

Jim Wayne was one of our returning authors to the Highland Summer Conference. Popular with students, faculty, and community members, he came four times as artist in residence, each time bringing fresh new insights to those seeking to entice their own

Jim Wayne Miller (photograph by Tor Mathiesen).

creative writing muse and to learn more about the excitement of Appalachian poetry and fiction. Sadly, his own muse deserted him and us far too early; he passed away from the ravages of lung cancer in 1996, leaving behind two novels, ten volumes of poetry, numerous essays, and educational materials. An anthology entitled *Every Leaf a Mirror: A Jim Wayne Miller Reader* is a collection of his best loved works, edited by Morris Allen Grubbs and Mary Ellen Miller, published in 2014.

Another writer of renowned stature who came to us four times was **Wilma Dykeman** (1920–2006), native of Asheville, North Carolina, and resident of Newport, Tennessee, with her late husband James Stokely. A fact about Wilma that has always awed me is that she actually knew Thomas Wolfe! She would have been a young girl when she met him, but clearly the experience influenced her and her life's work. She often told a delightful story about having to justify the existence of Appalachian literature at an elite literary gathering in New York. Never one to be cowed by such an exchange, she presented herself in learned circles all over the world, delivering speeches and reading from her work. She was a presence in and of herself, dressed impeccably in a fashionable pantsuit and broad-brimmed

Right: **Wilma Dykeman (courtesy Jim Stokely).** *Left:* **Robert Jackson (Jack) Higgs (photograph by Ricky Cox).**

matching hat. One could hardly ignore her—and one certainly did not wish to, for she had invaluable insights to share and beautiful words in both her fiction and non-fiction books. She published three novels and fifteen books of non-fiction. One of the best known of the latter group was her first publication entitled *The French Broad,* a lively amalgamation of history, geography, folklore, and environmental protest about the river (not a person!) flowing through western North Carolina and into east Tennessee. Her beloved first novel is called *The Tall Woman,* an appellation that might well apply to Ms. Dykeman herself.

Robert Jackson (Jack) Higgs (1932–2015), a consummate scholar and teacher, came to us from East Tennessee State University in Johnson City, Tennessee. Serving twice as author in residence at HSC, he entertained with hilarious renditions from the early Sut Lovingood tales of the 1800s. One of our greatest joys was watching Professor Higgs shake with laughter all over his massive frame from his own jokes and stories. He exuded a love of life that enveloped all of us who sat in his classes. A major contribution to the Appalachian canon was Dr. Higgs and colleagues' collection and editing of two anthologies of Appalachian literature, starting with the earliest examples of explorers' accounts of the mountainous region and moving to recent writings at the time of publication. The first book is called *Voices from the Hills,* and the second two-volume set is titled *Appalachia Inside Out.* Additionally, Jack had five other books to his credit, including one that

addressed his life-long interest in sport and religion, *God in
the Stadium.*

When **Peter Stillman**
(1934–2011) first showed up at
the Highland Summer Con-
ference, to us he was virtually
an unknown from New York
State. He came, however, with
high recommendations, and
his presence turned out to be
a great decision for our students. Peter brought a sense
of humor, an editor's skill, and
a savvy about publishing that
we all needed. He worked as an
editor and publisher for Heine-
mann/Boynton-Cook and was
himself an outstanding poet.
With a teacher's knack for
knowing what tools to use, he
coaxed creative work from students who didn't know they

Peter Stillman.

could produce what they did. Peter's talents were recognized by the RU
administration, and he was invited to stay on for a semester as visiting professor of creative writing. He developed quite a following among RU students and continued work on his own writing projects. His publications
include *Planting by the Moon, Families Writing, Write Away,* and *Writing
Your Way, Second Edition.* Peter was responsible for introducing us to Bill
Brown, a poet from Tennessee who has turned out to be one of our greatest
supporters and a frequently returning guest author.

James Still (1906–2001) is legendary in Appalachian literary annals.
Known by one and all as "Mr. Still," he lived most of his life in mountainous
eastern Kentucky where he worked at various jobs, including operating a
library book mobile on muleback. He was associated with Hindman Settlement School the last several years of his life and became something of a resident author/scholar for the Appalachian Writers Workshop held there each
summer. When we invited him to our own writing conference, he agreed to
come for a one-day classroom workshop and reading. Since we typically
asked the visiting authors to sit for a videotaped interview in the afternoon and then to give a videotaped reading in the evening, we requested
that of Mr. Still. He demurred on the grounds that there were videotapes

James Still.

already available of him talking, and they ought to do for our purposes. He had apparently suffered a bad experience with someone else's recording and did not want to repeat that. When we explained that ours were solely for in-house documentation and viewing, he finally agreed but not without reluctance. Our affable interviewer, Dr. Parks Lanier, had to struggle to get more than one-word answers from Mr. Still! Ultimately, however, his recorded interview and reading became some of the best known and most treasured ones in our vast collection. While not considered to be an especially prolific writer, he was a polished and revered one. He continues to be remembered most notably for his 1940 novel *River of Earth*. As the years passed, he produced more novels, short stories, poetry, folktales, riddles, and rusties from the little log house he occupied on Dead Mare Branch near Hindman. We in the Highland Summer Conference were enriched by his short but memorable presence among us.

When **Kathryn Stripling Byer (Kay)** (1944–2017) of western North Carolina spent a week with us in 2002, we knew we were in the presence of an excellent poet and an enthusiastic advocate for her craft. Not only did she read to us and tell us back stories of the many strong women that peopled her poetry, but she encouraged everyone in the class to dip into the magic of words, to write from their hearts, and to share openly with others. She was a caring and effective teacher whose lessons stayed with her students long past the time with her in the classroom. A few years later she was appointed by Governor Mike Easley as the first female Poet Laureate of North Carolina, a position she held for two terms from 2005 till 2009. At the time of her visit to the HSC, she had four books of poetry in her portfolio: *The Girl in the Midst of the Harvest*, *Wildwood Flower*, *Black Shawl*, and *Catching Light*. An engaging speaker who was much awarded by various organizations over the years, she would go on to publish five more collections of poetry, for a total of nine books, as well as several essays, before death claimed her in 2017.

Jo Carson (1946–2011) from Johnson City, Tennessee, came four times as a reader/performer for the Highland Summer Conference, beginning in the 1980s and ending in 2007. Widely known as a playwright and actor, she also wrote poetry, short stories, and children's books. One of her most loved collections is *Stories I Ain't Told Nobody Yet*, narrative poems based on tidbits of information she learned from eavesdropping on others' conversations. Jo suffered from hearing loss, but she heard well enough to glean hilarious nuggets of story from unsuspecting bystanders, which she then worked into "people pieces" that she shared in numerous presentations and performances in Appalachian venues and across the country. She also appeared several times to read these and other original works on National Public Radio, including her children's books, *Pulling*

Kathryn (Kay) Stripling Byer.

Jo Carson.

my Leg, You Hold Me and I'll Hold You, and *The Great Shaking.* One of her best known and longest running plays is *Daytrips,* a semi-autobiographical story of a daughter coping with her mother who has Alzheimer's disease. During later years of her life, she served as a community playwright and consultant, where her job was to spend time in a community learning what the major issues, joys, and sorrows were. She then collaborated with others in the area to produce and put on a play with a distinct local flavor. Jo Carson was known to say that one of her greatest ambitions was to be a storyteller. She accomplished that goal beautifully in every genre she attempted.

By the time we finally got around to inviting **Dot Jackson** (1932–2016) from Upstate South Carolina to HSC in 2010, she was in her late 70s and had recently published her first novel, *Refuge.* She told us the novel had been in the making, however, since the 1960s. Family obligations and work as an investigative journalist at *The Charlotte Observer* sidelined the novel for a long while, but her writing did not go unnoticed. She collaborated with newspaper colleagues on various nonfiction works, was nominated for two Pulitzer Prize awards, and won the award for National Conservation Writer of the Year. Finally in 2006 *Refuge* was published by Novello Festival Press of Charlotte, North Carolina. The novel garnered the Novello

Dot Jackson (photograph by Renee Ittner-McManus).

Prize for that year and also the Weatherford Award for Best Book of Appalachian Fiction in 2006. In her reading at the Highland Summer Conference, she entertained us with great rollicking stories about her mountain kinfolks who provided the fodder for her fiction. And she told us about her philanthropic work in the South Carolina mountains to provide a retreat for budding writers to create and showcase their work. The result is the Birchwood Center for Arts and Folklife which Dot and three friends founded and financed through grants they secured to promote the arts in Upstate South Carolina. Dot Jackson's legacy lives on through the ongoing work of this agency.

Our own **Dr. Rita Sizemore Riddle** (1941–2006) was a student in the Highland Summer Conference in 2000 and a reader in 2006, along with former student Jim Minick, who would later become an HSC leader himself. Rita had been a professor in the English Department at Radford

University since 1971. A couple of decades into her career, she began to seriously pursue her love of creative writing and to work toward developing those talents through participation in writing groups and writing conferences. She wrote poetry, fiction, and essays—all with passion and power. Her voice was that of a practical, sometimes angry, Southwest Virginia woman who knew hardship in her life story but recognized the rewards of struggling through to achieve a sense of completion. One of my favorite passages from her poetry comes from "Potted Ham and Crackers":

Next morning her mother
Put a paper poke in her hand.
"Potted ham and crackers," she said,
"It's all I have that'll keep."
....

Thirty years later, she opened up a can of potted meat
Which smelled of home, and him, and time.
Her mom was right. That's all there was to
    keep.

Rita Sizemore Riddle (photograph by Ricky Cox).

Rita published three collections of poetry and essays, including *Aluminum Balloons and Other Poems,* before her untimely death in 2006. Two years later Jim Minick, with support from the Southern Appalachian Writers Cooperative, of which Rita was a member, edited a collection of her poetry called *All There Is to Keep*, published by Iris Press in 2008.

Our beloved **JoAnn Aust Asbury** (1947–2013) served for more than fifteen years as assistant to the director of the Highland Summer Conference. In that role JoAnn communicated with and made friends of dozens of writers from throughout Appalachia. Sitting in the classes of the HSC teachers fueled her own creative writing talents, resulting in published poems, essays, and oral storytelling. Her laughter was infectious; her conversation lively. She met no stranger; she nurtured one and all. She advocated passionately for Appalachia and Appalachians. A native of Pulaski County, Virginia, she lived out her life there. Earning B.S. and M.S. English degrees at Radford University, she went on to teach in the English Department and in Appalachian Studies at Radford University for more than two decades. Her students loved her, and she loved them back, winning the most prestigious teaching honor at RU, the Donald N. Dedmon Award for Professorial Excellence. Believing in her students' capability to share their work beyond the classroom, she took them to many professional conferences as presenters, including the Appalachian Studies Association, the Appalachian Teaching Project, the National Council of Teachers of English, and the National Honor Society.

Her own work extended far beyond the classroom. Under her editorship, *ALCA-Lines*, the journal for the Assembly on Literature and Culture of Appalachia, an affiliate of NCTE, flourished. She also edited *Stitches,* the journal for the Appalachian Teachers' Network, an organization serving Southwest Virginia public school and college/university teachers. With Ricky L. Cox and me, she co-edited *A Handbook to Appalachia: An Introduction to the Region,* which continues to be used as a textbook for numerous students.

JoAnn Aust Asbury.

On a more personal level, JoAnn loved music of all sorts and was herself a singer in church choirs and informal music jams. A great cook and baker, she often treated her students and colleagues to delicacies of her own making. She loved color and creativity in art, in clothing, in home and office décor. Indeed, she lived a life filled with art of various kinds, the love of which she passed on to her family and friends. For most of the years I have been associated with Radford University, she has been part of my life: first as a graduate student, then a colleague, and always a friend. Her bubbly personality, her bright smile, her readiness to laugh, her quickness to nurture are traits that live on in our memories and give us comfort even as we continue to mourn this tragic loss of a dear personal friend and forever a champion for Appalachia.

* * *

Over the span of forty-plus years of the Highland Summer Conference, eleven renowned writers and treasured friends have left us. But we are not bereft, for every one of these has given us the gift of precious words to be read over and over, words that call up for us the faces, the voices, the wisdom, the humor of their creators. These eleven alone can attest to the value of an ongoing enterprise such as the Highland Summer Writing Conference, but the beautiful fact is that they have been joined in this enterprise by multiple others who continue to write and inspire legions of students, readers, listeners, and other writers. This book demonstrates the great success of the past and bodes well for ongoing success in the future.

* * * * *

Author's Note: Since this book went to press, we have lost another acclaimed writer/performer. The ebullient Anndrena Belcher died on August 27, 2020. She was a much-loved storyteller, singer, dancer, dress-up artist, and writer who performed across the country in venues ranging from grade schools to downtown bars. She served as leader or performer in the Highland Summer Conference three times and visited Radford University many other times for various events. Anndrena's liveliness and talent will be much missed in the Appalachian community.

Parks Lanier, Jr.

Highland Summer Conference:
The Beginning

Back when gas was sixty-five cents a gallon and *Grease* and *Animal House* were new movies, the first annual Highland Summer Conference came to Radford College in the summer of 1978. It was the brainchild of Dr. Deborah Dew, chair of the English Department. She had learned of a grant opportunity from the National Endowment for the Humanities that would bring writers and scholars to college campuses for two weeks in the summer. The $1000 stipend was attractive. The duties were not onerous. The purpose, ultimately, was to benefit both campus and community with readings free and open to the public.

Parks Lanier, Jr.

A committee of three, composed of Dr. Deborah Dew, Dr. Michael Sewell, and Dr. Parks Lanier submitted the grant proposal and rejoiced at its approval. Dr. Dew, department chair, wanted poet James Seay, novelist Sylvia Wilkinson, and regional scholar Dr. Cratis Williams to lead the first conference. She and Dr. Sewell put their heads together and decided they would assist the poet and the novelist respectively. It was left to me to assist the Appalachian scholar.

I cannot tell you how disappointed I was with that arrangement. All

I knew about Dr. Williams was that he came from Appalachian State in Boone, North Carolina. I knew the school well; I had grown up just down the mountain from Boone. In 1961 I had been the beneficiary of a summer science institute for rising high school seniors held at Appalachian State. Those fond memories paled, however, as I was denied access to the poet and the novelist. To make matters worse, the Appalachian scholar was offered less money than the literati, a further indication of his relative (un) importance. They would receive $1100 each; he would receive $800.

Totally unaware that I was dealing with the most eminent scholar America was ever to know in the annals of Appalachian studies (he was called "Mr. Appalachia"), I wrote Dr. Williams a letter introducing myself, explaining a little about Radford, and outlining his meager living quarters in Muse dormitory. With the consent of my wife, Mary Lois, I also offered him the hospitality of our dinner table as often as he would accept it. She was just a little pregnant at the time, but a brave hostess.

Summer came and so did our three guests from North Carolina. The Byronic poet James Seay arrived with a formidable eyepatch that made him ever so attractive and mysterious. Hovering in the background but invisible to us may have been—I emphasize *may* because I have no proof—his wife, a budding novelist named Lee Smith. It was not long after that she published *Black Mountain Breakdown* with a Radford College scene in it. Of course, she might already have known Radford more intimately than James did. It was the college destination of many women from her native Grundy and not far from her beloved Hollins to the north. The dynamic novelist, Sylvia Wilkinson, also made her arrival, bubbling with ideas about fiction or non-fiction describing auto racing. We hoped two weeks in our bucolic setting would inspire her muse and garner us mention in her acknowledgments. She went on to write thirteen such books for juvenile readers. More quietly from across the mountains came Cratis Williams (1911–1985), the retired dean. I do not recall where James and Sylvia lived those two weeks, but Cratis accepted our offer of a dormitory room and seemed quite comfortable there.

Nor do I recall the classrooms for the poet and the novelist. They probably were in Young Hall where our department offices had been newly located. I was told to take Dr. Williams to McConnell Library where we would use the beautifully carpeted, oak furnished Archives room in front. The polished tables and elegant chairs in a cool room were a perfect setting for a summer class. Up the steps I went, more dutiful than delighted, to assist in any way I could. Almost immediately, one student had an attendance problem. She could not attend the entire afternoon segment of our studies. I volunteered to tape record about an hour of lecture for her. Dr. Williams was agreeable, so we worked together to make all well.

The sociable Cratis enjoyed coming to our supper table. He warned Mary Lois that he was allergic only to butterfat. She was scrupulous about keeping her recipes free from it, but she slipped up one time. Cratis was good-humored about the slip since it caused little upset. Together he and Lois tracked the culprit to a measuring spoon. For my part, I kept a little of his favorite Kentucky whisky on hand to make our evenings more palatable.

Cratis's lectures about Appalachian literature and culture were very interesting. He used a textbook I liked very much, *Voices from the Hills.* It even included a selection from the disreputable Sut Lovingood stories I had enjoyed so much as a student and gave a nod to my distant kinsman, Sidney Lanier, a pioneer in Appalachian literature. Sidney had come back from The War in the 1860s and written an unreadable novel about mountain people who lived near Knoxville, Tennessee. I know it is unreadable because I have read it. His poetry fared much, much better and was, thankfully, the guaranty of his fame.

It was Dr. Williams's insistence on unique qualities of the mountain experience that nagged at me. He was supported by no less of an authority than Mr. Loyal Jones over at Berea, but it just did not seem right to me. The values and virtues Williams and Jones extolled were borne out in my experience one hundred percent, in my own family, but I was no mountain person. I was from the flatlands of Georgia. Eventually I had moved to the mountains of North Carolina at a young age, but I was Georgia born and Georgia bred. More than once I had had to translate what my father said for my wife who came from the Tennessee mountains. It was like translating Uncle Remus for Dolly Parton, my wife's high school friend. In class, I said nothing. I just listened and made my cassette recordings for the needy student.

The second week of the conference came. On a tiring Tuesday or Wednesday, I was going down the front steps of the library when a realization hit me. Only Saul on the road to Damascus was hit harder. I was not blinded, but I know I staggered a step or two. Of course, everything Cratis Williams had been saying seemed familiar to me. How stupid I had been not to remember. My maternal grandmother who all but raised me (we did not say "rear" in Georgia) was herself a child of the north Georgia mountains. Her ancestry, and by extension mine, was mountain. Her values were Cratis's values. Her "thou shalts" and "thou shalt nots" were identical to his. It was she more than anyone else who determined my view of the world. She never told me a Jack tale or a Mutt's Meg story, but her Bible was plumb wore out. If my grandfather irked her, she would threaten to move back to the mountains. Lordy, how that scared me. As a boy, I was never sure which mountains those were. She made us go see a movie about a mountain preacher, *I'd Climb the Highest Mountain* (1951). Those, she intimated, were her mountains. That's where she would go if sufficiently riled and either take us with her or leave us behind.

That movie came to haunt me later. We had monthly movie nights at my college in 1963. Since Pfeiffer was affiliated with the Methodist Church, showing *I'd Climb the Highest Mountain* was inevitable. It was based on books by Corra Harris, wife of a Methodist circuit rider. The funny part was that my Shakespeare professor, Dr. Hoyt Bowen, had a bit part in that movie. Returned from World War II and a student at Piedmont College, he had been recruited to play a mountain man reluctant to reach across the aisle, take his wife's hand, and renew his marriage vows. The reticence of mountain men was legendary in Dr. Williams's accounts, but also their superiority in the home. The mountain wife would never reprove her husband in public, he said. She would wait until she got him home and then burn his ears. My grandmother to a T.

Countless were the examples I had heard from Cratis about attributes of mountain character. Too quickly I had dismissed them. There on the library steps, my mountain forebears lined up and shook some sense into me. It was a moment that changed my life. It changed the trajectory of my studies. It informed and enriched my poetry writing. It enriched my reading a thousandfold. For thirty years after that moment, I was fortunate to count among my friends the distinguished Appalachian poets, novelists, and scholars who found their way to the Highland Summer Conference. In the first decade, Cratis Williams (KY & NC) was followed by Jim Wayne Miller (NC & KY), Fred Chappell and Heather Ross Miller (NC), Jeff Daniel Marion, Wilma Dykeman, and Marilou Awiakta (TN), Gurney Norman and James Still (KY), George Ella Lyon and Ron Eller (KY), Denise Giardina (WV), David Huddle (VT and VA), and Jack Higgs and Jo Carson (TN). Eventually guests from SC and GA would help round out the complement of southern Appalachians. Only Mississippi and Alabama remain, unless one counts James Still who was born in the latter.

The second Highland Summer Conference never happened. We were too late to receive a grant. After the successful third and fourth, the conference became self-sustaining. I made sure that when Cratis Williams returned in 1982, when Jim Wayne Miller came in 1980, or when Jeff Daniel Marion came in 1983, the Appalachian expert did not receive less money than others. True, the Highland Summer Conference had writers with no Appalachian credentials at all; it was never intended to be otherwise. Tom Bontly (1940–2012) from Wisconsin in 1980 and Max Apple from Michigan in 1982, for example, were noted novelists who came out of friendship with Dr. Sewell. Gradually, however, the Appalachian component became more dominant but it was never meant to be exclusive.

It was possible, the committee realized, to have a poet, novelist, or scholar whose work was closely identified with the mountains. The internationally acclaimed, award winning poet and novelist Fred Chappell from western North Carolina who came in 1981, for example, was always proud to be identified as a mountain person. So, too, the redoubtable scholar Jack Higgs (1932–2015) from Tennessee who first came in 1988, one of the editors of *Voices from the Hills.* Ol' Fred's friend novelist and poet Heather Ross Miller, also in 1981, made no secret of cherishing her ties to the Uwharries of NC as much as Chappell or Miller loved the higher, westward peaks. Poet, novelist, essayist Jim Wayne Miller (1936–1996) had left his (and Fred's) native NC mountains, taken a doctorate in German, and carved out a career in Bowling Green, Kentucky, where he later taught with Hoyt Bowen, the reluctant mountain man previously mentioned. Miller repeatedly returned to the mountains, however, to teach young and old alike. He led HSC sessions in 1980, 1987, 1989, and 1995. If he were still here, he would say one can be a scion of the mountains and a citizen of the world with equal ease.

Jim Wayne Miller's great friend, fellow world traveler, and mutual supporter was the renowned novelist and poet James Still (1906–2001) from Kentucky (originally Alabama). People sometimes hilariously confused Jim Wayne Miller and Jeff Daniel Marion, but nobody confused Mr. Still with anybody. James Still was the only Highland Summer Conference guest who disliked the format of our program. By the time he arrived in 1985, television studio recordings were a routine part of a guest's appearance. It was my privilege to do the interviews for many years, archived now in McConnell Library as the *Conversation* series. Mr. Still told Dr. Edwards he did not want an interview because a recent interviewer had been unkind to him. He had an antipathy to such encounters. Dr. Edwards insisted. A reluctant James Still came to the studio intent on thwarting me. For fifteen minutes I sweated. "No one ever calls the first-person narrator of *River of Earth* by name," I said. "May we call him Jimmy?" Mr. Still's curt reply was "No." By then, however, he had come to realize I meant him no harm, that I was genuinely an admirer, and that I had done my homework. For the next fifteen minutes, it was one of the best interviews ever. He took a taped copy back to Hindman, Kentucky, and showed it to all his friends. When I visited Hindman the next summer, James Still put me in his car, drove me all over Knott County, showed me his famous cabin on Wolfpen Creek, sang to me, introduced me to his adopted daughter, Teresa, and made me feel like a king.

Interviews with Highland Summer Conference guests were almost always completed in one take. I made certain I had done my homework, read the featured novel or book of poetry for the occasion, and knew to whom I was speaking. All the values Cratis Williams had taught us came into play. More than anything, I wanted each person to feel at ease and respected for his/her work. It was easy for me because I had some of the best people in the world to interview. There was, however, a small mishap with Wilma Dykeman (1920–2006). When Wilma Dykeman's clip microphone ever so gently and gradually slipped too far down her silk scarf, we had to "cut" and do a momentary re-take. I regretted having such a gracious guest suffer even the slightest pause. Other than that, I recall no problems with the interviews.

It is sad to think of many of those friends now gone. When Cratis Williams, who died in 1985, last came to teach us in 1982, he recorded the story of Mutt's Meg, told, he emphasized, in his native Kentucky mountain dialect. He could speak six languages, all of them English. I felt then he had a premonition he would not long be with us and wanted to leave behind a cherished part of his personal heritage. His grandmother told him that story, he said, when he was a boy in the 1920s. In eleven more years, Jim Wayne Miller would also be gone, and then Wilma Dykeman and Jack Higgs. Videos in the Highland Summer Conference archives in McConnell Library keep them with us.

With every single guest, I learned something new and significant. They may testify to how their writing or scholarship was enriched by contact with us, but we at Radford benefited enormously through the years. I know I did. My colleagues who spent time in the classrooms as their aides filled their own notebooks with brilliant ideas from these talented writers and teachers. The rich repository of creativity briefly assembled here could not help but shape our lives from year to year as we went back to our own students able to speak of those whom we had come to know so intimately. In our own classes, it was wonderful to be able to say "George Ella Lyon said…" or "Sharyn McCrumb said…" or "Denise Giardina said." My only regret is that I was never able to meet the elusive Lee Smith on our campus. She and I met elsewhere when I read a paper telling her what her novel meant. By then, I had become a brave mountain man. She might not have known who I was, but because of the auspicious beginnings of the Highland Summer Conference I knew very well who she was, kindred spirit to all the writers I had come to know and respect in the many years to follow.

Jeff Daniel Marion

The Chinese Poet Reconsiders Time

The little porcelain figure sat for years on a bookshelf in my living room, his long robe the traditional garb for a Chinese man of some centuries ago. He held some type of fruit in his hand, whether peach or lychee I could never be certain. Probably a talisman for good health and long life—and as I approach my eighth decade, I'd have to say this fellow traveler has fulfilled his promise as he journeyed with me from Radford, Virginia, to my house by the Holston River in East Tennessee. A treasured gift from some forty years ago after a splendid meal at a little Asian restaurant near the campus of Radford University, it was Parks Lanier who chose this gift from an array of items in the display case in the restaurant and it was Parks who had written me two or three years prior to that to inform me I was being considered as a potential teacher in a poetry writing workshop as part of Radford University's Highland Summer Conference.

Jeff Daniel Marion (photograph by Ricky Cox).

So here I was now in the early 1980s teaching a two-week poetry workshop to a group of eight or so students ranging in age from eighteen to the mid-forties. Max Apple, recently famous for his book of stories *The Oranging of America,* was there to lead a workshop on fiction, and Cratis Williams of Appalachian State University, dubbed Mr. Appalachia by many, was leading the first week of talks about the culture of Southern Appalachia. Loyal Jones, Director of the Appalachian Studies Center at Berea College, was to be there for the second week.

During that first week Cratis gave an evening lecture regarding the special qualities of the language of Southern Appalachians, and I recall distinctly his story about a unique but highly accurate string of words his mother once used when he was a child. Cratis had crawled underneath the dining room table to hide in his special nook—and in no uncertain terms his mother commanded, "Cratis Williams, you come *out from up in under there* right now!"

Later in the week Grace Edwards, Director of the Highland Summer Conference, invited Cratis and me to her home for dinner. Following a sumptuous meal prepared by Grace and her sister Lou Luckadoo, we all went to see the dress rehearsal of *The Long Way Home* performed at an open air theater down near the banks of the New River. As the arduous process of Mary Draper Ingles' escape from the Shawnees evolved in the rehearsal, evening and a chilling fog rose from the river. Cratis and I began to shiver until Grace remembered some blankets in her car. So there Cratis and I sat, hunched over and draped in blankets, looking a bit like old defeated and outwitted Shawnees! That scene remains my favorite image of Cratis Williams.

Shortly after our Shawnee adventure, Cratis invited me to his room for a nightcap in the dorm where we were housed. There he introduced me to his old and trusted friend Evan Williams and poured me more than a generous share of his libations. Then he launched into an incredible story of how as a young man he was travelling by bus in Kentucky when he witnessed another young man trying to flag the driver to stop so he could board. Cratis was able to get the driver's attention and the young man boarded to take the only seat available, a spot beside Cratis himself. The man settled into the seat and Cratis resumed reading the novel he'd brought along to entertain himself on the long journey. After some time Cratis looked up from his reading and saw that his companion had been studying him carefully. At that point the young man introduced himself by saying, "I see you're reading a novel. I've just had a story published in the *Atlantic.* My name is James Still." So it was that a young scholar who would someday come to be known as Mr. Appalachia met the young man who would become Appalachia's most distinguished writer! And so it was that Evan Williams kept me company as I listened to this amazing story.

Somehow I found my way back to my room that evening and actually made it to class on time the following morning, albeit a bit groggy and cursing the previous night's charm of Evan Williams. The two older students in the workshop later laughingly told me I didn't move the entire session but sat with my left hand propped up to cradle my head.

As the first week of the workshop ended, I headed to downtown Radford to the local bank to cash a check for the next week's expenses. When I presented my check to the cashier, she quickly informed me that I'd need some identification to cash an out-of-state check. I presented my Tennessee driver's license, and she exclaimed, "There's no photo ID on it!" I explained calmly that Tennessee did not include photos on driver's licenses, but this comment only sent her into a further frenzy of wondering why a state wouldn't include photos. I left the bank without having cashed the check. Later that day when I was telling Parks my experience, I saw a flicker of anger in his expression as he demanded, "Who told you that?" I described her and immediately Parks was on the phone speaking to various personnel at the bank. When I went back later to cash my check, I believe I could've written it for $100,000 and it would've been cashed, no questions asked, no photo ID required!

That weekend Parks and his wife Lois along with their daughter Wren were my hosts for a drive and picnic on the Blue Ridge Parkway. Once we had settled into Parks' car and were on our way, Wren, who was probably not more than four years old, looked over at me in the back seat and exclaimed, "You're in MY seat!" Before I could respond, Parks said, "Wren, he's our guest and we let him sit where he wants!" I quickly answered Wren by thanking her for the privilege of this seat of honor and promised to do my best to serve it well and fully enjoy its uniqueness. As we took in the beauty of the Parkway with a stop at Mabry's Mill along with a picnic lunch, Wren and I became fast friends even though I had usurped her honored seat. Over the following years I enjoyed finding little presents to send her, especially a set of bone china miniature figurines based on Mother Goose rhymes.

As our workshops entered the second week, Loyal Jones and his wife arrived and I enjoyed spending time with the two of them at various lunches. I especially delighted in hearing Loyal's signature storytelling and rendering of jokes. To hear and see Loyal tell a story or joke is a double delight—the pleasure of the story itself but perhaps more importantly the various joys of watching Loyal's own enjoyment of whatever material he's rendering as though he becomes lost in the sheer pleasure the story itself provides.

During the last week of my workshop I introduced students to the poetry of Ted Kooser, and the two adult members of the class, Kitty Stuart and Joan Short, seemed particularly drawn to his work. Over dinner one night, the three of us continued our discussion from class. That same evening I told them my story about the local bank's refusal to cash my check and jokingly added that because I didn't have a license with a photo ID, they must've thought I was a member of a marauding motorcycle gang! By the end of the workshop the laugh was on me when Joan and Kitty presented a "new driver's license" they had made complete with photo ID and listing me as a bona fide "member of a marauding motorcycle gang!"

Although the Highland Summer Conference drew to a close, it did not end—the following year Joan Short arranged for Ted Kooser and me to be visiting writers at Big Stone Gap High School where she taught. That was to be Ted Kooser's first of several visits with me at my house by the river in East Tennessee. So from that visit developed a friendship that endures to this day, some thirty-five years later. In essence that has been the gift of Radford's Highland Summer Conference—relationships, friendships, enduring memories. Another prime example was Mandy Luckadoo, daughter of Lou Luckadoo and niece of Grace Edwards, who often sat in my workshop and later did a study of my work for a national high school competition for which she visited and interviewed me at my home.

Over the years since that first workshop, I've had occasion to return to Radford for further work in the program, even to present a reading with my son Stephen when his first novel *Hollow Ground* was published. And most notable for me was that same year that Stephen and I read together, Christine Christianson was in my workshop and introduced me to her husband Scott, a member of the Radford University English Department. Scott and I quickly became friends discovering touchstones from our boyhoods—a fascination with baseball, a love of trout fishing, treasured objects remembered but lost over time. Unfortunately as our friendship grew so developed a serious illness for Scott. To try to cheer him in the face of a cancer diagnosis, I went about tracking the whereabouts of a former major league baseball player Scott had watched in the minor leagues during his boyhood in Minnesota, a player who had first honed his skills at Carson-Newman College where his team had won the NAIA National Championship in his senior year. Scott described in loving detail the fielder's glove he'd once had signed by Clyde Wright. But the glove was lost over the years and Scott had always regretted it.

I was able to find someone at Carson-Newman who was still in touch with Clyde Wright. She kindly contacted him and explained my wish to give back to Scott a replica of that lost childhood talisman. Wright signed the glove and also sent along a baseball signed by him and his son, likewise a major league player. I was able to mail these to Christine to be presented to Scott just after his surgery. To this day a photograph of Scott fishing on the upper Holston sits on a shelf in my river room overlooking the lower Holston. It's how I'll always remember Scott: smiling, alert, fully in one of life's joyful moments.

So—the Radford University Highland Summer Conference is a river of memories for me, an enduring source of sustenance and surprise. As I recall walking across Radford's campus that summer so long ago, the memory of Joyce Graham's voice calling my name from some hidden office or room brings back another of my most haunting memories: an afternoon fishing with my old friend Jim Wayne Miller on Joyce's farm:

"Late Autumn the Chinese Poet Invites His Old Friend the Brier Out to the River to Sit a Spell"

He remembers sitting on a smooth flat
rock by a trout stream in Southwest Virginia
watching the Brier's lines go out and out,

the reel's whisper taking up slack.
What the old bearded one retrieves
is a day the bluebells were in bloom.

He has carried that day like a pressed flower
in his secret pocket of memory, likes it
so well he believes today's October sky

is a bell of blue clarity ringing
across the miles to where
they now sit, their talk waist deep

in the river, studying the water,
reading its currents, casting to the dark
pockets for whatever swirls

to take the lure, silver spinner
or woven fluff of deer hair,
golden-backed bass or
sheen of rose-hued rainbow.

Loyal Jones

Words from a Legend of Appalachia

Editors' Note: The title above is supplied by the editors. Loyal Jones would never call himself a legend, but he truly is—an inspirational and hugely influential one. He came to the Highland Summer Conference to teach in 1982 and was joined that year by Cratis Williams and Jeff Daniel Marion, a trifecta of Appalachian "greats." Now 93 years old and living in a seniors' home, Loyal continues to write. His latest book is called My Curious and Jocular Heroes: Tales and Tale-Spinners from Appalachia, *published in 2017 by the University of Illinois Press. When invited to contribute to this book, he wrote, "Let me see if I can gather enough memory to say something about your successful Highland Summer Writing Conference." Here is his memory from thirty-eight years ago, as well as the poem he included.*

Loyal Jones (photograph by Ricky Cox).

One of my best experiences in Appalachian Studies was being invited to participate in the long-running Highland Summer Writing Conference at Radford University. The best of it was being with the aptly-named Grace Edwards, but I was impressed also with the high intellectual quality of the participants, one in particular, a teacher and Primitive Baptist who instructed us in the intricacies of her faith and had us singing a few of their beautiful hymns.

One afternoon, Grace took me to meet and interview the great banjo picker Kyle Creed. He sold me a new banjo head and signed it. Now when I see that fading autograph, I am reminded of that wonderful summer at Radford.

I am also including a poem.

*Tintagel**

Roaming through Cornwall, we saw
the sign of Tintagel and followed a
narrow road to the cliff-hung village.
The castle ruin, a long walk down, was
fornent a treacherous promontory
above the relentlessly pulsing sea.
But only crumbling walls stood fast,
with sea winds blowing through.
I visioned Arthur, knights, round table,
and golden Guinevere by his side.
But Arthur is not here, I thought,
nor romance nor token of chivalry.
Then in my mirror on the way back,
floated a man, helmeted and visored,
dark and inscrutable, sending a jolt
through my doubting heart.
Then he spurred his Honda 'round us,
and he, and we, and Arthur were all gone.

Love,

Loyal

---

*Tintagel Castle has long been associated with the legends of King Arthur in Britain from the late 5th and early 6th centuries.

Marilou Awiakta

Our Courage Is Our Memory

June 1984 / Night Flight to Virginia

As a seventh generation Southern Highlander coming to the Seventh Highland Summer Conference, I naturally expect a sign to appear unto me. At least a small one.

Already, unbeknown to me, the sign is on the way—and will be so stunning I'll have to stop writing in my journal. Meanwhile, for an hour or so, I gaze out the window, jot notes about natural events I watch evolve slowly. I wait.... (Mother Nature really knows how to calculate an entrance!) Sky is pitch black.

Marilou Awiakta.

Facsimile of Journal Page:
6/10/84 25,000 feet en route—Roanoke

I feel *irradiated*! Joyful! A bit stunned.

All the world waits for the sunrise, a celestial sign. And the sun has come, shining hope and blessing on all—including, I'm sure, the Conference and everyone involved there.

When I tell this story to other highlanders, some may respond with a mountain maxim and accent its wry ending with a wink. "The sun will come up tomorrow. The sun always comes up. The thing is … to be one of them as comes up with it." Doing so takes common sense and courage, with or without a blessing. The wink conveys that—and why the maxim is remembered. The first line is often quoted alone, as a good-natured reminder to keep a humorous perspective on life's minor ups and downs.

Sunrise at 25,000 feet! I sense more meanings in this sign than I'm yet able to grasp—so hum lines from "Farther Along" an old song: "Cheer up my brothers / Live in the sunshine / We'll understand it / All by and by."

The plane begins its descent to Roanoke. When I see the first blue mountain ridge rise up I feel at home.

Dawn Birth
Horizon dilates, water-pale
slowly widens to red-streaked cleft
in dark sky, where
like a baby's head
the sun crowns
birthing out...
birthing out...
I breathe deep
push along with strong rhythm
that brings forth the crimson face
the lusty cry of light.
I open my arms...

Musical Interlude
(Timing at the Reader's Discretion)

At this point, while I'm traveling from the Roanoke airport to Radford, you may enjoy experiencing the sunrise transposed to music. I recommend three selections via Internet links. For me, the *Finale* of the *Concerto for Cello* evokes the splendor that slowly intensifies from daybreak to sunrise. The two songs celebrate waiting for the sun and giving it a lively greeting when it comes up. (My friends and I often sing along—or even jig a step or two!). Enjoy at your leisure.

Finale: Concerto for the Cello in B minor, Op. 104
Essential Yo-Yo-Ma
Yo-Yo-Ma
Kurt Masur
Antonin Dvorak
New York Philharmonic Orchestra
Les Paul & Mary Ford: *World is Waiting for the Sunrise*
"Listerine Presents: The Les Paul and Mary Ford Show"
Here Comes the Sun
The Beatles
"Abbey Road Remastered 2009"
George Harrison

Radford University Campus

I savor the ride from the airport. The homey feeling continues as I settle into a cozy apartment in Buchanan House, a former residence. Made of peach-colored bricks, the house has several stories that are set on the green slope of a hill. I smile. "A hillside house for a Highlander Writer in Residence." Perfect. I'm sure my English professor hosts knew I'd appreciate the humor and comfort of their choice of abode.

Two memorable events are imminent.

By pre-arrangement, Dr. Parks Lanier, who co-founded the Conference, and Dr. Grace Edwards, who directs it now, will come, as they phrased it, "to pay you a welcome visit"—a traditional courtesy they extend to their principal writers and speakers.

I'm excited to meet them—and thank them. For some time they have taught my first book, *Abiding Appalachia: Where Mountain and Atom Meet* (1978), with great understanding and skill. As a result, many more people have come to appreciate my work and find it encouraging to their own pursuits.

Through frequent communication by letter and telephone we three have come to use first names informally.

A lilting voice calls through my front door screen, "Marilou … it's Grace."

"Welcome! Welcome! I have the kettle on."

"I've brought cookies."

Smiles and good talk. Grace shares with me her great admiration for one of the early Appalachian writers, Emma Bell Miles—who had lived in East Tennessee and she gives me a copy of Miles' book, *Spirit of the Mountains*.

"I want you to meet my boys too—Trent, Kyle and Zane—ages eight, five, and one. As soon as I can round them up." She chuckles. "How about going out for pancakes or burgers?"

"Sounds good to me!" (We do this during the week. A great time was had by all!)

Later in the afternoon I step out on the porch and see coming up the walk a tall smiling man and a little red-headed girl who is holding his hand with her right one—and in her left hand a large, luscious magnolia blossom.

"*O si yo*, Marilou. I'm Parks. And this is my daughter, Wren. She's five. When she saw the magnolia tree, she said 'I'm going to pick one for Ms. Awiakta.' And she did."

Wren holds up the bloom. "Welcome, Ms. Awiakta (in perfect diction)." Parks looks proud. I'm sure he's coached her.

"Thank you, Wren." I say, "Hmm, it smells so good! Let's go in and find a vase—and some refreshments."

Parks tells about the large copy of my Little Deer logo that he's making for our up-coming filmed interview. "And," he adds, "My wife Lois and I want you to come to dinner tonight."

I'm delighted. And touched that Lois, who teaches English at another college, has prepared a delicious meal. We have instant rapport. The four of us have a merry time, with Wren taking part. "Is my blossom keeping you company?"

"It is, when I go back to my apartment, as soon as I open the door its sweet scent will say 'hello' and I'll think of you and your folks."

Wren gives a slight nod of approval, as small children often do when a grownup gets it right.

Later I sit near the blossom, savoring memories of these two "welcome visits." Grace, Parks and Lois sharing their time and their families makes me feel at home, as well as connected to them in terms of life experience. Fifteen years earlier, I was where they are now: balancing care for a family (my husband Paul and children ages eight, six and one) with care for my professional responsibilities, weaving them together where possible. It inspires me to see them doing that so admirably. Grace and Parks tell me they have also factored that principle into the Conference, asking staffers to devise similar "welcome visits" for other writers attending. I'm sure this climate of courtesy and warm-heartedness will function as a matrix for well-being and creativity among all of us.

The Sunrise Sign is already manifesting. The sun will come up tomorrow. I'm eager to come up with it.

Experience of HSC

In their official capacity of founder and director, Dr. Edwards and Dr. Lanier open the Seventh Highland Summer Conference. Deftly, they set the tone: professional excellence woven with personal interest in the writers;

importance of upholding our Highland heritage in all its diversity; maintaining a friendly and co-operative spirit throughout.

To these purposes they have ingeniously designed what I experience as a Highland *Habitat*. (But I call it so only to myself.)

Instead of a typical writers' conference, which is often over-scheduled and reclusive, this one is integral to the Radford community and its environs. Through myriad activities, it draws writers/readers/teachers/students/musicians/dancers and other interested community folks and singers like the APPALKIDS.

For a week we celebrate each other, our talents, roots, dreams, stories, jokes. Although times for work and rest/relaxation alternate in a natural flow, we generate creativity that feels like solar energy because in spirit, we "live in the sunshine."

I feel so happy to be in my home mountains, among people who speak the same language. Not necessarily in words they say aloud but in the silent communing that rolls beneath the words from heart to heart.

Mutual understanding is a blessing. So I choose to share my new poem for the first time in public among homefolks, who know this philosophy—from their own experience, as well as from histories of their families and those of other highlanders.

"Out of Ashes Peace Will Rise"

Our courage
is our memory.
Out of ashes
peace will rise,
if the people
are resolute.
If we are not
resolute,
we will vanish.
And out of ashes
peace will rise.
Our courage
is our memory.

First appeared in *Selu: Seeking the Corn Mother's Wisdom*, Fulcrum Publishing, 1993.

The listeners and I share moments of silent communing as memories of ashes and survival roll among us. Then I say, in a softer, lighter tone, "But the sun will come up tomorrow. The thing is…"

Many people smile … wink … or give thumbs up.

We're of the same heart.

I feel its pulse, the creative energy that courses through everything in this highland habitat. For many of us participating in the Highland Summer Conference, the memory of it will become a "moveable habitat" that we can access for courage and comfort anywhere, any time.

I once overheard a veteran trucker put it another way to a driver at a Tennessee truck stop. "I'm from the Blue Ridge. I drive cross-country. Everywhere I go, I got my mountains inside of me. They're what holds me steady."

A "resolute" man by the look of him. And kind. A poet.

Lanier Filmed Interview

At the studio Parks Lanier and I have a preliminary chat. Our chairs face each other. Mounted on the set backdrop is his enlarged version of Little Deer (a white stag) leaping in the heart of atomic orbits—the logo of my life and work I designed to use in my first book, *Abiding Appalachia: Where Mountain and Atom Meet* (1978).

In the traditional Cherokee story their hunters in a long ago time were over-killing deer, the principal source of meat for the people. Little Deer, the small spirit chief of the deer, institutes a ceremony (which today we would also call a law). When the hunter kills a deer, he must ask its pardon and also express gratitude. And he must take only what he needs. If the hunter does this, Little Deer will bless him. If the hunter does not show respect through the ceremony, Little Deer says, "I will track the hunter to his home and cripple him so he never can hunt again."

Parks and I discuss this story a bit. "Let's begin the interview with this story and its relation to your logo—and the atom."

"I think that's a good idea. The law is very clear. Respect nature and receive blessing. Disrespect nature—ruin the balance—and you die. This law has been the same from time immemorial. By the way, Parks, your rendering of my logo is beautiful and so carefully done."

"Thank you. When I first read your *Abiding Appalachia* and saw the logo, I immediately understood the significance of the law of respect to the atom, to nature, and to humanity. I had to make this enlarged logo for our film interview. I just can't sit here with you without the viewers seeing the logo so they can have the same immediate experience. See how the technicians have lighted Little Deer up!" He gestures toward it.

I nod and smile—it's so exciting to have one's work understood—and to have such a creative and skilled interviewer.

"There's another thing," Parks says. "If you are agreeable, I want to ask about new work. Do you have another book in mind?"

"Well, it's not exactly 'in mind.' But something is stirring around. It may take a while to come clear."

Parks quips humorously, "Like seven years?"

I smile, laugh. "I wouldn't be surprised."

After the interview I say how much I've enjoyed it—and the Conference.

"Grace and I want you to come back soon," Parks says, "to work with us and our students—special visits, not Conference-related."

"I'd enjoy that. All week I've felt this place is a habitat. You and Grace created it that way. When you two call, I'll come…"

"Parting Thoughts"

I am grateful for
a week of blessings, as the Sunrise foretold.
I feel the genesis of new ideas,
new relationships that will deepen,
a gathering of strength and courage.
I also sense the Sign has been moved.
First it was given *unto* me.
Now it is *set* before me: a calling. I
step onto the path,
not knowing where it will lead.
Sunlight shines upon it.
In the far distance I hear
a cello *song* that sounds like *aaay-looo*.
I'll understand it—farther along.

Quantitative Thoughts—Requested by The National Endowment for the Arts

To: THE NATIONAL ENDOWMENT FOR THE ARTS
Literature Program: Residencies for Writers
July 27, 1984

Being at Radford University gave me courage to continue my work.

Why? Because, among the people there, I found an unusual combination of excellence, integrity and care, which gave all of us at the Conference the freedom to do our best. There was also an openness to my concept of the Cherokee and the atom as component (not sub-) cultures of Appalachia.

The maxim, "Attitude flows from the top," is true. Dr. Grace Edwards, Director of the conference, and Dr. Parks Lanier, Associate Professor of English, worked as a team in planning/executing the conference. They are first-rate professionals.

Advance preparations were thorough. Materials and audio-visuals for the course were ordered early. Publicity was effectively presented, astutely timed. Attention also was given to the *context* in which I would be teaching. A packet of suggested supplementary materials included information on the history and current interests of the Radford area. With this background I was able to custom design the course for the participants.

The same combination of excellence and care continued throughout the conference. Everything I needed was immediately supplied, from a prism to Georgia O'Keefe slides. And I was given many opportunities to orient to the community through activities planned with families of the staff. This holistic organization freed me to devote all my energy to the true subject of the conference—the men and women who came to study.

For me and my work, the results of our shared experience are these: I am strengthened to continue. I understand more deeply the nature and place of my voice in Appalachian literature and the audience for my work has been broadened. My notebook is filled with notes for new articles, poems, and the first sketch of a new book. Most important, the response and projected work of the staff and students renew my hope that survival is possible in this nuclear age. Appalachians will help lead the way.

I am grateful to the National Endowment for the Arts and to Radford University for the opportunity to be part of the Seventh Highland Summer Conference.

Marilou Awiakta

March 2019: Unexpected Catalysts

I've re-entered, resettled into the present—the digital, rushed, often unmindful world—where Spring and the sun always come up, regardless. And good friends come by. My grown children, who live elsewhere in Tennessee, call every day.

However remote the pre-digital 1980s may seem, primary friendships from that era are still close and the Highland Summer Conference convenes this year for the 42nd time. I still marvel at the ingenious design of it, which clearly seems to have been derived, on a micro scale, from Nature's vast Web of Life, where an immutable law is *adapt and continue.*

Is this conference design a prototype that could be adapted for addressing some issues today? I wonder. Tonight, as I savor warm blackberry cobbler and ice cream (a volt of sugar energy is good for the brain), I'm mulling other thoughts for Part Two, which I envision as a rather short epilogue. The conclusion will be my memory of the amazing 1990 conference with brief comments on the seven years I walked the "sunlit path" to get there.

From the perspective of 35 years, I can say that my "Parting Thoughts" in 1984 all came true.

"Farther along" I understood that the Sign set before me was calling me to undertake seven years of journeys and writings that would (and did) culminate in my third book, *Selu Seeking the Corn-Mother's Wisdom.* Along the way, I drew courage not only from the memory of the conference but also from other Radford experiences that accrued to it, like layers of nacre on a pearl. I was often invited to work with Dr. Edwards, Dr. Lanier and their quick-minded students, as well as with those of new English instructors JoAnn Asbury and Ricky Cox, who also became integral to my creative life. Relationships among us all deepened and widened—which led to my meeting other highland writers I admire.

Next, I plan to reveal the solution to the mysterious cello song (which is also the first two solo notes in Dvorak's *Finale*).

Tasting the last blackberry reminds me: Time to stop mulling and start writing…

A Funny Thing Happens on My Way to the Manuscript…

I flick the television on to PBS to catch a glimpse of what's going on elsewhere. The program is *Amanpour and Co.* (March 11, 2019)

An announcer is saying, "Tonight—surprising findings on brain/mind research as they relate to creativity. Author Steven Johnson will discuss these findings included in his new book, *Farsighted*, which is highly acclaimed."

I sit down. Reach for notepad and pen.

The author points to an enlarged photo of a standing group wearing white lab coats—one woman and four or five men. Johnson explains that they are neurologists who have conducted brain scans using PET and fMRI technology. When a research subject was focused on using digital screens or *iPhones*, one part of the brain was especially active. Alternately, when the subject was at total rest, with *no* overt focus, another part of the brain became extremely active.

"The guys thought the machine must be malfunctioning," Johnson says, then points to the woman in the photo, "but Dr. Nancy Andreasen, of the University of Iowa, said her research indicates that the part of the brain in question is the creative part—the part that daydreams, imagines, invents, composes poetry, music and so on."

Paraphrasing Dr. J.R. Binder, of the Medical College of Wisconsin, Johnson says, "When people are left to our own mental devices, the mind drifts into a state where it whirls together memories and projections, mulls problems and figures out strategies for the future."

Another way of avowing, "Our courage is our memory." Because we live in a high-tech world, I'm especially glad when science affirms wisdoms that people of the world have distilled through the ages. Communing with nature is another universal way of stimulating creative thought. "Be still and know…" is perhaps the most ancient admonition.

I am thinking, here, of how the Cherokee followed this wisdom to rebuild their nation after the destruction of the 1838 Trail of Tears. Their experience is implicit in the imagery of our theme poem, the phoenix being a symbol of the Cherokee Nation.

Worldwide, concerned people are trying to figure out ways to maintain the balance between the swift advance of Artificial Intelligence/Automation and the imperative of remaining human—creative, engaged with other humans as well as with the planet and all therein. We the people can work out solutions, "If we are resolute." *Crucial to this process*, as brain/mind research repeatedly emphasizes, is *the retrieval of long-term memory*. (Italics mine.)

You and I look at each other—reader and writer. Feel again the extraordinary creative energy the 1984 conference was designed to generate. Shout "A-ha!" Our minds take off running in the same direction.

Back to the Future: A Seed Thought

Two fundamental issues of our era involve time and space:

- for the creative mind/brain to function at its maximum
- for people to relate and communicate with each other *in person* (no wires).

What if the Edwards/Lanier conference design could be used as a prototype—expanded, adapted and specifically repurposed to meet these two needs? This is a practical possibility because the prototype apparently has been derived, on a minute scale, from nature's vast Web of Life, which adapts to an infinite variety of habitats—places where humans, animals, plants or things (entities) naturally grow and thrive.

Proposal for a New Balance

Image the design as a web, with the hub (or center) being the major emphasis: stimulating the creative mind, the *process* of thinking. For discussing specific aspects of solutions, participants could move onto radial strands of thoughts. The circumference—or matrix—strand, woven of relationships, would hold the web together. This type of conference might be called a "Habitat for Creativity" (the general public already being accustomed to the term "Habitat for Humanity.") The prototype's form and function can be adapted to many specific issues, and to diverse cultural ways of inspiring creative thoughts.

"That's all very well," you may say, "but we're already too rushed to take up that proposal." That's what I thought also until hearing this comment from an English economist on the BBC, who, on the subject of creative mind stimulation, stated coolly, "It's worthy of note that the elite Chinese, for some time now, have been demanding that universities where they send their sons, make specific time in their curriculums for stimulating the creative mind. Competing nations would be wise to consider this fact."

Harmonic Convergence of Creative Minds

SUMMER, 1988: SELU ARRIVES

The cello song (the first two strong notes) at last comes clear: "Saay looo"—it's coming from within me! A traditional story I learned as a child has been calling me to listen, delve deeper and write about the wisdoms abiding in the great teaching story, *Selu the Corn Mother*, the spirit of the corn.

The Cherokee have a profound concept of her. Selu signifies the Life Force, which she draws from Mother Earth, who receives it from the Creator. Provided the Cherokee respect her, Selu feeds the people, shares her strength, engenders good will, cooperation, unity in diversity. Cherokee women are her spiritual inheritors and help govern the people—to this day.

SEPTEMBER 1989—SELU CONSERVANCY LAND GIFTED

I am engrossed in writing about Selu when a stranger calls from Boston, John Bowles. He explains that his professor friends there (who had been my hosts when I was at Tufts University) had recommended me to name the conservancy land that he (John) was planning to give to the Radford people and to the University in honor of his grandmother, Kelly Bess Moneyhun, who had left the land to him—376 acres.

He said all of this in one breath.

Neither he nor his friends knew I was connected to Radford. And only I knew I was writing about Selu.

I send John the classic story of Selu. He pronounces that her character and spirit are in harmony with his grandmother's qualities, as well as with his own intentions of the purposes for which the land would be used. He asks me to be a consultant to him. I am honored by all of it—and agree.

Within *nine* months, the Selu Conservancy is officially birthed, named. Dr. Grace Edwards, as Director of Appalachian Studies, is to serve as part of a coalition of five department chairs to oversee major developments; I'm invited to be a Writer in Residence at the Highland Summer Conference...

JUNE 1990: HIGHLAND SUMMER CONFERENCE GATHERS...

...under the great oak on the Farm at Selu. About twenty-five of us gather enjoying the newly mown grass meadows and hills, the dreams that Grace, Parks and Ricky point out that will become realities: the Retreat Center on the hill, the farmhouse rebuilt around the chimney now standing alone. Ricky says the house will become a living museum, where school children especially will come to study what the life of their ancestors was like in the 1930s. Ricky Cox became director of that program. Dr. Parks Lanier will found the annual Selu Writers' Retreat in 1991.

Birds sing…. JoAnn Asbury directs the laying out of a picnic under the tree (her small daughter April sits under the tree writing in a notebook—she wants to be a writer, her mother says). Jim Minick, a graduate student and writer himself, is there—and John Bowles, smiling to see his conservancy dream coming true.

After lunch Ricky plays his guitar—we sing—break to walk awhile, write awhile.

Then we gather in a circle, jogging counter clockwise in silent meditations as I play my Taos drum steadily like a heartbeat. Everybody loves the dancing. Maybe Cherokee spirits of old are drawing near too.

"I Offer You a Gift"

The June sun bathes hill, meadow, tree and all in radiance.

…

Against the downward pull
against the falter
of your heart and mine,
I offer you a gift
a seed to greet the sunrise.
—Ginitsi Selu, Corn, Mother of Us All.
Her story.

First appeared in *Selu: Seeking the Corn Mother's Wisdom*, Fulcrum Publishing, 1993.

David Huddle

How and Why Radford University's Highland Summer Conference Was More Than Just a Teaching Gig for Me

"My great-grandfather was shot and killed in daylight in front of his store in Ivanhoe. The big boys picked on me in elementary school and later on the school bus riding to high school. Leon Jones pulled a knife on me and would have sliced open my belly if I hadn't been lucky and just agile enough. A hired man entered our home one night when we were all at the drive-in and rubbed poison oak all over the inside of my mother's swimming suit so that she spent all of July and August in a state of agony. A classmate from grade school, after he'd quit sixth grade at about age 17, quarreled with a neighbor, then went into his house to fetch a butcher knife, chased the neighbor, jumped on the neighbor's back, cut his throat, then watched him die right there in the dirt alleyway. Around 1990, when my parents were taking their fat old dog, Daisy, for a walk out on the dirt and gravel road from their house, two teenage boys with rifles coming the other way shot and killed Daisy, then ran away laughing. And finally, in an act that I can't help seeing in personally symbolic terms, an Ivanhoe pyromaniac set fire to my grandparents' home while it was empty and under repair and burnt it to the ground."

David Huddle (photograph by Molly Huddle Coffey).

44

—David Huddle
"Above My Raising: A Narrative of Betrayal"
*Walk Till the Dogs Get Mean: Meditations on the Forbidden
from Contemporary Appalachia,* edited by Adrian Blevins
and Karen Salyer McElmurray

It was my privilege to be a Writer-Teacher at Radford University's Highland Summer Conference in 1987, 1991, 2000, 2005, and 2011. In my first summer there, I'd been teaching at the University of Vermont for sixteen years, and I'd published three books, two of which were mostly autobiographical—a book of poems, *Paper Boy,* and a collection of short stories, *Only the Little Bone.* When I was first invited to teach in the HSC, the director with whom I spoke (Grace Edwards, I'm pretty sure) gave me to understand that the conference emphasized Appalachian writing. When I said that I didn't think of myself as an Appalachian writer, the director said, "You grew up in Ivanhoe, Virginia, didn't you?"

Well, of course, I had to say yes to that question, and when I considered my two books about growing up in Ivanhoe, Virginia, I realized—in that exact moment—that I was indeed an Appalachian writer. This may seem obvious to some readers, but it was news to me at the time. It was also news that, because of my experience growing up in the Appalachian hamlet of Ivanhoe, I didn't particularly welcome. I'd served in the army in Vietnam, and my first success as a writer was publishing stories about Vietnam, but I didn't think of myself as a Vietnam writer. I was born and raised in the south, but I didn't think of myself as a southern writer. And now I've lived in Vermont for nearly fifty years, and nobody, I least of all, would consider me a Vermont writer. The identity I have to accept, for better or for worse (and especially problematic after the 2016 election), is that of an American writer. And I'm certainly not easy with being categorized as an Appalachian writer.

I'm grateful to my family and to Ivanhoe for raising me and teaching me to value honesty, hard work, good manners and respecting people who aren't as lucky as I am. But if you ask me where I'm from nowadays, I'll say, *I'm from Vermont, but I grew up in Ivanhoe, Virginia.* What I disown from my Appalachian roots are racism, ignorance, complacency, and meanness. Those qualities are available just about anywhere in the world, but in the Appalachia I knew they were ingrained to such an extent that I don't think they'll ever be purged from the culture.

But to come back to my relationship with Radford's HSC, the weeks that I spent living on the campus and interacting with the students, faculty members, and staff—almost all of whom were from Southwestern Virginia—placed me in the matrix of the culture I considered stifling. But I enjoyed socializing with the HSC community in the campus dining hall and at BT's and Macado's—it was a rare occasion where I could hang out with "my people"—which is to say mountain folk with a desire to participate in the greater world.

Some background about my relationship with Radford University: (A) My childhood home in Ivanhoe is about 40 miles from Radford. (B) My Aunt Murrell (my mother's sister) attended Radford for a couple of years before she transferred to UVA's School of Nursing. (C) While I was at UVA in 1962, I had a romantic interest in Ruth Ann Reynolds, who was from Austinville (7 miles from Ivanhoe) and who was a student at Radford College (which became Radford University in 1979). Some fifty-six years later, I have a vivid memory of a gloriously extended goodnight kiss with Ruth Ann, among several other couples, on the big front porch of her dormitory in the last couple of minutes before she had to pass through the door to make her curfew—which I seem to remember as 11 p.m. All of which is to say that when I was invited to join the faculty of the HSC I was at least slightly familiar with Radford from far back in my childhood.

My teaching in the HSC in 1987 was a kind of strange "going home," in the Thomas Wolfe sense of "You can't go home again." I hadn't "lived" in Ivanhoe since 1960 when I began my studies at UVA, though of course I had visited often during those 27 years. But "visitor" was a relationship with Ivanhoe that I could manage—as a visitor I owed the place only good manners, respectful behavior, and at least the semblance of modesty. But as a visitor I always felt a weird combination of relief and shame over having outgrown it. Over having betrayed my raising. I also felt that Ivanhoe probably had no problem with my having made my life in the North. If I wasn't willing to own Ivanhoe, Ivanhoe was glad to let me go.

A notable fact about my upbringing is that neither I nor any member of my family ever walked through the town alone after dark. Another notable fact is that Ivanhoe was not incorporated—government and law enforcement were miles away. If you murdered someone or burned his house down, you'd have plenty of time to make your getaway. Or, since revenge was a strong current in the daily life of Ivanhoe, you might be murdered by relatives of your victim, and/or you might see your own house going up in flames.

So my teaching at the HSC, beginning in 1987 and coming back occasionally, was always a conflicted and illuminating experience. My colleagues and my students were educated and engaged in encouraging and nourishing the most positive aspects of Appalachian history and tradition. Many of them were aware of Ivanhoe and what I objected to about it—they had had similar experiences—but they had committed themselves to living in their hometowns and to making those communities desirable places to live.

The assignment I gave my students in the HSC was to write autobiography as rough prose to be used as raw material for their early drafts of poems, stories or essays. From my reading of their writing, I came to see how they embraced their upbringing rather than turning away from it as I had. Thus I saw a path that might lead me to forgive Ivanhoe for the meanness it had brought down on my family. I confess I haven't gone very far down this path, but through my students' brave and compelling writing, I came to see how I might grant myself some forgiveness—for being ashamed of where I come from. Maybe more usefully I came to understand how my own writing could become a means of liberating myself from the Appalachian victimhood I had used to explain many of my shortcomings to myself.

Of particular value to me were the Radford faculty and staff members who were living examples of citizens who had made their Appalachian grounding a source of strength, intelligence, and accomplishment. For years four of those people—Grace Toney Edwards, Parks Lanier, JoAnn Asbury, and Ricky Cox—probably unbeknownst to them—have been helping me put my Ivanhoe upbringing into a less painful perspective. All four of them seemed to me like cousins I hadn't met until I came to work for the HSC. They were well versed in the history and the traditions of Appalachia in general and Southwest Virginia in particular. They had educated themselves about their heritage in ways that I had not. To be frank, when it came to my regional background, they understood me better than I understood myself. Ostensibly a teacher in the HSC, I was more student than teacher and the learning I received was more personal than academic.

I've had a lot of good luck in my life (my parents and my brothers; my grandfather; my wife and my daughters), a superb high school English teacher (Arraga Young), a couple of extraordinary mentors (George Garrett and Peter Taylor), my day job (as a professor of writing and literature), and my calling (to write fiction, poetry, and essays). But one of luckiest events of the second half of my life was being invited to participate in the Highland Summer Conference. Here at the age of 77, I've come to realize that those weeks on the Radford campus were a necessary step in my growing up.

"Where Do You Come From?"

The cosmic speck of me joined the universe
by way of my mother and my father
my brothers and my Grandmother Akers
Granddaddy and Grandmama Huddle her
kitchen his tool shop his dusty office
the help Harvey Sawyer Monkey Dunford
Thelma Lucy Uncle Will Washington Peaks

work horses cows chickens a mule the food
they ate the way they talked my dad's music
my mother's reading books aloud to us boys
the Wytheville radio station daffodils lilacs
cigarette smoke the weather bumble bees
my grandparents' fighting at Sunday dinner
my parents' deep care for us and each other.

First appeared in *My Surly Heart*, LSU Press, 2019. Reprinted by permission of David Huddle and LSU Press.

"What Can You Tell Me About Your Father?"

Around people he was rarely at ease
but when he could settle into himself—
reading the *Roanoke Times*, watching TV,
or paying bills—he seemed comfortable.
I studied him when we had company.
He had nice manners, asked polite questions,
tried not to talk about himself—I think he
feared being the center of attention.
What he liked best was when mother's Uncle
Bo came to our house to play chess with him.
Reticent as a tree and deeply humble,
that man and my father played their slow games
saying almost nothing. Did they have fun?
I can't say. But those games went on and on.

First appeared in *My Surly Heart*, LSU Press, 2019. Reprinted by permission of David Huddle and LSU Press.

"What About Your Mother?"

Tempestuous, meaning *temperamental,*
hot-blooded, mercurial—long before
we knew the words we knew the individual
who embodied them. Of course we adored
her but we also feared her. Little boys,
my brothers and I couldn't know how young
she was or that before we were born she'd lost
a girl baby. A beautiful woman
in her mid-twenties in a big old house
at the end of a dirt road with the three
of us & no nanny to help—miraculous

she didn't just drive away to the city.
She spanked us with a hairbrush when she got mad,
but she was our mother—that's what mothers did.

First appeared in *My Surly Heart*, LSU Press, 2019. Reprinted by permission of David Huddle and LSU Press.

"Art for Money"

"It's a sad fact about our culture that a poet can earn much more money writing or talking about his art than he can by practicing it."

—W. H. Auden

A little boy, I'd pick dandelion bouquets
for my mother, who would then do her best
to feign delight over the droopy clump
of weeds I'd shyly handed her.
This lasted
a week or two. Then I caught on to her fake
joy, she grew tired of the game, so we stopped
and that was that.
I've been paid for poems—
it felt like money I'd found in the grass.
Truth is I like a regular paycheck
for work I've done in a classroom. Talking,
yes, but work nevertheless.
What's stayed
with me?
How my mother's blue eyes flashed that first
time I lifted posies to her in my sweaty fist.

First appeared in *My Surly Heart*, LSU Press, 2019. Reprinted by permission of David Huddle and LSU Press.

"What Are You Up To?"

What five syllables are more common more
friendly don't they insinuate an almost
familial affection between speaker
and spoken-to my father posed this question
if he came upon me reading of course
he meant to suggest I was a rascally
kind of boy and he loved me anyway

but he could see I was up to nothing
if anything I was down to zero
identity was entirely eyeballs
story and words innocent of even
the childish crimes I had in fact committed
but I liked it that he asked me that
question winking at me as he walked away.

First appeared in *My Surly Heart*, LSU Press, 2019. Reprinted by permission of David Huddle and LSU Press.

"*Elrica*"

Elrica is an Old German name that means "Ruler of all."
                    —http://scalar.usc.edu/works/wiki/baby-names/

My grandmother's sister, dead half a century
now, is the only person I've known
to have that name. Loud, obese, unschooled,
and opinionated, she was always

the center of attention. Uncle Jack Kent,
her husband, whom she treated like a servant,
did the cooking and house-cleaning, fixed her drinks, helped
her bathe and dress, was as sweet-tempered

a man as I've ever known. From age eight
to twelve, I found them disturbing, but I hung
around, studying them when I should have
gone outside to play. I think of them often—

those two perfectly content to be unhappy.
I can't name whatever it was they taught me.

First appeared in *My Surly Heart*, LSU Press, 2019. Reprinted by permission of David Huddle and LSU Press.

"*Some Kitchens*"

The average American family kitchen contains more then
ten thousand food or food-related items.
                    —*Culinary Miscellany*, Volume VI

Forever held in mind are my mother's
and Grandmama Huddle's in Ivanhoe;
Gran and Aunt Stella's in Newbern; the ones
Lindsey and I had in Roanoke, New York,

and Essex Center; Joe and Teresa's
in Winchester; Molly and Ray's in Winooski;
Bess and Nick's in Oregon (Wisconsin)—
I could, if ordered to do so or face

a firing squad, write my life history
in terms of kitchens I've known—where mother
kept the baking soda, the scent of fried
chicken Thelma made for Sunday dinner, Aunt
Murrell's iced tea. These particulars matter
only to me, to whom they're like scripture.

First appeared in *My Surly Heart*, LSU Press, 2019. Reprinted by permission of David Huddle and LSU Press.

"*Inez*"

My family sent my Aunt Inez to the asylum
in Marion after she pushed my brother off
the back porch one afternoon after Sunday
family dinner. They sent her home after some
years of receiving electroshock therapy.
She lived with Grandma Lawson until that
old woman died, then she lived by herself
in a dusty old house in the middle of town.
Dead maybe sixty years, Inez comes alive
in my thoughts occasionally though she
and I never talked—she spoke only to her
mother, my father, and the people we hired
to take her food and do some cleaning.
Inez cut her own hair, wore worn-out men's
jeans and a t-shirt, scared away children
who'd come to stare through her windows.
It's too bad Alfred Hitchcock never saw her;
he'd have put her in a movie where she could
have played the part of a little town's crazy
woman, supported by a family that wanted
nothing to do with her. In the falling-down
garage beside the house there was an ancient
Ford she'd driven as a teenage girl; inside
the house, in bureau drawers in her bedroom,
we found a collection of used menstrual pads
and band aids, and not much more—except four
astrological charts so elaborately drawn they

were works of what we'd now call "outsider
art"—one for herself and one for each
of her sisters—Ida, Elrica, and Dunkley.

I'm writing these words a thousand miles
north of that town in a house that's a palace
compared to the one in which Inez Lawson
lived out her final years. I think I must
be doing it to try to correct an injustice
that resists any correcting. I know I should
put my effort into helping my country heal.
Here in Burlington, at busy intersections
where cars must stop, there stand homeless
men and women holding handmade signs asking
for help. In Madison, Wisconsin, last month,
a block away from the state capital building,
in the 7 a.m. cold, walking from my hotel
to Starbucks, I stepped past a blue tarpaulin
covering an invisible human being sleeping
in a doorway, someone living like a dead
person in a culture that's siphoning wealth
upward from citizens who desperately need it
into the banking accounts of citizens who
live so extravagantly they'd think this is
a comedy I'm writing—a story about a madwoman
painstakingly creating charts of the stars that
aligned to give her and her sisters the lives
they had. And the lives they didn't have.

First appeared in *My Surly Heart*, LSU Press, 2019. Reprinted by permission of David Huddle
and LSU Press.

George Ella Lyon

Reflections: Community, Generosity and Magic

When I think of the Highland Summer Conference, three words come to mind: community, generosity, and magic. When I first taught there in 1986, I'd only published a chapbook and one picture book, but I'd had some poems in regional journals, thanks to the generous work of those editors. I'm not sure, but I imagine that Gurney Norman or Jim Wayne Miller or Jeff Daniel Marion suggested me to Grace, so there's another example of generous community. Wherever I went, whether to the Appalachian Workshop at Hindman or a rowdy gathering on Baber Mountain in West Virginia, or the Highland Summer Conference, I was welcomed, mentored, given room to read my work and to learn from others.

George Ella Lyon (photograph by Ann W. Olson).

I was told that my work had value, that folks wanted to hear it. There is no substitute for this!

As a freelance writer and teacher, such community was a saving thing for me. For the most part, in my adjunct work, I didn't have departmental colleagues, and I often felt isolated, lonely. But the HSC brought me rich friendships, deep learning—from participants as well as teachers—a sense of belonging to a large and varied circle of people who love the mountains that made us and who want to have a voice in how the past is portrayed and how the future is created.

Grace, JoAnn, Ricky: that first time around your humor, and knowledge, and steadiness steadied me. And didn't we have fun! Listening to writing as it happened, going to the Carter Fold, singing the praises of 11W. Gathering to make our own music in the evening. Getting to know one another and ourselves.

The magical part of that first year began as I drove from Harlan, where I'd been visiting my parents, over the mountain to Pennington Gap. Somewhere on the Kentucky side, my eyes were drawn to a hand-lettered sign at the edge of the highway: *Little Splinter Creek Church*. Since it was Sunday, I turned on the radio, thinking to catch the incantatory sound of mountain preaching. I did, but the preacher's version of salvation wasn't one I could listen to for long. It was all violence, with Jesus' arms torn from his body, a dismemberment meant to cement our redemption and guilt. I shuddered and turned him off.

As I drove on in silence, I longed for a different vision. And that night, when I was settled in my little apartment on Radford's campus, I reflected on the day in my journal. To my surprise, when I wrote about the sign by the side of the road, I extended it a bit to read: *Little Splinter Creek Church of the Mother Jesus*. It would be two years before I knew who those words belonged to, before I met Mamaw (Ada Smith), one of the main characters in my novel *With a Hammer for My Heart*.

Next time I drove that road, the sign was gone. Had I imagined it? Or was it an example of Creative Reading? Or had Little Splinter Creek Church itself splintered and taken another name.

Mysteries. The poet Lorca says, "Only mystery enables us to live."

Other visits to the HSC brought changes, of course, including the invaluable addition of Selu. My time there always nourished my spirit, connected me with new writers, and helped pay the bills. I've loved working with Theresa and Ruth, and cherish the reciprocity of learning that the Conference embodies. The circle we sit in that strengthens us all.

One final note of magic: when I came back in 1993, I was determined to work on my own words as well as those for the class. Having finished one journal, I went to the Radford Bookstore and bought a black and white composition book. On the first page, I began writing a poem called "Where I'm From" (which takes off from a poem by Jo Carson, another HSC presenter). Of all the things I've written, that little poem has made the most difference. Somehow by the power of poetry and place and teachers and the internet, it has gone around the world as a writing model. Just last week I received twenty-six "Where I'm From" poems from a high school teacher in Parma, Italy.

I know that the spirit of the Highland Summer Conference helped that poem happen, helped me be in right relationship to something longing to be said. Its gifts of community, generosity, and magic are beyond measure.

"All to Pieces"

It says this apparition
is easy to assemble
but be not deceived.

Parts are numbered, yes,
but the numbers vanish
in light strong enough

to read them. There is
a diaphragm, true, but
it is always doming

or billowing, so how
to read the picture
of the parts, I do not

know. Nor is it clear
that this apparition
is truly the one

we ordered. It arrived
all to pieces, as thin
and many as rain.

Bill Brown

Gift ... Beyond Measure

My relationship with the Highland Summer Writing Conference at Radford is complex and multifaceted. I'll start by saying that it changed my personal life and my writer's life in rich and important ways. Individual relationships and beautiful Southwest Virginia will never leave my memory, my dreamscapes or my poetry. In the early '90s my close friend, Peter Stillman, invited me to share a public poetry reading with him at Radford and spend two days with his HSC writing class. He wanted me to work with aspiring poets and observe a few terrifically promising writers. The conference was active, fluid and the two writers I specifically remember were Ricky Cox and Jim Minick. In summers to come, I would meet and work with Kay Byer, Ron Rash, Judy Miller, Darnell Arnoult, Rita Sims Quillen, Silas House, Wilma Dykeman, and Marilou Awiakta, among others. What can I say? Bless me, bless me, a poet's dream. I would also get to know our leader, Grace Edwards, a brilliant person with a generous soul. And JoAnn Asbury's sense of humor would kindly teach me to be a little more laid back while teaching at the Summer Conference for the sake of my students. We had some participants who just wanted to try their hands at personal writing and others who were submitting work for publication. Her attitude helped me find my way in the beginning of my time at Radford.

Bill Brown.

The friendship I developed with Ricky Cox over the years became deeply valuable to me. Often he was my guide to the countryside. He took me to his family graveyard perched on the top of a hill so graves would be open to the sky. Off the Blue Ridge Parkway we had lunch at a little café where I could get traditional pinto beans and corn fritters. I went back with my wife Suzanne to order the salmon croquettes. He taught me about the folklore of Floyd County, and I was a guest at his home in the shadow of Buffalo Mountain. Ricky's wit sometimes kept me in stiches. He said in Appalachia all things have a purpose. Your broken down pickup could be used to house chickens or hold up a broken back porch roof. He checked on the older neighbors on his country road to make sure they were doing well. An award winning writer, Ricky was also an outstanding musician. I've never forgotten one evening when two graduate students, Grace, Ricky and I met at a small apartment off campus. When Ricky sang Ralph Stanley's *Oh Death* a cappella, I thought I was at the Ryman in Nashville. I'll never forget his rat terrier and cat named Kitty.

The following is a poem I wrote for Ricky, published in the journal *Now and Then* and the collection, *Gods of Little Pleasures*.

"The Talk in Floyd County" (for Ricky)

Somebody studied that the tension
in a configuration of stars
struck a cosmic force
between Fred's Barber Shop
and the Floyd County Courthouse,
and soon a New Age Store sprung up
across from the City Café.
Next, California accents are heard
up and down the Little River,
the price of land is so inflated
that locals can't buy, and what's
worse, they wave funny.
Their kids sit square-legged
in the schoolyard staring at crystals,
and what the hell kind of card game
is tarot. You don't win nothing,
and what's the advantage of knowing
the future if you can't change it.
The waitress says they don't eat ham and eggs,

and Old Man Cox quips you can't trust
people who smile that much.
They're fair at gardening and carpentry,
my mother's measure of acceptance,
and besides, she says, if the stargazers
hadn't come, what would you boys
down at the feed store chew on
except the same tired lies.

During my time at the HSC I was often housed in a dorm with a group of women writers, The SELU Sisters. SELU is the name given to the Cherokee Corn Mother. These dear souls came to write and were articulate, well read and powerful. Luckily I became one of two men who were certified SELU Sisters. Isabel Zuber, Darnell Arnoult, Tamara Baxter, Heidi Hartwiger, Dianne Jordan, Jeanne Shannon and Harry Dean were true friends and cohorts. Professor Parks Lanier was our leader and provider. I was often the only poet in this group of prose writers. Therefore, I could steal their writing ideas and get away with it. To quote T.S. Eliot, "Good poets borrow, professionals steal." We lived in our rooms but shared a kitchen and meeting room. We took turns cooking suppers. The motto of the writing retreat was "You can never have too much garlic." Parks made a little laminated sign that we hung on our "Kitchen" door.

During one of the summers I taught at the Highland Summer Writing Conference at Radford an event happened that haunts me to this day. It was a large class that didn't seem large because the participants were cordial, supportive and willing to share inside and outside of class. Tom, an older teacher at a local school, seemed to set the tone because of his generous nature and desire to tell his Appalachian stories. On the third day we were reading mountain poems in order to write a prompt. Tom arrived late, sat in the back of the room and wiped tears on his shirt sleeve. The class stared at me with questions. I knew we couldn't continue. I gave the class a five minute break and asked Tom what was wrong. To skip traffic he had taken some back streets to reach campus. He noticed two animals in the distance at a stop sign. When he drove closer, one was a larger dog, apparently dead. Beside was a pup that patted the other's face trying to wake her. Both had collars and looked kin. A dark remorse entered him as he continued on slowly, trying to settle his emotions before reaching class. I asked him to share his story when students returned. That day we wrote animal stories and poems. They could be happy or sad but needed to involve deep personal emotions. Later, when we shared our drafts, a bond formed between writers that is rare. That week, that class, and its members are with me still.

Persona poem for Tom, placing it in winter instead of summer (published in *Yesterday's Hay*, Pudding House Press).

"Passenger"
(for Tom G.)

Frost on the dog
proves her dead, but
a pup crouched
beside sniffs her,
nudges, "get up
lazy bones," then
takes his paw
and pats her
face so softly
that I am filled
with a dark remorse
in the pit of my stomach,
and I pull away from
the stop sign, a eulogy
on my tongue, the steering
wheel so very cold
in my hands
as frost shimmers
on the windows
of solitary cars,
I release
the hard wheel
with my right palm
and for some nameless sorrow
pat my wool coat
in the passenger's seat
like the soft white hair
of my mother.

I have loved rivers, creeks and mountain streams since I was a child. Every summer my sister and I spent time in my grandfather's cabin above the Tennessee River. We also stayed at his rural farm at Bible Hills. I remember the time he put us on the back of his mare Neil and trotted us to the spring that started Cub Creek. He got us down, told us not to disturb the newts that helped keep the spring clean. He showed us the gourd dippers and taught us how to drink without clouding the sparkling, bubbling water.

During my teaching at HSC, my semester at RU as Poet in Residence, and my time spent in the dorm with my SELU sisters, one landscape joined these together—my jogging, walking and meditating beside the New River. I never had to get in a car, my feet, notebook and imagination, my transportation. My first stroll on the New took my breath. I identified three types of trillium and found a mulberry tree filled with Cedar Waxwings, one group passing berries down a limb.

How many poems and letters the New River birthed is hard to say, given the many summers I spent beside its banks and little tributaries. I wish to share two that were published during my time at Radford and later included in poetry collections.

"Learning to Be Quiet"

Learning to be quiet after a semester of talk,
I sit beside the New River, and watch a heron wade
off little island. The heron exists without words.
She relies on stillness, a snag left by April rain,
until she stabs a fish. Agitated by a kingfisher,
she lifts from the water, alights on a sycamore branch,
and scratches the morning with her cry.

I've known this rusty call since childhood.
My brother took me trotline fishing in the Hatchie Bottoms.
One morning as he baited a hook, he drove
a large barb in soft flesh between finger and thumb.
I grasped the weighted line that would jerk him
in the water. With his free hand, he clipped
the steel with pliers. I anxiously steered the john boat
between berms as herons lifted from limbs
painting the cypress sky with wings.

Even in meditation the mind strays from mantra
into memory. How easily the cry of a bird leads
to the realm of story. The heron has returned
to her fishing. Like my pulse, she performs
an adagio of measured steps before her posture
settles into sculpture, a note on a staff.

First published in *Asheville Poetry Review.*

How a landscape like a river or mountain takes one's imagination to another time and place that perhaps inhabits his or her dream-world is a wonder. See how it works in this poem:

"Otter Dream for Geron"

Jogging by the New River,
I noticed the summer streams
blue-green depth between white shoals.
Suddenly like a submerged bobber
the sleek head of otter
popped up and with his skilled body
swirled against a sycamore root
and lay on his back to eat a fish.

Brother, I thought of you in another time zone,
under the glare of an operating light,
gloved and masked, pinning
a fractured leg so that a child might walk.

I know about your harried life,
you rush from clinic to hospital to home.
You try to heal the sick and raise
grown children who will not stay grown.

I would have you like the otter,
who in his struggle to eat,
takes time to play. I would have
your life healed with this river,
nurtured by the soft fur of the otter's belly,
the joy of jogging by such freedom,
these shoals which roar a line of spray
one hundred yards across.

Thinking these thoughts for you,
I imagine that we wade into the stream together
and spying the feeding lips of trout,
cast our flies and watch fish pop the bait,
fling from the water like crone
sculptures against the sky.
I am not blind to the fact
that caring for others heals you.

Today my wish is that
a river seep into your dreams
like an otter among submerged trees
to bring you joy.

First published in *Metaphors*.

I've never been good at ending memoir writing. So let me say this: Grace's Highland Summer Writing Conference, Park's SELU Sisters, and the wonderful students at Radford created a mid-life gift to me beyond measure.

Rita Sims Quillen

Writing in the Highlands of Virginia

Editors' Note: Rita Sims Quillen also came to the Highland Summer Conference as a reader in 1992 when Wilma Dykeman led the workshop and again in 2001 when Bill Brown led the workshop. She has been one of the cadre of generous Appalachian writers that we have been privileged to call on again and again.

Rita Sims Quillen.

I am thrilled and honored to have been part of the long history and tradition of the annual Summer Highland Conference at Radford twice; the first time I had the opportunity to co-teach with my hero and mentor Dr. Robert J. Higgs in 2003 and then I taught again in 2015, the year after my novel *Hiding Ezra* came out. I remember that both workshops were filled with engaging and talented students, including now well-known and widely-published poet Charles Swanson in the first workshop.

I also recall that both workshops were not only richly rewarding for me from a teaching standpoint, but that I also got some serious writing done myself in both. In the first workshop, I devoted every spare minute I had each night after class to writing an essay that was due for a special issue of *Appalachian Heritage* magazine devoted to the work of Fred

Chappell. I wrote an article about the interesting women in Fred's poems, using Jungian ideas and images. The title was "Good Ol' Fred Wrestles His Anima."—probably my all-time favorite title for a scholarly essay.

In the more recent workshop, I was hard at work on what would become a book of poems called *The Mad Farmer's Wife*, a book that was a kind of echo and response to the work of one of the region's most gifted and most important writers and thinkers, Wendell Berry. The day we went to the Selu Conservancy—a tradition of the workshop that showcases a beautiful place and the importance of a retreat to nature to a writer's mind, body, and soul—I wrote the seminal poem in the collection. "A Woman Born to Farming" was the companion to Berry's poem "A Man Born to Farming" which is one of a couple of poems that had introduced his Mad Farmer poems to me years ago, and getting a woman's view from the same vantage point was central to getting my collection to gel into something cohesive. It's very fitting that it was at Radford, at the Summer Highland Conference and at Selu that the piece was born.

"A Woman Born to Farming" ## *(After Wendell Berry's "A Man Born to Farming")*

Skin soft as morning, the mother,
the woman born to farming,
her feet bare on God's green carpet,
gathers apples and pears and eats them.
Her heart is silent, too gentle to beat.
Sometimes it hums or vibrates along a scale,
waits for the call of purpose or need,
while she cans beans, looks for calves, plants seeds.
Sometimes it sends a code
delivered by hummingbird wings.
Her children will call her blessed, the Good Book says,
but mostly they are just too busy to call at all now.
It's not their fault any more
than the leaves that fall from the tree.
They call to her thoughts every day
like the cooing of doves at gloaming,
the whippoorwill reminding us it is dark here.
The farm is a man's world.
She cannot muscle the chainsaw or sick calf,

cannot pick up the heavy hay bales.
Walking in the woods and fields is her job.
Fox bark, turkey putt, buck snort

startle her to answer with laughter.
Words are no help on a farm.
How sad to be good at something unnecessary?
Like the hens and their grit
she has dirt in her craw,
keeps hatching out barren words for others to use.
The Cherokee say Corn Mother
grew corn from her backside,
fed humankind, but the Mad Farmer's Wife
knows it all comes to nothing—
to dark, quiet vastness.
Now it's only the waiting
for the rain, the sun, the next moon change.

Accepting the briers' price,
she gathers raspberries and blackberries,
the stains' temporary tattoo
her only recognition for her work.
She has only the stains

of many things on her empty hands,
the whistled song of days passing in her head,

First appeared in *The Mad Farmer's Wife*, Texas Review Press, 2016. Reprinted by permission from Texas Review Press, Huntsville, Texas.

Robert Morgan

Experience at Radford: Connecting with the Indigenous Roots

In 1999 I conducted the writing workshop at Radford University for the Highland Summer Writing Conference. My happiest memories of that workshop concern the diversity of that group of participants. Normally in an undergraduate or graduate workshop the members are roughly the same age and from similar backgrounds. But in the Summer Conference at Radford I was pleased to work with some undergraduates and graduate students, but also folks who were retired or coming back to school after long absences. At least one had worked for a newspaper, and others at non-writing professional jobs. Some were raising families, or had raised families. This mixture of participants with a wider range of backgrounds and life experiences enriched the discussions and the work submitted for discussion.

Robert Morgan (photograph by Chris Kitchen, Cornell University Photography).

One special advantage of the Radford workshop was that Radford faculty also took part, with Grace Edwards, JoAnn Asbury, Ricky Cox, and others on the staff of the Appalachian program joining us in the workshops. The Radford community was very welcoming to writers and writing groups. Faculty such as Parks Lanier and Donald Secreast took part in summer programs, and a large number from the university and the community attended the evening readings. One group of women writers, called the Selu Sisters, present that summer week, had been meeting there for several years.

I have also happy memories of the lunches with Grace and other members of the faculty, and our conversations about Appalachian history, Cherokee history, and teaching. This was the summer before my novel *Gap Creek* was published, and the last time I would have the leisure for that kind of conference.

Radford is situated in one of the most beautiful spots in the mountains of Virginia. It was a treat to spend time in the New River region, with all its history from the frontier era. The Warrior's Path, *Athiamiowee*, which would become the Great Wagon Road, passed nearby. The Wagon Road would become United States Route 11, and then would be superseded by Interstate 81. One cannot spend time at Radford without thinking of the early settlers, Daniel Boone, and explorers of the Blue Ridge, Allegheny, and Cumberland Mountains.

Two highlights of the week of the Highland Summer Writing Conference were the visits to the homestead in the country nearby, called the Farm at Selu, or the Selu Conservancy, with the seven-sided Cherokee Retreat Center, and to the Carter Family Memorial. I was not able to include the latter during my stay, but I did have the good fortune to visit the farm and the Cherokee center. It was refreshing to get away from campus one afternoon and walk the grounds of the 375-acre traditional homestead, look at the heirloom crops, the farm equipment and animals, the barns and outbuildings, and to be reminded of the agrarian roots of Appalachian culture and writing.

Most memorable to me was the connection to the Cherokee past and the exhibits at the Retreat Center, to be reminded of the rituals of the Corn Mother *Selu*, and to recall that these mountains were part of the vast Cherokee hunting ranges. I grew up on a farm in the mountains of North Carolina, and when hoeing corn or weeding, often turned up arrowheads and pieces of Native American pottery. It seemed the ground itself, and the nearby streams and waterfalls, were haunted by Indians, both the Cherokees and the Woodland peoples who had preceded them.

The visit to the Retreat Center near Radford confirmed that the religious and cultural traditions of the mountains go far back, beyond the first churches and white settlers. Long before Bishop Asbury arrived, there were holy men and holy women conducting rituals, offering prayers, performing dances, and asking blessings on crops, crafts, children, and all the community undertakings. Connecting with the indigenous roots and routes of the area was an essential part of the Highland Summer Writing Conference experience.

Lost Lead Mine of the Cherokees

All my life I'd heard stories about the lost lead mine of the Cherokees. When I was growing up on Green River, old folks would tell how the Mayhew family up the river had lead for bullets even during the Confederate War when nobody else could get lead of any kind. My Uncle Avery liked to tell how in the dark days of 1864 a Confederate colonel and a detail of men brought a wagon all the way from Greensboro two hundred miles away, and under cover of night hauled away a load of ore. One of his sergeants was a Mayhew who must have told him where the secret mine was.

"And I'll tell you something else," Uncle Avery said and aimed tobacco juice into the fireplace where the spit hissed in the flames like a riled cat. "Wherever there's lead there will likely be silver. There's more than lead been dug out of that hole."

"How did the Mayhews know about the mine?" I asked.

Uncle Avery looked like I'd spoken out of turn, as if a boy of ten had no business asking questions when a subject so grave and mysterious was discussed. He grunted and continued, as I knew he would.

"The Mayhews was loyal to the crown of England, and during the Revolution they come up here in these mountains to hide out when things got too hot for them down in the Piedmont, about the time of the battles of Kings Mountain and Cowpens. They got to be special friends with some of the Cherokees that was also loyal to the king, and they furnished gunpowder to the Indians. And the Cherokees in turn showed the Mayhews where to find lead. And all these years later the Mayhews have had lead whenever they needed it. And my guess is they have took a lot more than lead out of that mine."

I attended grammar school with a number of Mayhew kids and once on the school bus I asked Nathan Mayhew, who was about my age, if he knew where the secret lead mine was. But he just turned away and didn't answer. And I didn't know if I'd insulted him or embarrassed him. Uncle Avery had said none of the Mayhews would ever talk about the mine. He also said Peter Stilson, a well-known trapper and hunter and poacher in these parts, had vowed he would find the lead mine if it was the last thing he ever did. But he disappeared and there was muttering that the Mayhews had a hand in his disappearance. But his body was never found, and some folks hinted Peter had been killed by moonshiners or rival trappers over in the Dark Corner of South Carolina. Still others said an angry husband had killed him, or that he'd fled to the Far West after a crony's body was found in a car sunk in a lake on Gap Creek.

As the years passed the story of the lost lead mine was not exactly forgotten, but the community changed, as new factories moved into the county, and television, and later social media, replaced the story telling by the fireplaces. I went away to college and then took a job with a Raleigh law firm and only got back to Green River at Christmastime and sometimes for a long weekend. My wife and children preferred to go in the other direction, to the beach in summer, so we didn't return to the mountains as often as I would have liked. After my dad and then my mother died, I regretted that I'd not visited them more often. They'd lived near their own parents all their lives, and never understood why I'd moved away and stayed away.

Maybe it was guilt that made me return to the mountains more as I approached my own retirement. Every weekend I could get away I began to drive up there, sometimes with Sharon, sometimes by myself. I'd inherited the old house and my excuse was that I had to check on it, make sure the furnace and plumbing were working, that the grass had been cut by the caretaker I'd hired. The valley was now very different from the world I'd grown up in. There were many new houses, some owned by retirees, and gated communities, as well as trailer parks in old pastures and hollows where Mexican workers lived. One of my cousins had stashed a necropolis of industrial scrap and waste on his land, tons of metal, glass, plastic heaped among the pines and hemlocks of the house site where many of our ancestors had been born.

It was another cousin who reminded me of the lost lead mine story. We were lamenting the changes in the valley and the loss of good farm land to golf courses and the wide interstate highway. "They've bulldozed everything," he said. "It's a wonder they ain't dug up the lost lead mine of the Cherokees."

"Do you think there ever was such a place?" I said.

"Course there was, and the Mayhews are still guarding the secret."

"Then where is it?" I said. "This valley is not that big. How could they keep the location of a mine secret for over two hundred years?"

"They say it can only be reached by water," my cousin said. "The entrance is somewhere in the river."

"But where in the river?"

My cousin looked at me like I was being a pushy city lawyer who'd gone off to college and lived in Raleigh for forty years. I was no longer exactly one of the boys.

"If I knowed where in the river it was, I'd go there myself," my cousin said.

As you near retirement you look for things to hold your interest. Some people play more golf, some volunteer for community service, or help at the SPCA. I decided I'd spend more time fixing up the old home place, set out fruit trees, maybe start a new garden where the old one had gone to scrub. I'd buy a little tractor, get my feet in the dirt again. And I'd poke around the river valley, reacquaint myself with the haunts of my childhood, delve into local history. Uncle Avery was long dead, but somebody should be keeping that history alive. Once I'd known every foot of the valley intimately, and I'd get to know it again. I would do what I was inspired to do, and one of the things that suddenly inspired me most was the story of the lost lead mine. It was a mystery and a legend, and if there was any substance to the legend, I meant to find it out once and for all.

I couldn't get out of my mind the one detail my cousin had given me: that the mine could only be reached through the river. From its source near Blue Ridge Church down to the head of Lake Summit, the river flowed about seven or eight miles through woods and then farm land and by housing developments. If the mine was buried under the lake there was no chance of reaching it without diving equipment. Near the housing developments the banks had been smoothed off and walled. So the only likely places were through the farmlands and in the forests near the head of the river. But the stream was so tiny up there, before it was enlarged by the addition of Rock Creek and Cabin Creek and other tributary branches, it was unlikely to conceal the entrance to a cave. That made the most probable stretch of river the one through farmland, where river birch and sycamores and hazel nut bushes lined the banks.

I thought of Peter Stilson, the trapper and poacher who'd vowed to find the mine decades ago and then disappeared. Besides catching muskrats and mink along the river, he'd trapped foxes and bobcats in the hollows and the Flat Woods near the head of the river. To supply wealthy clients with venison he'd killed deer out of season, as well as other game, furnished rattlesnake hides, and living animals for pets for whoever could pay. Rumor had it that he'd served as a hit man for various interests, and that he had a special relationship with the police in both North and South Carolina. There was one story, as I said, that a jealous husband in South Carolina had done him in. But always lurking in the back of people's minds was the thought that one of the Mayhews had something to do with his vanishing. He'd gotten too close to the secret mine.

So I made up my mind I'd tell no one I was looking for the lead mine. I'd fish the river along the three-mile stretch of farmland and wooded banks, looking for any evidence of a cave mouth under water. If I could spot such a cave entrance, I'd return later with swimming trunks and snorkel mask, a flashlight wrapped in plastic, and try to enter the cave, calling as little attention to myself as possible.

Logic told me the cave entrance, if it existed, had to be in a deeper part of the river. The larger pools were at the bends where the turning current scooped out the river bed and kept it deep. There was the Lemmons Hole, the Bee Gum Hole, Avery's Hole, and Lucian's Hole, among others. The most promising was Lucian's Hole because the bank was highest there. In fact the Cicero Mountain came right down to the water's edge at that bend. My distant cousin Lucian had owned the land there, and in the summer we boys fished in the hole. But it was not a preferred swimming spot because the current was so swift where the river narrowed in a trough and there were jagged rocks to skin your knees and toes.

With my waders and fly rod and fishing hat and vest I entered the stream near the old foot-log several hundred yards above Lucian's Hole. Luckily the bank there was lined with sycamores and river birch. It would be hard for those on the river road to see me, and even if they did spot me, I was just whipping the water with my line and Royal Coachman fly.

As I eased downstream, moccasin snakes slipped off limbs into the water and, with a scribble, disappeared. A muskrat plunked into the river and shot away like an underwater cannon ball. Sand spun in the lees of rocks. The river sang at the shoals like a choir. Water arced over buried logs and circled in eddies. It was the river I'd loved as a boy, the musk smell of rotting vegetation, a faint fish smell. The sound of insects in the weeds beyond the trees thrilled and soothed me.

I stepped around rocks and waded through lengths of lullwater. When I reached the bend, it would be hard to wade where the current concentrated into a chute between rocks before crashing into the pool. Most of the river passed through a channel there about four feet wide. That was why we had trouble swimming in the pool so narrow and lined with sharp rocks. It was too deep and the current too strong to wade through. Looking into the turbulent depths, I tried to think of a way to probe under the bank. My fly-rod could not be risked in the churning current. I'd have to get out on the bank, find a pole eight or ten feet long, and see if I could find an opening under the overhang.

Just as I was about to wade out of the river, I heard a metallic thump and splash and voices. Turning upstream I saw a green canoe paddled by two teenage girls and behind them three or four other canoes, paddled by younger girls. Most of the paddlers looked to be about thirteen. The two in front were older, probably counselors. I guessed it was a group from one of the local summer camps. They paddled over rocks and between rocks and sometimes bumped into moss-covered boulders. I pulled in my line and stepped into the shallows to let them pass.

"Any luck?" one of the counselors shouted.

"Not yet."

Some of the girls were wearing shorts and sweaters and some wore bikinis with their sweaters tied behind their backs. It always surprised me to see how mature the bodies of adolescent girls could look. They were just girls, but already women too.

"If it's less than six inches put it back," one of the girls called, and they all giggled. It was an old joke, usually printed with a picture of a fish on a pillow in a guest room of a hunting lodge.

"Watch out for snakes," I answered.

When the canoes dipped out of sight around the bend, I laid my rod on the rocks and mounted the steep bank. It took me several minutes to find a fallen sapling among the grapevines and briars. I broke off the top and trimmed away the twigs. Standing on the rocks at the water's edge, I plunged the pole into the deepest part of the pool, aiming it back under the bank. The current was so fierce it almost jerked the pole out of my hands.

The pole hit rocks and trembled in the vigorous current. Leaning as far out as I could I pushed the pole back under me and found that sure enough there was an opening down there. Working the pole around, I probed the gap. It seemed at least a foot and a half wide, maybe two feet. There was no way to tell how deep the opening was, but there was definitely some kind of cavity there.

As best I could tell the cave entrance was right at the bed of the river. Because of the strength of the current it would be hard to reach and enter. It was possible that the opening or chamber it led to was filled with water, in which case I wouldn't be able to stay under long enough to search for anything. I had to go back to the house to get my swimming trunks, a snorkeling mask, a rope and flashlight, and a mason's hammer.

But just after I reached the house a thunderstorm came up over the top of the Cicero Mountain. There was a good deal of rain and thunder, and lightning blew the top out of an oak on the knoll across the road called the Squirrel Hill. When I returned to the river with my equipment after the storm, the stream had risen and was the color of dishwater. I could wait until the next day for the water to recede, or I could go ahead with my plans. I decided to plunge in, in spite of the high water.

First I tied the rope to a tree a little upstream from the pool. I'd wrapped the flashlight in clear plastic and taped it tight. With the snorkeling mask on, the flashlight in my left hand, and the mason's hammer tied to my waist with a nylon cord, I grasped the rope with my right hand and waded into the pool, bracing myself against the force of the current. My feet hit sharp rocks and I lost my balance and dropped the rope and had to swim. Luckily I didn't lose the flashlight.

Wading along the shallow side of the river, I worked my way back to the rope and tried again. This time I slipped the flashlight into my trunks and grasped the rope with both hands. With my head under water, gripping the rope, I backed into the pool slowly. When I reached the bottom of the pool, I saw the opening was about eighteen inches high, maybe two feet wide. I pushed myself into the blackness and bumped my head on a rock.

Still holding the rope with my right hand, I took the flashlight from my trunks with my left and switched it on. All I could see was a kind of tunnel, a throat through rock, that tilted upward. With elbows and knees I pushed forward, hoping I wasn't invading a nest of snakes or rabid minks. Every move I made stirred silt on the tunnel walls. My elbows and shins scraped on the sharp rocks.

The tunnel widened after a few feet, and I raised my head above the cloudy water. I seemed to be in a chamber maybe four feet high and ten feet long. I tore the mask off to see better. The walls were powdered with a kind of white dust, and marks made with charcoal were just visible under the powder or dust. Surely Indians or cave people had been here long ago. I played the flashlight over the walls looking for signs of metal. Lead is usually found in galena, a lead sulfide, that looks gray or dark gray.

Something shone in the corner, glistening like beads or sequins. With a start I saw it was a snake, or a snake skin. When I looked closer, I found it was a dead snake, the skin dried and shriveled. Where there was a dead snake there might be live ones also. I turned the flashlight to the other side and saw something gray and round. It was a skull. The hollow eyes had been watching me. The teeth gaped in an awful grin. Hair was stuck to the skull and rotten clothes covered a skeleton. My elbow touched a moldy, decayed shoe.

Obviously I was not the first to find this hidden cave. Whoever had preceded me had died there. It was probably not a Cherokee, or not an ancient Cherokee, if I could judge by the remnants of the clothes. Could it be someone who was murdered and whose body had been hidden there? Had I stumbled on a crime scene? I tried to examine the bones without disturbing anything. There were no signs of a fracture in the skull.

A kerosene lantern lay in the dirt beside the skeleton, its handle and sides scaly with rust. And near the lantern lay pieces of half burned sticks. A fire had been started and then put out. It was impossible to tell if the remains of the fire were older than the skeleton. Had someone found this cave even earlier than the deceased lying before me?

If I'd stumbled on evidence of a murder it was my duty to report it. And once the body was reported the cave would no longer be a secret, whether or not it was the lost lead mine of the Cherokees. But while I was there it was also my duty to find out as much as I could before going to the county sheriff or anybody else.

The air in the cave tasted bitter, like some ancient salt or corroded metal. I spat to clean my tongue, but the taste wouldn't go away. My eyes burned a little. As slowly and carefully as I could I tried to find the pockets in the pants on the skeleton. The fabric was so rotten it fell apart at my touch. Through the cloth I touched bone, hip bone and thigh bone. Finally I found what seemed to be a pocket and felt slivers of metal. Pulling the pieces out of the dust I saw they were keys on a ring, old car keys and house keys. Bending over the skeleton, I found the other pocket and drew out a rusted pocket knife and some coins that turned out to be two dimes and a quarter, thirty years old.

If there was a wallet there might be some identification. It was too much to hope for that after all this time paper would have resisted the rot and dampness. Fishing under the skeleton, shaking the pelvic bone loose, I found something thick as a wallet or small book. Grasping it carefully, hardly daring to move it, I drew the object into the light.

It was covered with rotted leather and I thought it might be a small Testament. But then I saw it was indeed a wallet. Inside were faded bits of paper. Some were dollar bills, the ink melted and blurred. Some were cards with numbers and words on them. One piece of paper was encased in plastic. The writing printed there had melted. But holding the flashlight closer I could make out "Department of Motor Vehicles" and the name "Stilson." It was the driver's license of Peter Stilson, the poacher and scoundrel, rumored to be a murderer. Had he, like me, found this cave, or had he been killed and the body stashed here?

There was one other pocket to look in, the shirt pocket. I fumbled with the disintegrating cloth and found a piece of folded paper, so decayed it seemed to melt in my hands. Examining the bits, I saw it was a page torn from a textbook or encyclopedia describing lead ore and the process of mining and refining it. Stilson had almost certainly come here looking for the lost lead mine.

I wondered if Stilson had been carrying a weapon. According to rumor he'd always gone armed. I reached to the other side of the skeleton thinking there might be a holster with a pistol in it, either a side holster or a shoulder holster. As I reached behind the bones, I felt something round and hard in the dirt. It was about the size of a pistol barrel or a rifle barrel. I pulled and the object came loose. But what I saw in the beam from the flashlight was not a revolver but a bone. It was much older than the bones of Stilson's skeleton. I reached into the dirt and found other bones. When Stilson had found the cave he must have seen the bones of others, either animals or human, who had come here and left their skeletons. Who had they been? Was it a place of Indian burial?

Sweeping the light over the walls again I tried to make something out of the lines scratched there. Was that an "S" scraped in the dirt? Had Stilson tried to write his name on the wall before he died? He had the lantern, and it looked like he'd even made a fire to help him examine the rock for signs of lead ore.

I tried to think what to do next, but for some reason couldn't focus my thoughts. The sight of Stilson's skeleton had distracted me, and finding the additional bones had confused me even more. Had I found the secret lead mine, or just a cave where bodies had been hidden? Was the dark stuff on the walls galena, or just ordinary granite?

It seemed I could hear voices. But of course there were no voices. It was just the sound of rushing river water coming through the short tunnel. The sound of roaring water always seems to contain voices. My Uncle Avery used to say that if you listened closely to a waterfall on the creek or shoals in the river you could hear Indians talking or chanting. He said the Indians had been here so long the river and all the creeks and even the wind still spoke Cherokee.

It seemed someone was calling me through the sound of the water. But I knew I was being silly. It sounded like the voice coming through the tunnel said *You too have come here, you too.* I'd not realized how tired I was. The effort of fighting the current and climbing through the tunnel must have worn me out. I was tired and even sleepy. I just wanted to rest a little, and then I'd think about what to do next. I needed to lie down and think about what it all meant: the cave, the bones, the writing on the wall.

I was so sleepy I leaned back against the wall. Crumbs of dirt and mold fell on my shoulders. I just wanted to rest a minute until I could decide what had to be done. My arms were heavy and my head was heavier. My eyelids weighed so much I couldn't hold them open. Black things like shadow bats flitted wherever I looked. I leaned against the rock and felt I was floating. A warm ocean was rising in my veins and I didn't want to move.

What woke me was the sound of the flashlight falling out of my hand. When I opened my eyes there was nothing but blackness. I felt around in the damp dirt, among the rags and bones, but couldn't find the light. With a shiver I realized how cold I was. I was naked except for the wet swimming trunks. The dirt and rock were damp. I shuddered and felt farther around the floor for the flashlight. It was only when I touched a stick of half-burned wood that it occurred to me why I was so sleepy and weak, and the probable reason Stilson had died here. There was limited oxygen in the cave and the fire had eaten it all up. Stilson had died of oxygen deprivation. And someone long before him had probably died the same way. The cave was a death trap. There might even be natural gas seeping into the cave and poisoning the air. I remembered the awful taste on my lips and tongue. But more likely I was weak and confused from lack of oxygen. I'd heard voices because I was on the verge of passing out. Only the fall of the flashlight had wakened me.

The light was nowhere to be found and I guessed it had rolled back down the tunnel. When I put my hand on something round and slick, I thought it was a snake, but with relief realized it was the rope. I'd forgotten about the rope. *Take charge, take charge now*, I said to myself, trying to focus my strength, fighting the drowsiness. Grasping the rope, I tried to pull myself into the tunnel. Not only were my muscles weak, but my legs felt heavy as logs of lead. It was all I could do to move. With sheer will power I made myself crawl forward, and bumped my head on the rock, forgetting how low the passage was. The pain woke me a little more, and with my head lowered against the rope I pushed and pulled myself, an inch at a time. It was only when my face touched the cold river water that I remembered the snorkel mask I'd taken off in the cave. Rather than back into the tunnel to retrieve the mask I decided to just hold my breath while I crawled out through the water into the river.

Taking as deep a breath as I could, I closed my eyes and mouth and heaved myself forward. Knees and elbows scraped on rocks. My knee hit the flashlight, but I couldn't grasp it. I pushed myself an inch, another inch, another. I needed to open my mouth. My chest felt like it was going to explode. Meteor showers passed before my closed eyes. I had to breathe and water churned against my face and up my nose, burning my sinuses. I made one last effort to pull myself forward.

And then I don't know what happened, for I lost control and a great force thrust me aside and rolled me over and pummeled me from all directions. I was spun around, and tried to cough so hard my eyes burned. My shoulder hit a rock and I rolled in somersaults and scraped my head on something.

Then I was thrown against gravel and sand, gasping so hard I threw up. But when I opened my eyes the sun sparkled through the trees above the river. I was lying in the shallows and I vomited again. After a while I stopped heaving and sat up. I was about a hundred yards down the river from Lucian's Hole. The current had given me a beating as soon as I emerged from the tunnel. My shoulder was bruised and bleeding and there was blood on my forehead. My knees and elbows had been scraped raw. But I knew I was lucky not to have suffocated in the cave or been drowned in the powerful current.

As I rested before trying to stand, I wondered what I should do about the bones in the cave. Should I contact the sheriff and tell what I'd found? Or should I let that rascal Peter Stilson sleep on in his own secret sepulcher? And should I tell folks there probably never was a lost lead mine of the Cherokees? Would they believe me, or continue to cherish the legend? What would Uncle Avery say? These were things I had to think about. At the moment I just needed to get cleaned up and dressed, bandage my wounds, and rest. I was glad, damned glad, to be alive. And in my heart I knew I would let the legend continue as it had, and I would leave the bones to rest as they lay.

Diane Gilliam

How I Got to RU, and What I Found There

I keep a clear memory of the night Grace Toney Edwards called my house to invite me to teach at the upcoming Highland Summer Writing Conference. I was standing in the kitchen and my younger daughter was in there with me—we were on a streak, she and I, of good things happening for me when we were together. Grace's call was good news, extraordinary to me, though I'm sure she'd made such calls scores of times before. It was the first time in my relatively new poet-life that I had been asked to teach, and it felt like a welcome into the Appalachian literary tradition that I had hoped for.

I am one of those writers from out. My mother is from Mingo County, West Virginia, and my father from Johnson County, Ken-

Diane Gilliam (photograph by Deborah Boardman).

tucky. But I was born in Columbus and have lived all my years in Ohio. I took my first poetry workshop in my late thirties, as my academic career was proving unlivable. There I met my friend poet Jeanne Bryner who, after I read a first attempt at a poem with junebugs tied and flown like kites, brought me a pile of books including *The Dollmaker, Fair and Tender Ladies,* and poems by Irene McKinney and Kay Byer. That was the first I knew there was such a thing as Appalachian literature. It was love at first page. Whether or not I was a writer, where I would belong if I were—that I did not know.

I followed the poet path and after a few years I had some books of my own. Like all writers with new books, I wanted to get mine into the hands of people who I thought would be their best readers. I met Grace at Hindman shortly after *Kettle Bottom* came out. I was there as a participant and she was teaching the Appalachian literature class. I especially loved her talk about Emma Bell Miles, starved as I was to know all I could about writers from the region. I told her so when I introduced myself and told her about my books. If I remember rightly, I did so in the Ladies Room. She took it in stride and kindly, and I went on once the moment had passed to consider that maybe I needed to learn a little restraint. Still and all, she brought me in with the invitation to come be part of that summer's workshop.

I also sent Parks Lanier copies of my books after reading *The Poetics of Appalachian Space*. On a morning when I learned that I had not won a prize I thought I ought to have won, I decided to go yank some weeds out of the flower bed. It helped a little, but it was a note I found from Parks when I came back in that put me back into myself. He had gotten my books, sent thanks and was also sending a check to cover the cost of the books, plus a little bit more. If he could, he said, he would do as he had done for *River of Earth*—carry a box of the books around in his trunk and put them into people's hands. His old Subaru, however, was no longer up to that task. With the money he sent, I was to send copies of my books to someplace they might not otherwise make it. I sent them to high schools in Mingo County. The weeds in the flower bed were safe after that. I didn't need a prize—Parks had given me something truer.

When I think back to the first classroom I was in at Radford, I have a sense of light and air. I was nervous about this first creative writing class, so I prepared and prepared. I expect I tried to spell out most anything I might want to say. The light and air and energy in the room wasn't coming only from the summer day. It was also coming toward me from the circle of writers who made me feel welcome from the start. There was a togetherness in the reading and work we did and in the talk that rose from the circle which changed the way I thought about teaching. I saw that it could be both grounded in and a source of community—a community of writers that I might belong to after all.

I have been back to Highland Summer Writing Conference several times since. It feels like coming home. There has always been time on the porch at Selu, and often on the porch with Grace. There has been music with Ricky Cox, and bags of his home ground corn meal to take home. There has been talk with Theresa L. Burriss and Ruth B. Derrick, Parks Lanier and

JoAnn Asbury, whose presence I always feel, and with all the writers who come with their work and their trust in what can be accomplished together. All that light and air, all those voices and all that welcome—no wonder when they asked us, we came.

"Said the Girl to the Boy"

Paul Simon is getting old,
or so he says in the song my friend
played for me on Youtube.
We watched Joan Baez too,
and she wept when Joan sang
about the swinging low, for we
are nearing the head of that line,
of that particular taxi stand, my friend
close enough now
to hear the singing.

Which is how I've ended up
this Saturday morning, when I have
better things to worry about,
with Simon and Garfunkel playing
over and over on my computer, the way
their voices spun around and around
on my record player for months on end
that last year of school.
Do you remember
how I came into homeroom
every morning and reported
what I'd done the night before,
those three words, that made you laugh
the laugh of someone who asks
the question just to hear the answer

he already knows,
those three little words—
Simon and Garfunkel.

But why not, I would ask,
it's poetry.

I argued for dreamers and you
for the doers. And there were other songs,
you argued, besides those
that I rode around and around

the year I was sixteen, because oh, what love—
by which I mean, how I loved you—
and oh, what words I found for it there.

And this morning, thinking that I have never
ever written a love poem, I have to wonder
why not. Why not a love poem for you
before I go? For you, and for my own heart
back then, as it broke and kept on breaking,
as even now it circles and keeps circling
those songs that promise there is such a thing
as love, that the chariots that bring it
will swing low, that always
there will be singing,
and that never, ever, can it be wrong
to listen for that song.

PART II

More Inspiration

Ron Rash

Words from Ron Rash

Editors' Note: Ron Rash came twice to the Highland Summer Conference as short-term leader of the writing workshops, once in 2003 and again in 2006. When invited to take part in this book project, he asked if he could submit a short reaction paragraph and a poem. Of course, we were delighted to have anything he wanted to contribute. During the process of our soliciting contributions, he sent the email to editor Donia S. Eley. Because we so loved the creativity of his "excuse note," we asked for permission to reproduce it here.

Ron Rash.

From Email:

Because of a back injury that has me hanging like a bat, assuming amphibious poses on the floor, plus being hopelessly behind on a plethora of deadlines, so unable to do blurbs, etc., for worthy folks, plus being no big fan of electronic communication anyway, plus my amazing ability to hit wrong keys, buttons and therefore erase, displace, replace, deface whole paragraphs, please forgive any response that may be any/all of the following: days, weeks, eons late, and /or brief, illiterate, gnostic, perhaps even runic. RR

Reflection on Highland Summer Conference

What I most treasure about being a part of the Highland Summer Conference was the strong sense of fellowship. Friendships began there for me that continue, for which I am grateful. That sense of fellowship was largely because of Grace Toney Edwards' leadership. Dealing with writers is like herding cats. Looking back on my time there, I realize Grace had to have been exhausted from such a task, yet she was always smiling and patient, and made every individual feel special. I and so many other Appalachian writers have had their lives enriched with the time we spent in Radford.

Canning

(For Grace Toney Edwards)

It wasn't enough to taste
June's bright-berried abundance.
My grandmother scratched specifics
measured in hardening parafin.
Sometimes a date or initials,
sometimes something more:
a neighbor's birth or death,
a daughter's recent visit.
Months or years would pass
before the past was unsealed
solidly still above
the jelly's murky quiver.

Ron Rash
308 S. Mechan
Pendleton, SC

Ricky Cox

My First Highland Summer Conference

Unless we count captions in a high school yearbook, my first published writing began with a prompt offered by George Ella Lyon during the 1986 Highland Summer Conference, the first of two in which I was a paying customer, the first of more than twenty in which I had some part as a staffer or hanger-on. My memory is that George Ella led the conference for two full weeks, and in the first day or two asked us, before attempting action or dialogue, to describe the clothes and habits and voice of someone we knew well. I thought first of a much admired uncle, who smoked unfiltered Pall Mall cigarettes, wore green or gray work pants and shirts every day of the week, and who, in discussing virtually any topic, was to swearing roughly what Emily Dickinson was to hymn meter, both servant and master. I could hear his voice clearly in my head, but wasn't comfortable then (or now) putting on paper or reading aloud the colorful words it was using. So I began instead to think of my maternal grandfather, who had then been dead only two years, but whose voice, both words and sound, I discovered, was already lost to me. When I tried to play in my head the cadence of his speech, the tone and the timbre of his voice, there

Ricky Cox (photograph by Lora Gordon, Radford University Photography).

84

were no cuss words, not my name or any other, no expletives, exclamations, or bywords, no words at all that I could hear him saying. So I set out to capture what was left before it, too, disappeared.

I pictured my grandfather in a brand new plaid flannel shirt, one of the dozen bestowed on him every Christmas and at every birthday in the gray-paneled living room of a brick ranch home, with a walk-in basement and a tiny, useless front porch, miles from the 150-acres he had farmed for fifty years and the German-siding frame house he had built there. By the second week I had settled down to write about his last summer, about hot days spent mostly asleep in a recliner in front of an oscillating electric fan, in a white cotton t-shirt, slacks, and unlaced shoes, recovering each morning from a night spent back on the farm, working behind horses long dead, cradling wheat in fields grown up in woods, shouting instructions to men whose sons were gray headed.

It felt a little bit like dabbling in the occult, working out with a dot matrix Ouija board the incantation for calling my grandfather back to life. By the end of the two weeks, I thought I had succeeded. Encouraged by George Ella and Grace Toney Edwards, the long-time director of the Highland Summer Conference, I sent the finished piece, half essay and half short story to the editor of *Appalachian Heritage*, the quarterly literary journal still published by Berea College. I reread it, just now, for the first time in years. The image it holds is only a snapshot, lacking in depth, poorly composed and badly focused. Nonetheless, it still looks, to me, like my grandfather. The lines that form the image seem overwrought and self-conscious. Nonetheless, they still sound, to me, like me.

Where Are You Now, Marlos Perkos?

I didn't realize how much Floyd County had changed until the day I saw a llama in a blue nylon halter sniffing at a neighbor's potted geraniums. When I stopped for a closer look, the llama trotted on toward the main road, and I turned and drove the half mile back home to report the at-large llama, as I would have done if it were a horse or a cow. Since I didn't know who owned the farm adjoining the lot where the neighbor's trailer stood, I called the real estate agency that had recently listed and sold that property.

The realtors' receptionist knew nothing about llama ranchers, but did give me a name and phone number from the far end of the county. The new owners of the farm seemed glad that their neighbors were keeping an eye on things and promised to get word to their son, who lived on the farm and was supposed to be taking care of the llama.

Except for occasional comments from other people who saw the fugitive llama that same day, that was the last I saw or heard of it. But I still hadn't forgotten about it when I heard a few weeks later that emus had been seen running loose in our community.

I thought about the llama and wondered briefly if this might be more than coincidence. Maybe llamas and emus are the venture capitalists of the animal world. Anticipating that northward migration would be the next big trend in real estate, thanks to global warming, they might have been getting in on the ground floor, staking out prime chunks of habitat. Or perhaps continental drift had slipped up on us while all the scientists were looking up at the ozone layer.

An hour or so after being alerted about the emus I was raking dead grass and weeds along the edge of my mother's yard and looked up and saw four six-foot birds pacing nervously up and down the bank of the creek that forms the front boundary of the yard. It's pretty strange to see four grown emus, even when you're kind of expecting them, in a place where no feathered creature bigger than a twenty-pound turkey has been since the last ice age. My mother, who was helping me with the grass and weeds, said that if I hadn't been there to tell her better, she might have thought they were big turkeys, which made me think to myself that all the collie dogs and brown ponies in Indian Valley were lucky that she had never taken up rabbit hunting.

Having watched a lot of nature specials on public television, and read several Tom Clancy books, I can best describe these birds by comparing them to ostriches who had pledged their lives to an obscure and underfunded terrorist organization. Their bodies were covered with dirty grayish feathers, but their necks, beaks, heads, and legs, looked like dull black leather. Traveling late at night, these avian commandos would look like soot-smudged butterball turkeys cruising below the radar horizon.

In spite of their sinister appearance, these birds seemed harmless enough. They talked to each other with soft, inquisitive chirping noises, and if you didn't have in the back of your mind what four ordinary chickens, given enough cracked corn from a Chernobyl grain cooperative, would do to flowers or a vegetable garden, you'd want to invite them over to keep you company for awhile. And it did seem like they wanted to come and pass the time with us, but couldn't figure out how to get across the creek, even though there was a newly planked wooden bridge right in front of them. Instead, they paced up and down the far bank, like a dwindling flock of broiler hens around a bloody chopping block, trying to calm themselves by rehearsing a few steps from a beginner's class in country line dancing.

While we were watching all this, a green and white van stopped in the road about 60 yards away, sat for a minute, then backed enough to turn and come up the driveway to the house. I recognized it as the old telephone company vehicle a local tree farmer had provided for his Mexican laborers to drive back and forth to work. I leaned my pitchfork against the hood of my pickup and moved toward the van, walking slowly to give myself time to dredge up a few fragments of college Spanish. Only a few weeks before, the Spanish word for "suitcase" had popped into my head and I had used it in a sentence for my wife. She was impressed, and said she felt sure that this word must come up frequently in conversations between Spanish speaking people. She gave examples: "Gosh, I guess you'll be taking suitcases when you go on vacation next July." Or, "Manuel and I want to start saving money for the children's suitcases."

My Spanish was never very good, but I was determined to compose a greeting more sophisticated than, "Hello. How are you?" On such short notice the best I could do was, "¿Piensan que ellos son aves grandes?" I think that means, "Do you all think those are big birds?" If this went well, I would continue, "Estan muy mas grande que unas maletas, no?" I believe this means, "They are very much bigger than suitcases, wouldn't you say?"

A young man with a goatee came out the passenger side door while five other men of various ages waited inside the van. I was preparing to hit him with my big birds question when, pointing toward the four pacing emus, he asked in perfect English, "Are those yours?"

With his help I reconstructed what had probably taken place back at the Emu Ponderosa the night before or early that morning. After a short but intense argument with the four emus that were now standing by the creek, a fifth emu had decided to strike out on its own. As they were driving to work, the Mexicans had come upon the renegade emu standing alone in the middle of the road, and had jumped out and caught it and loaded it into their van. While the man with the goatee was telling me this I looked back across the creek at the legs and necks and beaks of the other four emus and asked the young man if the emu had been hard to capture. "Oh no," he said, and the men in the van nodded and smiled in agreement. From where I stood I couldn't tell if the captive emu was still in the van. The young man continued, "We can catch these others if you like." Again, the other men smiled and nodded enthusiastically.

To be honest, I did want to see how they would have organized that campaign, but it was already mid-morning and hot, and I knew they had other work to do. Plus I didn't know what to tell them to do with the emus once all five were in custody, which I was pretty sure would happen if these men made up their minds to round them up. I asked them to wait while I went inside and dialed the mother of the man on the llama farm.

I identified myself as the person who called before about the llama and asked if she was missing any emus. I was not surprised to learn that she and her husband had dropped off five emus the day before, when they had come to retrieve their llama, which I assumed without asking was the one I had seen contemplating my neighbor's geraniums.

This woman was pretty much certain that the emus were theirs, even though I hadn't given her a detailed description. She said she was glad that the Mexicans had caught one of the emus and asked me to tell them to put it back inside the gate to the property. Regarding the four still at large, she promised to call her son when he got in from work and made a point of giving me his number at the farm where the two breakouts had taken place. Before letting her go, I asked if emus were a threat to a vegetable garden. She conceded that they might be, but didn't say if there was any one thing they were especially fond of.

I told the Mexicans what the woman had said and they left us with a promise to catch the four emus if they were still around when the Mexicans finished work later that evening. Then I told my mother that the emus might eat her garden, implying that she ought to keep an eye on them while I went off to unload the grass and weeds we had piled on the back of my pickup. When I came back twenty minutes later, one of the emus had jumped a drainage ditch at the lower end of the meadow and crossed the culvert over to my parents' property. The other three had fallen into formation behind it, and struck out for an apple tree near the potato patch.

"What do you think they eat?" I asked my mother.

"Fruit, roots, and herbs," she answered, explaining that she had looked up "Emu" in *The World Book Encyclopedia* while I was gone. Forty human years is probably a very long time to an individual emu, but it's not much at all from an evolutionary perspective, so we figured that even the 1968 *World Book Encyclopedia*'s description of the diet of the emu would still be pretty accurate.

To my mind, "herbs" means parsley, sage, rosemary ... that sort of thing, which my mother didn't have except for a few dill plants in the garden and some wild peppermint along the edge of a swamp. For roots, I thought about the potatoes growing right there under the apple tree. Technically, potatoes are tubers and not roots, but I didn't expect the emus would know that since I didn't myself until a few months ago.

There were plenty of little apples on the ground and within easy reach on the tree, but we weren't surprised when the emus showed no interest, since we never ate any of the apples ourselves. The emus circled around in the fence corner while we pondered what to do, experimenting first with getting in front, and then with getting behind them, neither of which was very promising.

Maybe because their gene pool comes from below the equator, they had different concepts of in front and behind. They seemed to want to be in front when we were trying to keep them behind. When we agreed that they could go in front, they would dart and bob around enough to get behind.

The only other technique we knew to get them under control was to give them a taste of something they liked and lure them along to wherever we wanted them to go. While my mother stayed between the emus and her garden, I went back to my house for some cracked corn. I leaned over and set the bucket on the ground in front of them, but when I stood up it was behind them. I backed away and they stopped, turned around, and eyed the bucket. My plan was to get them interested, set the bucket on the tail-gate of the truck, and hope they would follow back to where they were sup-posed to be.

Two of the emus tasted the corn and moved on. The third stuck its head in the bucket and pecked around a bit, but came up empty. The fourth showed no interest at all. By this time I had decided that the birds were skit-tish but not completely wild, and might be approached if one were cautious. I thought briefly of making a grab for the smallest one, but remembered something from a PBS documentary about vicious kicking and pecking. I made a mental note to be in front of the television the next time they show a special on emus.

This train of thought led me naturally to remember Marlin Perkins, host of *Mutual of Omaha's Wild Kingdom*, which I think came on for half an hour each Sunday when I was a kid. Marlin and his assistant, Jim, would stake out an isolated water hole or salt-lick for about five minutes, then leap out of the bushes or off a low growing tree branch in front, behind, or on top of whatever dangerous animal was in the script for that week. Then they would try to subdue it, sometimes with the help of natives or a zookeeper on holiday, so a local game biologist could do some emergency surgery or attach a radio transmitter. When the biting and kicking and scratching reached a climax, the cameras would fade to a commercial where Marlin talked about accidental disability and the need to plan ahead for unfore-seen situations. When the program resumed, the animal would be tied or drugged with Jim on top of it and Marlin's hair would be all messed up. The plot of the second half of the program hinged on whether or not Jim and Marlin and the game biologist could do what they had to do before the anesthesia wore off, or some of the animal's friends got there.

Only a few years ago I heard one of the older men at home say he wished they'd put old Marlos Perkos back on the air. I wish they would too, but right then I'd have been more satisfied with a 1–800 Wild Kingdom Hotline: "If you are calling from a touch-tone phone, and are being stalked by a nocturnal carnivore, press 1 now. If you wish to speak to an operator, please hold until the next available associate can take your call. Your call is valuable to us."

But old Marlos wasn't around, and there wasn't any hotline, so I resigned myself to dealing with the situation without even the Mexicans to help. I looked again at the eight powerful legs, and the four sinewy necks topped by four fuzzy black tennis-ball heads. "Even if I could handle one of them," I thought, "four would be too many." True, the Mexicans had caught one easily enough, but there were six of the Mexicans and only one of me. And maybe they had a bucket of Purina Emu Chow in the back of the van.

So it was a standoff. But neither my mother nor I had time to sit and watch them all afternoon, so we went to get Heidi, a large, biscuit-eating German Shepherd, intending to fasten her chain to the rear bumper of my dad's pickup truck. By the time we returned the emus had disappeared, but we could hear twigs cracking in the grove of pine trees above the potato patch. Heidi sniffed around and barked a few times, then jumped up in the back of the pickup which had an eight-foot camper shell temporarily installed on its six-foot bed, giving the whole thing a very homey sort of portico-aluminum awning look.

Heidi guarded the potatoes from the back of the pickup truck all afternoon but the emus were gone. I knew that after so narrowly escaping me and my mother and Heidi, they would move cautiously, keeping out of sight of roads, risking discovery only to steal the occasional root, fruit, or herb pie cooling on a farmhouse window sill, or, in a moment of desperation, to hotwire something with good tires and a full tank of gas.

The next week the local paper ran a picture of two emus someone had trapped inside the chain link fence surrounding a cemetery about two miles from my house, with the intention of keeping them there until the owners came to claim them. If I'd had Marlos and Jim and the six Mexicans to back me up, I'd have gone and taken them into custody right away, and maybe even fitted them with radio transmitters or clipped their toenails. Since it was just me, I decided I'd better stay home and mind my own business. But I have been reading up on dingo dogs and picking out spots for the eucalyptus trees.

This essay first appeared in *Draft Horse: The Literary Journal of Work and No Work*.

Ruth B. Derrick

Fun, Terror, and Gratification

I can say with certainty that I'm one of the few fortunate folks who have been on more than one side of the Highland Summer Conference. My first experience was as an undergrad who "stumbled" into the conference serendipitously when my other summer class was cancelled. I had not heard of the Appalachian Studies Program previous to my

Ruth B. Derrick.

first HSC opportunity, so the conference was my introduction to the program, the creative writing experience, and the wonderful staff who would eventually become dear friends.

My first time as an HSC student was a mixture of glorious fun, terror, and gratification. The fun came as Silas House introduced me and my fellow classmates to the possibilities of writing fiction. The terror gripped my heart when I realized that the second week of the conference would be given to exploring and writing poetry. I had never written anything but a few awkward rhyming verses, and now I would have to produce something that others would read. Poet and teacher Cathy Smith Bowers encouraged all the students that summer, but I personally felt her teaching was a gift to me. Through her many pithy statements ("Go to the white hot center, and don't flinch") and her exploration exercises, she coaxed long-buried thoughts and emotions onto the page and helped me write a poem about a topic I had struggled for years to give voice to: the loss of my father at a young age.

I followed up year one with two more HSC stints as a student while in graduate school. Each year brought me in contact with different author-teachers, and each one enriched my life as they brought their own personality and individual style to the classroom. Darnell Arnoult worked us hard during the fiction week. We produced many pages of text, and we attempted new approaches to fiction that stretched creative writing muscles: try writing a short story using only one-syllable words! Crystal Wilkinson guided us down paths that challenged us to create characters with depth and history, and to bring those people to the page. Bill Brown and Frank X Walker helped us hone poetry skills with word and phrase acrobatics that taught us to view language in new ways and deliver that to our readers.

After three years as a student, I was a vocal cheerleader for the Highland Summer Conference. I told anyone who would listen what an amazing opportunity the HSC offered. Then my experience shifted. I joined the Appalachian Studies Program as an adjunct faculty instructor and general staff member with the responsibility of facilitating the creative writing conference which put me on the "other side," giving me a very different view of the conference. While I had many and varied responsibilities as part of this position, I also sat in on classes every summer, joined in the creative writing process, and enjoyed the benefits without having to worry about submitting work for a grade. My HSC cheerleading routine became even more enthusiastic as I told friends and students alike why the HSC was my favorite week of the year. Yes, I was working. Yes, I put in long days of set-up, cleanup, and errand-running. But I reaped the benefits, sitting in with the students and joining them in responding to numerous prompts and participating in workshop activities that propelled me to think creatively 24–7.

The conference has changed format in recent years. Two weeks of afternoon classes have been shortened to one week with class morning and afternoon. Two teachers, one focusing on fiction and one on poetry, has changed to one teacher who has published and taught in multiple genres. A strictly credit bearing experience has been opened to non-credit students. And our most recent change: moving the whole week and housing it at the beautiful Selu Conservancy (we used to spend just one day at Selu). The quiet, natural setting, removed from the hubbub of the Radford University campus, is a perfect spot for quiet reflection and releasing the flow of creative juices.

There are also things that have not changed about the Highland Summer Conference. First, the quality of teaching was and *is* outstanding. Each year, we bring highly respected, published authors to teach at the HSC. No fewer than five of the teachers over the years have been Poet Laureate of their states. These include Cathy Smith Bowers, Joseph Bathanti, and Kathryn Stripling Byer of North Carolina, and Frank X Walker and George Ella Lyon of Kentucky. Our teachers have won many awards for their works including multiple winners of the Weatherford Award for the best writing in Appalachian literature, Book of the Year for the Appalachian Writers Association, and the Sherwood Anderson Award. In general, these author-teachers bring years of classroom experience from university courses to workshops and seminars. It is indisputable that this conference offers a quality experience for the students who participate.

Another thing I have observed over the years is something I experienced my very first time as a student: the safe environment this seminar provides for newbies and veterans alike. At the time I first attended, I had no idea of the caliber of some of my fellow classmates. There was no sense that some had "arrived" while others were just getting by. We were all welcomed, and our work was given respect from the greenest of writers to those whose work was known and recognized in the creative writing world. I found out later that some of the students in my first HSC had already been published and were highly regarded. This situation is one I have seen repeated year after year. Students of all levels come together, and each one is given encouragement and the opportunity to bring their writing to a higher level. No one is esteemed above another.

Evening readings by the teachers and invited guest authors are one of the aspects of the conference that has remained constant and has provided many memorable moments. As a young inexperienced writer, I was in awe of the talent I witnessed during these presentations. As the years went along, and I attended more of these events, my respect and admiration only grew. I recall Sharon McCrumb coming with musicians who brought an added measure of entertainment. I remember an aging Jo Carson, hard of hearing and needing someone to help her during the Q&A, and yet full of energy, her spirit unflagging. George Ella Lyon read but also brought her guitar some years and sang original songs for her appreciative listeners. And I'll never forget the hush that fell over the room when Frank X Walker finished reading from his gripping work, *The Unghosting of Medgar Evers*. The poetry, written in the voices of Evers' widow and assassin, left the audience stunned and unable to speak.

Again, my experiences as both student and Appalachian Studies staff member are rich enough to fulfill all the measure of what makes the conference great in my eyes. But I also have deeply personal reasons for my gratitude. The conference introduced me to the Appalachian Studies staff: Grace Toney Edwards, JoAnn Asbury, and Ricky Cox. JoAnn eventually returned to the English Department, and a few years later, I assumed her role as HSC facilitator. When Grace retired, Theresa L. Burriss took over as Chair of the

Appalachian Studies Program and Director of the HSC. These gifted and committed individuals were amazing colleagues to work with and over the years have become dear friends.

Additionally, that initial verse I wrote in that first conference as an undergrad opened up the world of creative expression through poetry. It led to many more poems about family, childhood experience, and the depths of grief and pain. And it was the kernel for a chapbook collection called *Remnants* that I was fortunate to see published in 2017. Over the years, my experience of "sitting in" on the Highland Summer Conference helped me give voice to many personal stories and emotions, and a number of those became part of that collection. So in very tangible ways, the Highland Summer Conference changed my life.

I was fortunate to witness the Highland Summer Conference turn forty in 2017. It was fitting that Jim Minick was our teacher. Jim had been a student at the HSC in his younger days, and he had also taught at Radford University in the English Department. At that important milestone, Jim helped us witness the HSC come full circle, and I firmly believe there are many more circles to be traced.

"The Sweater"

I can't part with it.
Its history consoles me.
A garment smoothed
by many wearings
and washings.
The deep green faded,
the cloth supple in my hands.
The image often present
in my recollections of you.

So it hangs,
a sentinel.
Your other clothes are gone.
Your shirts long donated.
Your coats protecting others.
Your uniforms mothballed.

Some days,
I gather its softness,
drape it around me,
inhale its musky spice—
warmed by its memory of you.

First published in the chapbook *Remnants*, 2017.

"Taken"
(for Dad)

Borrowed.
Stolen, really
Images of you.

Me, held close in your arms.
Us, together, feeding a lamb, your gentle hand
guiding the bottle to its hungry mouth.

Box social suppers
purchased and abandoned
till you found the one
you'd spend your life
with. Your humor that left
its dimpled imprint on its listeners.
Movies missed
to avoid those sentimental tears
you easily cried.
Grandchildren longed
for but never

met. Secondhand memories
taken from the albums of others'
claimed as my own.

First published in the chapbook *Remnants*, 2017.

"Body Language—1918 Family Portrait"

The man is seeded in you, child.
Your future
is masked by pressed white knickers,
blonde curls,
and a stiff frown—
but it's all there.

Feet to dance
you to countless parties.
Eyes to flirt
girls into your arms.
A mouth to drink
your body to disease.
Hands to grasp
cold steel
and end it.

First published in the chapbook *Remnants*, 2017.

"Life Cycle"
Four Poems in One

Waves pounding the shore	balance	the turquoise numbers pulsing his heartbeat
Current teeming with vigor	gives	contrast to the ebbing of his mortal frame
Never still, ever speaking	truth	while his voice is silenced
Vibrant cerulean water	counters	eyes once bright with mischief
Breakers racing to the sand	waning	vision now dimmed by ruthless loss
Tides' relentless motion	life	marching toward a knowable end

First published in the chapbook *Remnants*, 2017.

George Brosi

Appalachian Mountain Books and HSC

I have forgotten when Appalachian Mountain Books, the traveling Appalachian bookstore that my late wife, Connie Fearington Brosi, and I created, first started coming to the Highland Summer Conference. It was probably in the 1980s. We would come for one day, a day when one of the authors was making a major evening presenta-

George Brosi.

tion. We would set up our book display so people could see how many great books were coming out of our region. We came every single year up into the two-thousand and teens.

That trip was a highlight of each year for us. The Highland Summer Conference provided us with an opportunity to be with old and dear friends, especially Grace Edwards, Ricky Cox, and JoAnn Asbury. Both JoAnn and my wife Connie, were diagnosed with the same terminal cancer, multiple myeloma, in 2012. JoAnn died in December 2013, and Connie died in June of 2015. Ricky Cox was the only person in all our travels who could be depended upon to help us load and unload our books! And Grace Edwards was the only person who ever provided travel money and a place to stay when we brought our book display to an event!

We often either came to Radford via the Blue Ridge Parkway or left that way. And we also created many different routes between our home in Berea, Kentucky, and Radford, going and coming. They included driving past the predominantly African American coal camps on U.S. 52 in West

Virginia and driving through Burke's Garden. A favorite route was Virginia 100 from Dublin to Pearisburg. Yes, I know that road runs perpendicular to a line between the two towns, but that just shows the priority we put on the scenic value over travel time, and it isn't nearly as much out-of-the-way as the Parkway is, especially when we took it all the way to or from Cherokee.

Once we got to the Conference, sometimes our book display was in the same room as the conference sessions, or in a locked room, so we would get to hear the presentations. Of course Grace Edwards was always her gracious, rather formal, always excruciatingly polite, self. But JoAnn Asbury felt no such need. I won't name names, but there was one guest speaker in particular who wasn't her favorite. Connie and I both had to restrain ourselves from falling on the floor in laughter as JoAnn, in the back of the room by our book display—how can I articulate it for this venue?—"complained" about how much extra time this presenter was taking.

One year when the sessions were not in the same room as our display—regrettably!—Connie held the fort while I held forth in a classroom the one time that Dr. Edwards asked me to give a presentation to the Conference. I felt very comfortable with the people there, having seen many of them at the Highland Summer Conference more than one year, and some at other regional conferences and celebrations over the years. My comfort level was enhanced by the fact that my dear wife—whose expectations of me were always of the highest order—was absent. I must admit that my presentation veered into a little gossip about the authors that I considered and was accentuated by a few little naughty words. Always graceful, Dr. Edwards took it all in stride. She cared deeply for Connie and our seven children and continued to pay our way to the Conference. I, however, was never again asked to say so much as one peep to the gathered Conference.

Not many people think about it, but any effort, including Appalachian Studies, requires—or at least is enhanced by—an institutional support structure. Campus Appalachian Centers like the one at Radford, now called the Appalachian Regional & Rural Studies Center, are local manifestations of this need. Their work is reinforced by additional region-wide resources. For generations, starting in 1913, the Council of the Southern Mountains provided a network and annual conference for people who cared about the region. Berea College set up its Mountain Collection of regional books and other materials the very next year, 1914. In the early 1960s, the Council set up the Appalachian Book and Record Shop near its headquarters in Berea, Kentucky, providing a place for those interested in the region to find a wonderful display of regional books and records. I first worked for the Council in 1963 and again in 1967, and I depended upon that bookstore to deepen my awareness of the region. In 1968, Cratis Williams established the W.L. Eury Collection of materials about the Appalachian Region at Appalachian

State University in Boone, North Carolina. In 1970, the Council sponsored the very first event to be called an Appalachian Studies Conference. It was held at Clinch Valley College, and I was the representative to the Council Board from the Education Commission that proposed the event. That same year, Loyal Jones became the director of the first campus Appalachian Center, located at Berea College. In 1973 *The Appalachian Journal*, a scholarly journal devoted to regional scholarship, was established at Appalachian State University. That same year, Al Stewart founded a literary magazine, *Appalachian Heritage*, designed to highlight the creative work of people in the region and sponsored by Alice Lloyd College in Kentucky. Before long, it was moved to the Hindman Settlement School nearby, and then to Berea College. In 1978 the Highland Summer Writers Conference was founded by Parks Lanier at Radford University. That same year Al Stewart founded the Appalachian Writers Workshop at Hindman Settlement School. The Appalachian Studies Association was established in 1978. It provides crucial support as a scholarly organization with an annual conference. In 1979, my late wife, Connie, and I were hired to run the Appalachian Book and Record Shop in Berea. In 1982, after the Council moved its headquarters to Clintwood, Virginia, and began preparations to establish a coal mine, we were fired and established our own book business—Appalachian Mountain Books—which carries out-of-print books as well as new books. Soon thereafter the Council bookstore went out-of-business, and the Council itself closed down in the 1980s. In 2002 I accepted a half-time position at Berea College as editor of *Appalachian Heritage*, a position I held until 2013, while continuing to keep Appalachian Mountain Books afloat.

In September of 2018, Appalachian State University held a celebration, which I attended, for the 50th anniversary of the W.L. Eury Collection of Appalachian materials, the 45th anniversary of the establishment of *Appalachian Journal,* and the 40th anniversary of the opening of their Appalachian Center.

The Highland Summer Conference is still thriving, and maintains its focus on our region, though the Appalachian Writers Workshop at Hindman no longer exclusively features regional writers. *Appalachian Heritage* no longer exclusively features the work of writers of the region. Berea College's Mountain Collection, named the Weatherford-Hammond Collection in 1964, no longer keeps up with its field nearly as well as the Eury Collection does. Appalachian Mountain Books is still going strong with a traveling book display and its own website—*apmtbooks.com*. I would argue that the support structure for Appalachian Studies currently consists primarily of the Appalachian Studies Conference, the *Appalachian Journal,* the W.L. Eury Collection, the Highland Summer Conference, and Appalachian Mountain Books.

Grace Toney Edwards, the founding Director of Radford's Appalachian Center, and Theresa L. Burriss, its current director, have been active in the Appalachian Studies Conference in many ways, including Grace's service as its chair.

Radford's Highland Summer Conference is the only writers' conference and the Radford Appalachian Center which sponsors it is the only Center which has provided travel money to Appalachian Mountain Books to attend its events. This demonstrates a singular commitment to the infrastructure of Appalachian Studies. And, of course, I personally deeply appreciate it.

Pamela Duncan

In the Blue Ridge of Virginia

In June 2010, I was lucky enough to spend a week teaching and writing in the Blue Ridge Mountains of Radford, Virginia, as part of the Highland Summer Writers Conference. The conference gave me the opportunity to work with some excellent writers in the classroom, and I got to spend time with the delightful writer Dot Jackson. It also provided an inspiring place to work on a novel set in the mountains and dealing with Appalachian identity. I met some wonderful folks there, especially Ruth B. Derrick, Ricky Cox, Theresa L. Burriss, and Parks Lanier, Jr. What I remember most fondly, though, was spending time with Grace Toney Edwards, former

Pamela Duncan.

Director of the Appalachian Regional Studies Center at Radford University, and her husband, John Nemeth, scientist, educator, and raconteur extraordinaire. I had never been to that part of Virginia, so Grace and John took me under their wings and became my tour guides. They showed me historic places like downtown Radford and the Farm at Selu. We spent an evening in Floyd, Virginia, enjoying good food, music, dancing, and people-watching at The Floyd General Store. But best of all, they welcomed me to their own beautiful home, Loch Ranchnoch, in nearby Christiansburg, Virginia.

We visited, shared stories, laughed a lot, and a friendship was born. I will always be grateful to Grace and John and to the Highland Summer Writers Conference.

Real Life

It begins on the bus, on the brink of everything possible.

Not at home in the red tarpaper house in Morgan Village where your husband works at the plant and you keep house and raise chickens and children and sometimes work at Morgan's yourself, not making furniture but in the cafeteria cooking and serving, just like at home

Not in the bedroom where you made all those babies, and this new red dress, pumping the treadle on that old Singer to make it go; the bedroom where every Saturday before you go to town you bring a pan of warm water to wash with—a bird bath, you call it; a whore's bath, your mama used to say; the bedroom where getting into this red dress takes a stout girdle, an 18-hour longline bra, and—almost—a shoehorn.

Not in the mirror as you put on your lipstick (Avon Red Velvet) and check that your wig (midnight sable), hat (a red straw Juliette cap), and clip-on earrings (the bird's nest ones with fake pearls the kids gave you for Mother's Day) are straight.

Not in the kitchen where your least girl, the only girl still home in a house full of boys, is washing the breakfast dishes before she gets on with the cleaning. Such a pretty girl, nearly fourteen, and a hard worker. But her time'll come and she'll find some man and get married and go off just like the other two, even though you'll warn her just like you did them.

Not in the living room where the oldest boy still at home has the three youngest lined up on the couch playing I Spy with My Little Eye to keep them out of the way, and because they're bored he tells them how one time he played with Grandma Calloway and she said, "I spy something starts with a A," and after they guessed and guessed every A word they could think of, she cackled, held up an orange from the fruit bowl, and said, "Ha! It's a airnge!"

Not on the front porch as you holler, "Bye!" and tell them to mind their daddy, who's down in the garden turning over the ground, getting ready for planting, unconcerned with you leaving, unconcerned with you at all since he took up with that strumpet down the road, thinking he's getting away with something, thinking what you don't know won't hurt you.

Not when you walk real slow and careful on your new red heels through the gap in the hedge, down the rock road, over the bridge, past Morgan's, and up the hill to the highway to wait by the TB hospital for the bus to Asheville.

Not when you climb on the bus and make your way to a seat without seeing a soul you know, nobody to talk your ear off, nobody wanting anything from you.

Not when you're sitting on the black vinyl seat, red leather pocketbook on your lap, eyes glued to the window, smelling sulfur and exhaust as the bus pulls away, leaving the sanitarium and the plant and Black Mountain behind.

Not when you pass through Swannanoa, Azalea, Oteen, down Tunnel Road past Buck's and Wink's and Babe Malloy's, drive-ins where the teenagers—yours included—go of a Saturday night to check the drag, which you figure means they're seeing who all else is out and about for them to get in trouble with.

Not when the bus goes in the dark hole of Beaucatcher Tunnel and comes out in downtown Asheville and stops finally at the station and you wait until everybody else has stood up and walked forward before you stand, smooth your skirt down like you have all the time in the world, and make your way to the front of the bus.

Only then, when you stop for a minute on the top step, looking out at the city like a movie star holding still to have her picture made—only then does it begin.

Now you're Ava Gardner and just like in *Mogambo* it's jungle hot already and bound to get hotter and sweat trickles down the middle of your back and out from under your sable hair and you don't care because sweat makes Ava glow.

Now you are young and beautiful and rich in the city and you walk through Belk's and Bon Marché and Winner's proud you can afford anything they've got because your money is your own and you earned it.

Now, just for something different, you have lunch at the Woolworth counter instead of going to the Grove Park and you eat chicken salad with nuts and grapes—lady food like you never had growing up in the country—and then you walk up and down the streets looking in the store windows and noticing people noticing you.

Now you try not to think about the 4:00 bus you need to catch so you can get home in time to fix supper.

Now you try not to think about changing out of your town clothes into one of the sleeveless mumus you wear around the house that makes you look like a sack of flour and has pockets full of safety pins and buttons and matches and hard candy, the mumus you make from cotton remnants bought on sale at the dime store.

Now you try not to think about how these red high heels you had no business buying are murdering your bunions, and you walk back to the bus station, go into the women's restroom, pay a nickel to get into a stall, and put each foot—shoe and all—in the toilet and flush and flush because the cold water feels so good and walking in wet shoes will stretch them out and those toilets are cleaned twice a day and who cares what people think.

Now you climb on the bus and sit in the back corner and you're Audrey Hepburn in *Roman Holiday*, royalty hiding in the riffraff, a runaway princess having a big adventure, just a little bit of freedom before you have to go back to real life.

Grace Toney Edwards

Yesterday's Voices, Today's Visions: The Power of a Teacher's Influence

Editors' Note: This essay was begun in the early 1990s in response to a prompt given in the Highland Summer Conference. As administrator and teacher of record for the HSC credit course, I always sat in the visiting author's classes and wrote as often as possible with the students. Frequently unable to finish an assignment because of other duties, I carried the beginnings of this one into a later Radford University writing retreat sponsored by the Center for Teaching Excellence. I finished it there and shared it in an internally published collection called Tales from the Classroom *(Radford University, 1993).*

Remember those fold-down wooden seats that we sat on as kids in schoolrooms of the 1950s? Each one was attached to a writing surface and desk compartment behind the seat so that the child who sat on the seat had to work on the surface of the desk in front of him. Perhaps some sense of community developed as a result of two children sharing parts of the same piece of furniture. Of course, in today's thinking, the students and teacher were disadvantaged by the linear row arrangement, necessary in order for the concept to work. Recently I saw one of those old desks in a friend's tastefully decorated study; the desk appeared to be right at home, and well it should, for my friend lives in a converted schoolhouse, much like the one I remember so vividly from my North Carolina childhood. As I stood gazing at Roberta's desk, with its seat carefully folded up, a strident voice rang in my ear: "All aboard, children. This train leaves in one minute!"

It was the voice of Mrs. Wilson, my fourth-grade teacher. Her favorite subject, and therefore mine too, was geography. She worked magic on those little wooden seats and in the heads of those little country boys and girls. Seated in twosomes on the fold-down wooden boards, we felt them transform into the plush, upholstered armchairs of trains, planes, cruise ships, automobiles, and even rickshaws to take us all over the world.

105

Wilma Dykeman and Grace Toney Edwards (courtesy Radford University).

Mrs. Wilson always had us sit in the rows nearest the tall, multi-paned windows so that we could look out of our transporter, whatever it might be, to see the sights outside. Never mind that in reality we gazed on the same giant cedar tree, the same green grass, the same little store that were permanently rooted there. In her mind's eye, and therefore in ours, we spotted slow-moving anteaters and upside-down sloths hanging from tree branches. We heard strange drums echoing through the jungle and glimpsed a fleet-footed native. We marveled at the mighty Amazon. From our lofty second-floor perch, we surveyed the rain forests below us. We checked out the beans of the cacao tree to learn where our much-loved chocolate came from. We were explorers, roaming far and wide to study the world's wonders. To enhance our vision, she hung colorful travel posters around the room, but the major prop, and the only one we really needed, was Mrs. Wilson's imagination, which fired our own.

As I consider Mrs. Wilson's influence in my own teaching, I realize that she whetted my curiosity to see and know people, places, and cultures from around the world. She pushed against the walls of that schoolroom and urged us to flee the insularity of our little community. I did—again and again by her side. What makes her gift even more special is that she was herself physically limited. Standing scarcely more than four feet tall, she suffered partial deafness and spoke with a noticeable lisp—but as she captained our ship or engineered our train, those impairments disappeared through the same magical transformation that happened to our wooden seats.

Mrs. Wilson's cultivation of the imagination in geography class prepared me well for Mrs. Hamrick's promotion of reading and writing in the seventh grade. A lover of books herself, she read to us each day after lunch, a chapter a day, from classics like *Giants of the Earth, The Adventures of Huckleberry Finn, Anne of Green Gables*. Though we were fully capable of reading those books for ourselves, she believed in the value of reading aloud, of sharing orally in a community of learners the experience of the printed page. That activity quickly became my favorite part of the school day; I waited for it with great anticipation. In fact, it spilled over into my home life, for I was a "walker"—that is, I walked to and from school and also went home for my midday meal. Because our reading session came right after lunch, I was always racing to get home, gobble my soupbeans and cornbread, and race back so as not to miss a single word from Mrs. Hamrick's melodious reading voice. I was apt to dash out the kitchen door with fried apple pie in hand, devouring one dessert from Mama's kitchen while en route to an even more lasting one.

Mrs. Hamrick used the oral reading as a starter for our own writing. She assigned us to write stories that took off from an episode in the novel she was currently reading to us, or she had us to rewrite a scene that we especially liked or disliked. She invited us to create our own fictions—and made us believe we could. I remember that one of my stories had to do with freed slaves working on a Southern farm (wishful thinking on my part, no doubt—I grew up on a small farm where the only workers were my parents, my siblings, and I!). One day during the after-lunch reading session, Mrs. Hamrick read my story aloud to the class, complimented it lavishly, and remarked especially on the appropriateness of the names I had chosen for my characters.

I don't remember what John Paul and Martha Ellen plotted in that seventh-grade story, but I recall very clearly that they carried their author to a moment of glory, thanks to Mrs. Hamrick. Through her nurturing she offered me confidence in my own abilities to create a fiction that might entertain in the same way that the classic novels entertained each day after lunch. She opened the door just wide enough so that I could see the possibility of entering the world of books I loved so well.

That love carried me through high school and into college into, quite appropriately, an English major. The voice that resounds in my ear from those days belonged to Dr. Cratis Williams, who gave me the gift of my own culture, although I didn't recognize what he was giving me until I had finished college and was well into my teaching career.

Dr. Williams was an American literature teacher from an Appalachian background, the Big Sandy region of East Kentucky, to be exact. He loved every piece of good writing—and some bad—if it told a good story. The oral stories and ballads of his own past greatly enhanced his ability to bring to life literature on the printed page. He was as apt to break into the keening notes of a Scottish border ballad as to declaim the revered verses of Bobby Burns, or of Edgar Allan Poe. His greatest love, though, was to teach about his own people; he considered himself "100% Appalachian." And he made it his life's work to tell the story of Appalachian folkways, of Appalachian literature, and to connect his story—always—to the larger American and global stories.

The gift he gave to me was two-fold: first, the model of his own teaching, which included comprehensive knowledge, genuine care and consideration for his students, and his belief that all students are capable, eager, and industrious. Beyond that, he was simply a charming person, easy to know and like. The second gift he gave was of greater magnitude than I can yet measure: a direction for my career and my life. He showed me the riches in my own culture, the hunger that others have to share in those riches, and the ways that I might help to feed those hungers. It is Cratis Williams, then, that I must thank for the joys I have experienced over the past fifteen years and more* in my pursuit of Appalachian Studies.

Not until the writing of this essay did I see linkages among the three teachers I have just eulogized, but today I recognize that their influences come together every day in me as I teach my own students and chart a course for each day's existence. To Mrs. Wilson I am grateful for curiosity to know the exterior world and for imagination to visualize and conceptualize

---

Now, more than forty years!

it; to Mrs. Hamrick I am grateful for the wonderful interior world of read-ing and writing, for a means of making sense of that which I imagine and conceptualize; to Dr. Williams I am grateful for the legitimizing of my own culture, for the treasures he showed me in my own backyard, for the path he pointed me to and the walk he shares with me daily. These legacies have followed me into my own classroom, and with a little luck, they'll go out again—into other classrooms, other lives. "All aboard, children. This train leaves in one minute!"

Robert Gipe

Words from Robert Gipe

Editors' Note: In 2015 Robert Gipe came to the Highland Summer Conference as an evening speaker. He joined Rita Sims Quillen, who was the workshop leader for that week. Gipe read from his first novel, Trampoline, *published earlier that year by Ohio University Press. This illustrated novel features the author's own pen and ink sketches which become part of the text. His sequel novel follows a similar pattern of illustrations; called* Weedeater, *it is a continuation of Dawn Jewel's and eastern Kentucky's contemporary stories, published in 2018 by Ohio University Press. OU Press has now published his third novel in the trilogy entitled* Pop. *He has generously contributed a segment from that work for this collection.*

Robert Gipe.

In an email to the editors of this book, Gipe remembers his evening at the HSC.

I enjoyed talking with Rita Quillen's students while at Radford in the summer of 2015. And so did my mother. She came with me to the workshop. It was very reassuring to have her there. I believe my niece and nephew came to the reading that night. Rita and everyone at Radford made me and my whole family welcome. A lot of places would have made them wait outside in the vehicle. But not Radford. That's what I appreciate about Radford.—RG

The Hide-Behinds

Hubert told me about the hide-behinds. Told me they only move in the pitch dark. Only move when you stop moving. When you're in the pitch dark, it's hard to keep moving. It's hard to stop. But when you stop, that's when the hide-behinds come out and get you. Eat you up.

Hubert said when a hide-behind gets ahold of you, they're nice about it. Apologize for crushing your neck, act sad the whole time they're devouring your flesh. Hubert said he caught a hide-behind one time, kept it on a leash. Said they'd holler all night, make it rough on you to sleep, pore old hide-behind.

I told that man had the TV show about the hide-behinds. He come up on the ridge with his cameras, made a show of us. We saw the show. Said I was a witch. Said I made a pop had a spell on it. Said it was the best pop ever made.

They said when you drank my pop, you only wanted one. Said when you mixed it with liquor, you only drank one or two drinks and you didn't want no more. They said I done that cause I wanted people to not drink so much pop, not get sugar, not be such drunks. They said I was trying to get people to be healthier, that I was a good witch, a mountain angel, but with a pisspoor business model.

They said I was in congress with ghosts. They said I lived wild. That I lived inside a tree trunk. That I was a feral girl. That meant I didn't have no raising. Which of course is ridiculous. Which of course hurt Momma's feelings.

They said my business model was flawed cause people'd drink way more of my pop if it didn't have a spell on it. Cause it is delicious pop. Comes in all the good old mountain flavors. Sassafras. Honey straight from the beegum. Sorghum and wintergreen, honeysuckle and jellico. I mix it so it don't taste too weird. Unless you want it to taste weird and then it does. That's part of the witchery. It tastes the way you want it to. That's what that man said on his television show.

He said my pop is special, like pop used to be, when they called it sodey-dope, when a kid might grow up and never have a pop to theirselves their whole childhood. Which I think is cool.

But people said the problem is I wouldn't never need no trucks with pictures of my pop on the side, bottles laying sideways in piles of ice cubes big as bales of hay. People said I wouldn't need no dudes in Timberlands and short shorts needing help through the store door cause they were packing carts with big huge stacks of my pop. They'd said I'd be small time till the day coming soon when I'd be out of business, to which I didn't pay much attention cause I just like making pop. I like walking through the woods hunting pop ideas. I like wood walking and smelling things—I like little brown jug. I'm thinking right now about how to make a pop out of little brown jug—one you could tell from root beer, which little brown jug puts some people in mind of.

That talk about money and how we weren't going to make any—it flew all over my girl Pinky. She burned herself up thinking about how we was gonna make money. It was her decided I was going to call my pop Feral Girl. It was her decided I was going to do things exactly the way I wanted to, that I was going to make a butt ton of money, that I was going to do it my way, and that me and her was gonna sit on our money mountain and eat popsicles and smoke cigars and tell all them people to kiss our foot.

So off Pinky went. She got this boy she knew up Drop Creek to start drawing pictures for the bottles and the t-shirts and the billboards. She got him to draw a comic book based on the legend of the Feral Girl. Which Pinky wrote. She sat at Tilda's kitchen table and read it to me as she made it up, and Tilda would turn the TV down when I couldn't hear and I'd tell Pinky it was perfect even when sometimes I hadn't quite made out what she said.

* * *

One time I took Pinky out gathering with me. We was in this cloud of honeysuckle billowing up both sides of a red rope of dirt trail that snaked back away from the river.

I said, "Pinky, watch out for snakes."

She said, "Always."

The honeysuckle vines tangled around sassafras and pine, kudzu and tulip poplar, and Pinky'd waded off into that mess, snake-fearless and whistling. I couldn't bear the thought of Pinky hurt, or poisoned, and I said, "You know what, Pinky? We don't need the whole vine. What we need is them blossoms."

She said, "Don't matter. This is the last time I'm coming out here with you anyway."

I said, "What?"

She said, "I'll be in the office making money."

I said, "What office?"

Pinky said, "Our office. The Feral Girl office. With its file folders full of orders set in metal cabinets. Shipping invoices, accounts receivable, me lording over ever bit of that shit."

Pinky yanked a stretch of vine taut above her head, took her hog sticker lock blade, cut the vine loose, jammed the whole thing down in the big black garbage bag she had strung by a shank of clothesline across her shoulder.

I said, "Why aint we gonna keep all that on the computer?"

She said, "We are gonna keep it on computer. But we gonna keep it on paper too. Cause we aint bullshitting, Nicolette. We gonna show them dingleberries we aint scared of money."

I went to pinching off honeysuckle blossoms.

Pinky said, "That's right, aint it?"

I said, "What?"

Pinky said, "That we aint scared of making money."

I said, "I don't reckon."

Pinky said, "I aint scared one bit of it." Said, "I aint scared of nothing."

When I told Pinky me and Hubert had killed my uncle Colbert cause he tried to hurt me, cause he tried to "make a woman out of me," you know what Pinky said? She said,

"Yeah. I got uncles." And when I told Pinky I thought I was ready to go back to my house, that I was ready to sleep by myself, you know what she said? She said, "Aint no point to that."

I said, "Pinky, you scared of sassafras?"

She said no.

I said, "Get it, too."

Pinky mashed up a sassafras leaf like I'd showed her how to do, and smelled of it.

She said, "Mmm. That's good smack." Pinky slapped her neck, said, "Bugs eating me up."

I said, "Smoke your cigar."

She took out the skinny cigar Tilda gave her, had a plastic mouthpiece made it look like a child's whistle. Pinky struck her lighter, fired it up, stood there smoking. Stood there not gathering honeysuckle, not gathering sassafras.

She said, "You want this?"

She held the cigar out. I took it, said, "Too strong for you?"

She said, "There's things worse than bugs."

She picked and I picked, quiet for a while. The cigar smoke smelled good to me, reminded me of listening to old records with my papaw Houston, sitting behind the counter with Hubert at the store.

Pinky said, "Why don't you put that thing out?"

I did, asked her why.

Pinky said, "I hate them things," slapped her arm, said, "I'm going back."

Pinky put her headphones on, didn't hear me say, "What happened?"

And so it was I was out there, pinching blossoms, to the very edge of pitch dark.

Richard Hague

Jesus of the Hills

In what legendary Appalachian writer and mentor Gurney Norman says "belongs on any list of the greatest one hundred American poems of all time," the speaker of Jim Webb's "Get In, Jesus" is hitchhiking not far from Virgie, Kentucky, when he is picked up by some boys in an old Chevy. "Get in, Jesus," they say, grinning, and the long-haired, bearded hippie leaps into the back seat. He is welcomed, offered some cheap wine, which he trustingly sips without wiping the bottle, and generally has a good time as they travel down the road, alternately joking and seriously discussing what it is like to be Jesus. The speaker realizes "A body could do worse,/bein Jesus might be/ better'n I'll be." It is a just and sobering realization.

Richard Hague.

Apropos of this situation is a theological term I stumbled upon once, undefined, just floating out there in the cloud of discourse I have stumbled through for roughly seven decades. This term is a mouthful, and certainly a head-full, and I have resisted doing any homework. It is so powerfully evocative to me that I don't want to risk emptying it of its power by knowing too much about it. And since the context of the term is always religious, pertaining to Jesus, a bit of mystery and uncertainty feels right.

The phrase is "the scandal of particularity."

It has named for me the cost

of believing in the humanity of Jesus, because with that comes the burden (to some, the *scandal*) of the fact that the Divine arrived and dwelt, as a human, among us. To be human means to be subject to injury and disease: the baby Jesus might have caught the mumps. The boy Jesus possibly had acne. The young man Jesus experienced nocturnal emissions. The mature Jesus may have felt the stirrings of sexual desire. To some, this exact, particular humanity of Jesus is unacceptable. It's scandalous, dangerous to faith and belief, to entertain the notion that Jesus may have undergone nightmares, or sleeplessness, or diarrhea. But we have no such hesitation in believing that the mature Jesus, man-God, was, like some common upstart radical, nevertheless detained, beaten, stabbed, pierced, mocked, spat upon, and finally executed.

Difficult as it is, "the scandal of particularity" seems to me to be the very heart of the Christian mystery. Jesus came as a living embodiment of God's love for humankind, while at the same time subject to all "the slings and arrows of outrageous fortune" that Shakespeare's flawed Hamlet (and the rest of us mortals) have had to endure. I speak here not as a theologian, God knows, but as a writer: Jesus was God's way of entering his own creation and understanding it, actually experiencing it, first hand. The original Creator in *Genesis* looked down upon his work and saw that it was good. But is it too outrageous to wonder whether or not He had to come down from up there ("the Word was made flesh and dwelt among us") and be incarnated as Jesus to fully comprehend what He Himself had wrought? That He had to get down and funky, had to eat his bushel of dirt, had to know pain and hunger and rage in order to fully realize Himself (and therefore realize what it is to be us?)

So when three writers, myself and two others, all of us friends and of a similar age, and all associated with Appalachian literature, turned to writing poems about Jesus, we risked being misunderstood, thought of as loutish, blasphemous disbelievers—accused of causing scandal ourselves.

For example, not long ago, I had occasion to bring Jim Webb's "Get In, Jesus" to what just happened to be an all-female poetry class in a small denominational college in northern Ohio. I read the poem aloud to them. When I got to where the boys in the car ask Jesus, "what's it like to be/ hung up/ on a cross?" and Jesus answers, "It ain't for shit," the backs of many of the young women stiffened. The room tingled with silent vibes of disapproval.

But to my way of thinking, we have somehow to get our heads around the possibility that Jesus, the actual Jesus, would have said this, not just Jim Webb the poet, not Jim Webb the hirsute hippie, but Jesus himself, his jeans covered in dust, his lips still wet with the cheap wine from a just-shared jug, his actual being in that road-wise old car, that actual hot afternoon near the Kentucky-Virginia line. "The willing suspension of disbelief which constitutes the poetic faith," as Coleridge put it, requires me not only to affirm the humanity of Jesus but also to believe this: Jesus was not out of touch with the poor and working men and women: he was as deeply embedded in their world as surely as were spitting camels and the stink of Galilee fish. Jesus spoke these people's truths and cared for their hearts, and celebrated the dailiness of life with them. Jim Webb's poem is the latest Gospel news, arriving from where the incarnated Jesus lives and speaks.

Of my own contribution to this body of contemporary Jesus poems, I have little to say other than a thank you to Jim Webb, and then to Michael Henson, for establishing the poetic space into which I humbly stepped with my poem "Jesus H. Christ," which begins with an apology for the blasphemous, cursing way it is titled. But as poetic disciples of a tangible, earthly and earthy Jesus, I hope we have done as Hasidic tradition believes is the work of humans: to assist in the Creation. Dragging Jesus back from the clichéd and commercial sanitized versions, from the pink-and-turquoise clouds under the ascending, white-skinned, blue-eyed Jesus, we scruffy poets reclaim him. We are the boys in the pickup ourselves; we stop and invite him in, bedraggled, thirsty, soon-to-be blood-stained, thorn-scarred, stabbed, strung up on a tree.

Michael Henson's "The True Story of the Resurrection" is, I think, the most audacious of these contemporary Jesus poems. Its wicked satire cuts in several directions, risking censure from those who acutely feel "the scandal of particularity" in the religious context, and those whose values, habits, and capitalistic addictions are sledge-hammered by Henson's far-reaching cultural indictment. In his poem, Jesus has been abducted on the third day of his entombment by a vast corporation

> consisting of cosmetologists,
> kinetic specialists,
> Biblical scholars,
> and some very sharp marketing minds.

They conspire to pull off "the most stunning makeover of all time." They appropriate the great mystery and wonder of the Resurrection and transform it into a marketing opportunity, intending to present the resurrected Jesus as a "brand." Thus, to appeal to the widest possible market, they have to take off all his edges—"they cut off the beard (of course)/then trimmed the hair, and gave it a little shape/ then a nose job to make him look a little less ethnic."

Henson's satire turns even more sharp as this modern, sanitized Jesus nevertheless begins to subvert the terms of his brand. "And if they didn't watch him close, he was gone." "Fishing," he told them as they cleaned him up. "I went fishing with my friends.'"

The Fisher of Men, the calmer of the stormy waters of Galilee, the radical advocate of the poor and the outcast, the dismisser of Philistines and letter-of-the-law conservatives, is re-emerging. This terrifies the marketers and their insidious combine. "They had to bail him out of jail one night/ for doing the woe-unto-ye thing/ on the steps of city hall." Soon, He was out to ruin it all unless they could get him under control.

In 21st century America, Jesus in his original state is unacceptable—too unpredictable, too "crazy," too revolutionary. So in the poem's terrible ending, the Jesus of the New Testament, God become man, undergoes the ultimate correction. The marketers do the

> only thing they knew would work.
> They fetched him back to the Golgotha mall.
> They built a new cross
> and they nailed him down again.
> And again.
> And again.

What would Jesus do? wonders a recent facile question in popular culture. Henson's poem produces a sharper, more pertinent question—What would *we* do if Jesus appeared again among us? What would our crass, co-opting, profiteering, divisive, bullying society do? Henson's hypothetical answer is devastating. Jim Webb suggests we'd stop and pick Jesus up along the road, share cheap wine, ask respectful questions—*empathize*. My own poem suggests that Jesus might catch on to the fact that we are tempted to want to demean his presence among us, and so He hides in the woods. "Next thing you know,/they'll want him on the school board or for scoutmaster/ or judge of the sheep competition at the county fair." By the end of the poem, the speaker knows there are more consequential things Jesus could do for us:

> fix the sky and rivers and air.
> Keep the poor poor but comfortable,
> teach the rest of us to live like them.
> With holy dread,
> he could lead the Great Eating of the Rich,
> the transubstantiation
> of the world.

But "The True Story of the Resurrection" imagines—if love and justice in the particular form of Jesus promise to reign on earth—what we might do, woe unto us, again. And again. In these times of immigration and asylum resistance, the systematic transfer of wealth to the rich, the dismantling of environmental protections, the demonizing of the innocent, the scandal is what *we*, not Jesus, are doing. *(June–October 2018)*

Postscript

The three poems discussed, "Get in Jesus," (*Get In, Jesus: New & Selected Poems* by Jim Webb, ed. Scott Goebel, Wind Publications, 2013),

"The True Story of the Resurrection," (*The True Story of the Resurrection*, Wind Publications, 2014) and "Jesus H. Christ," (*Public Hearings*, Word Press, 2009), all of which were published much earlier in journals, further incandesce when read with "Parabolic," by David Armstrong, a short story with a similar premise—Jesus returned to the present day. It recently won the 2017 fiction contest sponsored by *Slippery Elm Literary Journal*. (One of the little miraculous blessings arising from pairing this story with the three Jesus poems was learning that Armstrong teaches at—of all the most impossibly perfect places—the University of the Incarnate Word, in San Antonio, Texas.)

My Week

My week at the 2018 Highland Summer Writer's Conference was as satisfying as any I have attended or staffed. The participants were an inter-generational group, some boarders, some day-trippers, all willing to work hard. There was the added delight of being able to introduce a few essential Appalachian writers to them, and to draw from them responses to Appalachian literature and to their own lives as citizens of the region. The final reading of work drafted during the week was inspiring, and many participants vowed to become more active writers and members of the Appalachian literary community. For me, it's always a gauge of good luck when I get some new writing myself while working with others; the essay I include above is the direct result of a study we embarked on at one point during the week and which connected to the various "alliances"—with, among other things, "the religious traditions, human families and communities, and the essential stories and songs" Wendell Berry insists we form. These alliances served as the touchstone concept throughout the week. For all, I am grateful.

Heidi Hartwiger

There Is No Such Thing as Too Much Garlic

Whether on purpose or by accident those stepping from the elevator on the third floor of Norwood Hall encountered a laminated sign which said, "THERE IS NO SUCH THING AS TOO MUCH GARLIC." This was the portal, the sacred entry into the creative space belonging to a colony of vibrant Appalachian writers known as The Selu Sisters. We set aside two weeks of every summer for sixteen years to gather at Radford University for the Selu Writers Retreat named for Selu, the Cherokee corn mother and fertility goddess.

Heidi Hartwiger.

Yes, I was a deer in the headlights the first time I walked into Norwood Hall with my suitcase and Smith Corona typewriter. Parks Lanier, the retreat sponsor, greeted me, and my amazing journey began. My corner room turned leafy bower as I gazed into the sheltering pine waiting for other writers to arrive. Would these Appalachian writers who probably knew each other be my people? I answered their question I prayed would come. "We know where you live, but where are you from?" Yes, they were my people! Although I live in Yorktown, Virginia, I am from West Virginia, the other side of the mountain. My strength is nonfiction, yet I challenged myself to write a novel. I was among poets and fiction writers honing their craft. They encouraged me.

Our group connected on so many levels. Together we celebrated births, deaths, marriages, successes and rejections. To this day we remain loyal and beloved Selu Sisters. Darnell Arnoult, Tamara Baxter, Judy Miller, Isabel Zuber and I were there from the beginning. Poet Bill Brown joined us and became an honorary Selu sister. We welcomed Parks Lanier as our Selu Sister.

Through the years a number of dedicated writers joined us when they could. Chelsea Adams, Evelyn Bales, Harry Dean, Dianne Jordan, and Jeanne Shannon became Selu Sisters. As an assortment of creative souls, we did our best to bring a modicum of structure to our days. We wrote, we walked, and oh my, did we enjoy our meals! Twice a week we made ourselves presentable and went to the evening readings at the Highland Summer Conference.

As the first Selu Writers Retreat ended, the Appalachian Writers Conference began right there at Radford University. Since herbs were a key component in my novel, I searched for herb books among the booksellers. It was there I met Jerry Bledsoe of Down Home Press, and my writing life took off. I asked him if he had anything about herbs. I was stunned by his reply. He thought I was proposing a book about herbs. I went back to the Selu Sisters. We sat up into the wee hours as they helped me brainstorm an herb book idea.

Jerry Bledsoe's response to my idea was, "Send me a chunk." I sent him a chunk in September, and he requested the entire book. By February he had *A Gift of Herbs* manuscript. He located an illustrator. We were in business. Legendary Dot Jackson was his editor, and we began a long friendship. *A Gift of Herbs* (Down Home Press 1993) was the first Down Home Press book to receive national acclaim. *The Herb Quarterly* and *Herb Companion* reviewed the book. It became a 1995 Rodale Book Club selection. Then came *All Join Hands: The Forgotten Art of Playing with Children.* (Down Home Press 1994) Pleased with this book as well, Jerry called it "ever green." *All Join Hands* gave me credibility when I proposed my Natural Parent~Natural Child monthly series which has appeared in OVParent, a WV parenting magazine for over twenty years. The Selu Sisters helped me write the proposal for the first article.

In my leafy bower at Norwood Hall the idea for another nonfiction book, *Keeper of the Stories* (Parkway Publishing, Inc. 2002), was born. It was a guide for older beginning writers. To this day I use the book as a valuable resource for my family stories course offered to older beginning writers in Christopher Newport University's LifeLong Learning Society.

During various summers I began rough drafts for Appalachian themed novels, *The Secrets of Indian Knob* (Frog Hollow Press 2001) and *Fire in Progress* (PublishAmerica 2012). I spent many happy hours researching in McConnell Library. Little did I know that years later I would be invited by

Grace Toney Edwards and librarian Gene Hyde to archive my work in the Appalachian Collection at the very library I called my home away from home. I never dreamed when I began my literary odyssey twenty-six years ago among the Selu Sisters I would earn a place at the table among Appalachian writers I so greatly respect.

Meeting James Still was on my Appalachian writers wish list. That never happened. However, Parks Lanier shared his James Still stories with me. Parks also spoke many times over the years about the writer, Marilou Awiakta. I nearly gave up hope at meeting this legend. Then came exciting news. Marilou Awiakta would read at the HSC. Everything I had learned about her was truth before my eyes.

Early in the days of our retreat at one HSC evening reading, I had the pleasure of meeting Jim Wayne Miller. His health was failing, yet he managed to be an engaging pen pal. Sharyn McCrumb became my advisor on how to keep smiling until your face is stiff at book signings. One evening I was invited along with some others to Sharyn's home. We discussed a plotting issue frustrating her in one of her Ballad series books. That experience was a priceless writing lesson.

Listening to George Ella Lyon kindled my interest in writing for children. My current work for younger children is *The Incredible WOW Factor Women*. These are stories about six Colonial American women who lived quietly until called upon to use inner resources to remedy a situation. A national publisher suggested that it would be of regional not national interest. That's okay! I am a Selu Sister and an Appalachian writer with perseverance.

Another Appalachian writer with perseverance was the late Tennessee poet Jo Carson. During an HSC I was invited to have supper one evening with Jo Carson. Although her hearing was failing, we had a conversation that I think about to this day. I teach in a place called Yoder Barn. Christopher Newport University acquired a tract of land from the Yoder family, Mennonite dairy farmers. After the dairy closed, the barn was converted into a Mennonite church. Then CNU converted the barn to classrooms. During dinner I shared with Jo Carson that I was currently teaching in the milking room of a barn. Some milking apparatus still hung from the ceiling. She asked the location then smiled. "Upstairs is a large auditorium with a stage," she said. In the course of conversation I learned that she wrote living history dramas for communities. She had been right there in the Yoder barn a number of times gathering Mennonite stories. Sometimes while I am teaching, especially my "Keeper of the Stories" class, I feel Jo Carson's presence. It is a powerful moment for me to share her *Stories I Ain't Told Nobody Yet*. Although she is gone from this earth, her essence remains with me in the barn.

Since I am a member of the Advisory Council for CNU's Annual Writers Conference, I am often tasked to find quality presenters. Because of my HSC connection, I knew Jim Minick, Virginia poet, novelist, and memoirist. His memoir workshops are real crowd pleasers for our conference-goers. Both Jim and Bill Brown, another conference favorite, have sewn unforgettable literary seeds during their workshops and talks at CNU's Annual Writers Conference, just as they have at the Highland Summer Conference.

There is a standing request by local poets and writers for Bill's poetry workshops so he has been with us several times. Scheduled for a February CNU Writers Conference, Bill and Suzy, his wife, arrived a day early ahead of a big snow storm. The snow came. Restaurants, groceries, gas stations … everything was closed. When we found that their quaint motel on the York River would not be serving meals because the cook couldn't get to work, I invited them to dinner. My husband's trusty Ford 150 made it through the snow. The Browns are gracious people. I knew they would be satisfied with a warm meal, but I wanted this to be a spectacular meal. We would be serving supper to the Selu Sister chef extraordinaire. Thank goodness we had a well stocked freezer. For me the Selu Sister magic transcended years and miles during that snowy afternoon and evening by our cheery fire.

So what exactly is Selu Sister magic? Although we were writers, we were also eaters. As a rule I put on the morning coffee and went for a walk before the others were up. Bill Brown went running. Dianne Jordan acquired our morning newspaper. As we lingered over breakfast, Bill came in from his run to report ideas for half a dozen poems, and literary magic began. Our daily culinary magic started around 4 p.m. When it was Bill's night to fix supper, the Selu Sisters were oh so happy to savor the aromas coming from the tiny kitchen. He planned his menu, did the shopping, and all the preparation. One occasion he discussed his concern with garlic in a particular dish. Isabel sat up very straight, adjusted her glasses, peered at us and then at Bill. She said with great dignity, "There is no such thing as too much garlic." We gave her the Selu Sister salute.

Two notable writers dined with us while they were part of HSC. Katherine Stripling Byer took many meals with us and offered me a special friendship which lasted until she was called home. The night Silas House came to dine with the Selu Sisters the stories flowed. I am thrilled that I shared a meal and also my family zucchini bread recipe with the young writer on the cusp of Appalachian greatness.

While Bill was a fish and pasta chef, Tamara Baxter was top chef concerning all things chicken. All her recipes she carried in her head. In the tiny Norwood Hall kitchen she could prepare a full Sunday dinner. One of her specialties was roast chicken with lemon, garlic, and rosemary. We coveted her chicken curry. Of course with all these good meals, we had leftovers. Isabel was the mistress of leftovers. We often commented that she could prepare an entire meal with a half a cup of leftovers. Every Selu Sister had a role. Darnell added her culinary magic with amazing hors d'oeuvres for our social hour. She could stretch an avocado and a tomato into sumptuous garlicky dips and spreads. Judy and I were the cleanup crew.

On evenings without HSC readings, we strolled the beautifully landscaped campus. After writing all day, we needed companionship. It is a good thing our conversations never moved beyond the sealed lips of the Selu Sisters. Sometimes our retreat coincided with the Summer Solstice. One summer we moved about the campus after dark with candles which were strictly forbidden in the dorm. With glowing candles and a bag of corn we strolled to the fountain in the center of campus. Our ritual we dedicated to Selu, the corn goddess. We planted our corn in the flower beds that encircled the fountain. We don't know if a single kernel germinated, but we could dream. Another Summer Solstice we again strolled the campus with glowing candles. Our destination was The Nest of Life. Evidently this huge dome woven from sticks was a student project which received awards and much acclaim. People tucked messages and wove flowers, herbs, and other memorabilia into the structure. I believe there were five Selu Sisters standing with flickering candles in the Nest of Life. The lightning bolt struck us simultaneously. If we weren't careful, in a heartbeat the Nest of Life could become an inferno. We carefully departed, and the stick structure survived our Solstice visit.

The Selu Writers Retreat is in the rearview mirror now, but the Selu Sisters remain connected in spirit. Sometimes as I shuck corn, I thank the corn goddess. When I break open a garlic bulb and too many little cloves spill out, I smile and think of my Selu Sisters. It's true. There is no such thing as too much garlic.

An Incredible WOW Factor Woman

Editors' Note: The following, a story from history about a colonial woman, Ann Wager, is written for young readers.

In 1716 Williamsburg, Virginia, was a prosperous town under British rule. By the late 1760s many people grumbled about strict British laws. Rumors of higher taxes swirled. Some people worried, and others did not.

Nevertheless people continued the daily routine. They went to church on Sunday. Early every week morning they shopped at the Market Square for fresh eggs, meat, fruits and vegetables.

Many rich, educated men became ministers or lawyers. Wealthy and middle class women organized the household, embroidered beautiful linens, and served elegant meals. If a woman became a widow, her world turned upside down. How would she support her children? If she were lucky and had a formal education, she could teach.

Suppose a tragedy happened to you? How would you support your family? Would you choose to earn lots of money teaching fancy dressed children of wealthy Williamsburg families? Or would you rather make a little bit of money teaching raggedy children of enslaved parents? In this story set in 18th century Williamsburg before the Revolutionary War you will discover the choice Ann Wager made.

Ann Wager 1716–1774

She could embroider beautiful shawls, she could serve delicious meals, and she could read. At this time it was usually just boys who could read, write, and cipher. Ann's father made sure she was as educated as any boy. Then a sad day happened. Ann's husband died. Now she must make a plan to support her family. With her good education she became a teacher. Sometimes she taught the wealthy children in their homes. Other times students came to her home for lessons.

One particular afternoon the little boys had gone home, and Ann was relieved that school day was over. Shadows of night began creeping across the road. As Ann lit some candles, her heart flip-flopped a bit. Mary, her grownup daughter, had not returned from the daily errands. "Where is that girl?" She listened for the familiar clip clop of horses' hooves and the creaking carriage wheels on the cobblestone street. As she scrubbed and chopped potatoes and carrots for tonight's stew, she thought about a school problem. "I need a better way to teach Psalm 23. I can't get beyond saying, 'The Lord is my shepherd' without the boys leaping and baa-baaing like sheep. This behavior is getting on my nerves."

At last Ann heard Mary's voice rising above the clatter of the carriage wheels. "Mother… Mother…" Mary shouted and waved from the carriage. Wiping her hands on her apron, Ann hustled to open the door. This was unlike Mary to be so loud. Mary didn't wait for the carriage driver to put the carriage step in place. Leaving the parcels in the carriage, she lifted her blue woolen skirt above her shoes and jumped to the cobblestones. With her brown eyes as round as saucers she grabbed her mother's hands. "I stopped by William Hunter's Print Shop to pick up your order and something unbelievable happened!"

"Whatever it was must have been more exciting than watching Mr. Hunter set type for the next issue of the *Virginia Gazette*."

"He had a visitor from Philadelphia. Guess who?" Mary's brown eyes danced. "Here's a clue. Who was so curious about electricity that he flew a kite with a key dangling on it during a thunderstorm?"

"Benjamin Franklin? Benjamin Franklin is here in Williamsburg?"

"Indeed! From what I saw, Mr. Franklin and Mr. Hunter are really good friends."

Ann thought for a moment. "That makes sense. They work in the printing business, and both are postmasters."

Mary smiled. "I'll bet Mr. Hunter quotes from Mr. Franklin's *Poor Richard's Almanac* in the *Virginia Gazette.*"

"Do you remember Mr. Franklin's words I tell my little scholars every day?" Ann smiled.

"'Tis easier to prevent bad habits than to break them." Mary knew this quote by heart. "My manners were not the best. I confess I listened to their conversation. I think Mr. Franklin was asked by people in England to find a location for a school ... a school for children of the enslaved."

As it turned out, a major reason Benjamin Franklin visited Williamsburg was to locate a place for a school to educate children of the enslaved and indentured servants. In many of the thirteen colonies the enslaved and indentured servants were forbidden to read and write. In Virginia this was not so.

Williamsburg would be the perfect place. At The College of William and Mary young men studied to become ministers. The Brafferton School where nine- and ten-year-old Native American boys received a Christian education was located on the college campus. So, in 1760 a third school called the Bray School funded by an English clergyman, The Reverend Thomas Bray, and his associates opened under the care of The College of William and Mary. The directors of the school wanted the very best teacher. Since boys and girls would come to the Bray School, the directors decided a woman would be perfect. Their number one choice? Ann Wager! The little house that would be the school was near the College. Ann moved into the school, and Mary stayed at the family home to take care of it. As she made her lesson plans, Ann probably had many visits with the Reverend Thomas Dawson, the President of the College of William and Mary. He was her supervisor.

"Mrs. Wager, as you see," he pointed to one area of the main room, "we have arranged benches for student seating. When the benches are full, the younger students may be seated on the floor."

"How many students will attend?" she asked.

"You could have anywhere from twenty to thirty boys and girls who live in town. They will arrive early in the morning and will walk back to their homes before dark."

"And their ages?"

"As young as three and as old as eight," he said. "The plan is for them to attend a three year term. I want dedicated students. I don't want the children coming and going willy-nilly." The Reverend Dawson was a no non-sense person. "The Bray School is for education not child care. As part of their Christian education, your students will learn to read and recite scripture. Every Sunday you will escort your students to church."

To Ann's thinking, the Reverend Dawson seemed rather stern. She knew teaching would be a challenge, but it was a challenge she happily accepted. It was exciting to be arranging and organizing a classroom. The classroom had lots of light streaming through the windows. Ann sighed and moved her hands along the rough wooden benches. "I wish there were desks for the older children."

Along one wall was a big brick fireplace to warm them on winter days. "I love this room." She dusted the shelves along another wall. "I will put the slates and slate pencils for writing on the lowest shelf. The books for religious training will fit on the middle shelf along with food they might bring." Ann chose to keep the sewing basket filled with fabrics, colored yarns, and needles on the top shelf. She knew children were curious. Embroidery needles could be an unnecessary temptation. She looked all around the room. Something was missing. "Apples! That's it! I'll keep a basket of crunchy red apples in the corner. I'm not required to feed my students, but I know children. Hungry children can't learn, and they won't behave."

She planned her school activities according to the guidelines from the Reverend Dawson and the Bray School sponsors. The boys were to learn reading, writing, and math called ciphering along with catechism and scripture. The girls had a similar path except that embroidery would take the place of ciphering. "I will gladly add the challenge of teaching social skills," she thought. "These children will be more successful if they have good manners. I certainly don't need books for that."

The sunshine's fading fingers danced around the classroom floor. All was ready. Tomorrow the room would hum with children's voices and maybe even laughter. "How shall I settle the students and get each day off to a good start?" She thought for a moment. "Bible stories. That's it! I will tell them the story of 'How God Told Noah to Build an Ark,' and then we can read it in scripture." She smiled. I will make it clear. The classroom is not Noah's Ark. Animal sounds are fine. Save the leaping and bounding for outside. Would thirty voices bark, meow, cluck, and moo? Make little lamb sounds? Whinny like horses?

Knock.... Knock.... Knock. The sound jolted Ann from her daydream. She opened the door. It was the Reverend Dawson. "I've brought the list of children who will be attending school tomorrow. Your students have parents who serve some of the best families, including Peyton Randolph and Robert Carter Nicholas households. I understand Christiana Campbell will send children from her tavern. No doubt Jane Vope will want to get the children at The Kings Arms Tavern out from under foot."

Ann checked the list. "Perhaps I'll recognize some children. They may be in the group I see playing along Duke of Gloucester Street. I fear one day they will fall under carriage wheels or be trampled by horses."

"I wish you well, Mrs. Wager," the Reverend Dawson said as he stepped outside. "Don't worry about firewood. I will see that someone from the college delivers and stacks firewood. You will always have a good supply."

In the blink of an eye it was the first day of school. Ann was awake at sunrise. Her breakfast was biscuits and boiled eggs. For an extra good start she drank two cups of hot tea with honey. School was about to begin. Thoughts were a jumble in her head. Would the children be happy or anxious or wild? Wrapping her favorite hand embroidered shawl tightly around her shoulders, she read and reread the list of more than two dozen names. Matching names and faces would be a challenge.

Before she could see them, Ann heard children's voices coming closer and closer. Smiling, she stood by the open door with a special greeting for each child. "Good morning and welcome." She extended her hand to shake the hand of each child. "I am Mrs. Wager, and your name is?"

She looked at the children, then looked at the benches. No benches right now. Some children were too shy to speak. "Ok, everybody find a place on the floor to sit." Younger children snuggled up to the older ones. That worked well, so each morning the children sat together on the floor to begin the day. What do you suppose the boys and girls heard on their very first morning and every morning? After a Bible story, scripture reading, and prayers, Ann passed around slates and pencils. The chorus of children recited Benjamin Franklin's words with her, "Tis easier to prevent bad habits than to break them."

In 1763 Benjamin Franklin returned to Williamsburg because his good friend Mr. Hunter died. No doubt by this time the Bray School was very successful. Certainly Mr. Franklin would check on things with Robert Carter Nicholas who took charge after the Reverend Dawson died. If Benjamin Franklin visited her school, Ann may have been delighted and a bit nervous. Can you imagine giving Benjamin Franklin a tour of your school?

Through the years educated, well-mannered children graduated from her amazing school. All was going well until the day gloomy Robert Carter Nicholas stopped by the school. "Mrs. Wager, I am sorry to say we have very little money. We have no choice. We must close the Bray school."

This news was worse than being caught outside in a thunderstorm. "Surely there must be a way to continue ... these students are doing so well," she said.

Robert Carter Nicholas shook his head. "Taxes are increasing. Things are changing, Mrs. Wager. Money to support the school stopped coming from England."

Ann looked around the room. She thought about the children. She heard their voices reciting Psalm 23. "My needs are few. I can live on little or no salary."

Robert Carter Nicholas accepted Ann's offer to work for very little money. Now it was possible for the school to stay open until 1774. The school closed when Ann, the beloved teacher who made a difference in the lives of so many children, died.

Old school records are not always accurate; however it is believed that Gowan Pamphlet was one of the children from the Kings Arm's Tavern. When he grew up and was given his freedom, Gowan Pamphlet was greatly respected as the first African American Baptist minister in Williamsburg. Do you suppose sometimes when he preached, he thought about Ann Wager and Noah's Ark?

What do you think was Ann Wager's incredible WOW factor? How do you know she loved teaching? Why was she eager to accept this challenge? In what ways did she help students become the best they could be?

Sources and Further Reading

Brendan Wolfe, "The Associates of Dr. Bray."
www.encyclopediavirginia.org
www.historyworld.net
www.localhistories.org
www.ushistory.org
www.womenhistoryblog.com

Jeff Mann

HSC Memory

What do I remember about the 37th Annual Highland Summer Conference, during which I was the featured author?

I conducted a workshop on using regional folk culture in creative writing, handing out poems by Maggie Anderson, Irene McKinney, Louise McNeill, Jeff Daniel Marion, and Robert Morgan as illustrative texts. Folk culture has always interested me, so it was fun to study references to it—food, tools, proverbs, superstitions, legends, and dialect—in Appalachian literature.

Theresa L. Burriss interviewed me about my 2014 novel, *Cub*, and Ricky Cox filmed us. I'm a big fan of Theresa's, so I enjoyed

Jeff Mann (photograph by L.S. King).

fielding her questions about the novel. Several months later, they sent me a DVD of the interview, but I'll never watch it. I hate to see myself on video or hear myself taped.

The evening of June 26 (my late mother's birthday), I gave a reading in McConnell Library, on the Radford University campus. One element of that reading made it a particularly memorable one for me.

I am, admittedly, an odd mixture of elements—gay, Appalachian, Southern, country, cosmopolitan, pagan—a contradictory amalgam that some people find difficult to handle or comprehend. One thing about me that many people find perplexing is that I don't, on the whole, like children. To quote from the Misfit in Flannery O'Connor's "A Good Man Is Hard to Find," "children make me nervous." Their erratic movements, hyperactivity, and noisiness distract and annoy me. I'm of the very strong opinion that parents should not bring children to literary readings, and a few times in the past I've gotten pretty close to asking audience members with kids to leave. Badly behaved, noisy children have sometimes destroyed my focus at public readings, which meant that I was unable to give the audience the kind of poised, entertaining reading they deserved.

Soon before that Radford reading, I had a little epiphany. Not only do I not want children at my readings, I want to read what I please. Much of my work is frankly homoerotic. Though I'm too much of a polite Southern gentleman to read in public detailed depictions of man-on-man sex, I'm enough of a rebel, contrarian, and iconoclast to read work that's mildly erotic. I have, after all, carved out a small literary reputation by writing about being gay in Appalachia, and writing about being gay means writing about my erotic predilections and preferences, even in a region as blighted with conservative Christianity as my native Highland South. To leave the homoerotic entirely out of my readings would be to censor myself, just as leaving honest portrayals of gay sex out of my fiction would be metaphorically castrating it. For too long, homosexuality was "the love that dare not speak its name." I and many other contemporary queer writers intend to speak our truths. Rather than being ignored or silenced, LGBT Appalachians need their lives positively depicted in the literature of the region.

So how to deal with this double desire? How might I read edgier work and also avoid the presence of children?

Folks at the Appalachian Regional and Rural Studies Center at Radford had created a very handsome poster for my reading (though in my photo, the gray in my beard looks a little like powdered sugar or doughnut glaze). In order to insure that (1) no squirming, chattering kids would be there to distract me, and (2) I could read R-rated material if I chose to, I warned my hosts that my publications could be spicy and it might be best if children were not to attend my reading.

Who knows what went through their minds? For all they knew, I was poised to read a detailed scene in which gay men frolicked about in an orgy. (That would be fun to write. I'm imagining several nicely built, bearded country boys with copious body hair.) At any rate, when I got to campus that rainy night for the reading, someone, to my delight, had affixed to all the posters big red sticky notes that said, in capital letters, "PROGRAM NOT SUITABLE FOR CHILDREN."

Hooray! Just what was needed! The only underage people at the reading were a little clutch of high-school students that their teacher had brought. I joshed with them a bit, pointing out the warning on the poster, and they promised me that they were up to the challenge.

So they were. The reading went well. Folks were gracious, asking intelligent questions during the Q-and-A, I didn't have to punch any angry fundamentalists, and no one delicate fainted with sanctimonious outrage and puritanical shock. I still appreciate being invited to participate in that conference, and I think I'll have a stack of "PROGRAM NOT SUITABLE FOR CHILDREN" sticky notes produced for future reference. Seeing that phrase on those posters made me feel like one of the true Bad Boys of Appalachian literature, and that gave me and still gives me profound and defiant pleasure.

"Country Kitchen—Christiansburg, Virginia"

Sweet iced tea with lemon, yes.
Country-fried steak with peppered
milk gravy, yes. Fried okra with Tabasco,
buttered limas, butterscotch meringue pie,
yes, yes, yes, praise the Lord, yes.
The waitress and I share the same
vowels, the same mountain cadence
and lilt. "Thanks very much, ma'am.
This looks great!" "You're welcome,
honey. Here's more tea. Y'all enjoy."

I had a lover's quarrel with the world,
said Robert Frost. I the same,
though more specifically with
my native region. And Lord God,
how I love you, my sweet Southland.
Let me today forget your toadish
preachers, your devout Republican
majority, your swinish family values,
your vicious crusades against
same-sex marriage, how you refuse
to love your queer children back.
Let me fill my mouth with the tastes
of home, share bites with my Yankee
husband. I belong here, though

you will not believe it. Outside,
among November's blowing leaves,
my pickup truck cools among all
the other four-by-fours. Picture-
framed over our table, my hero Lee
rides, victorious at Chancellorsville.

The restaurant radio's playing my
Nashville favorites: Luke Bryan,
Chris Young, Kathy Mattea, Tim McGraw.
In the far corner sits a black-goateed,
burly country boy in cowboy boots,
Mountaineers baseball cap, and camo
pants, younger version of myself
whom I would gladly woo and ravish.

Appalachia, I want no other place:
no traffic-snarly gay ghetto, no over-
priced noise-wormy urban warren.
Beloved Baptist-blighted hills, can't
we forget the other's supposed sins
for an hour? Put down your vengeful
cross, and I'll sheath my flaming sword.
Let's avoid religion or politics, speak instead
about the crown of frost on Draper's Mountain,
the silver fog of meadow milkweeds,
the persistent green of autumn kale,
what brands of livestock feed are on sale
at the nearest Tractor Supply Company.
Once my butterscotch pie is done, then

truck out the woe of Leviticus, cast out
the unrighteous and the wild, and once
more I'll be the godless freak and you
again will be my batshit-crazy mad-dog foe.

First published by Lethe Press, Amherst, MA.

"Gay Redneck, With Baby Stroller"

Mid-October weekend, back in his hometown
of Hinton, West Virginia, for the Railroad Days
street fair, he's threading the swarm of leaf-peeper
city folks just off the train, catching up with family,
admiring a few hot bearded boys in dirty camo,
and gobbling in rapid succession two hot dogs,
slaw-topped barbeque, and one country ham
sandwich. "You look like a West Virginian!"
says his classy cousin, in from the Bluegrass State,
in reference to his Justin boots, Western drover,
Shady Brady cowboy hat, *Hill Billy* T-shirt, bushy
gray goatee grown down to his breastbone.
"I am!" he says, flexing an arm and tipping his hat.

While his sister slips into a produce market
to fetch tomatoes, rat cheese, and creecy greens,
he stands by her baby stroller and watches over
his nephew while he sleeps. The two no doubt
look like just another redneck daddy and his son,
living the safety and the ease of those born
normal, those with less to hate and less to fear,
an existence he can barely imagine, only
thirty years and a block away from the spot
where Shorty Bennett called him *Queer*, stopped
the truck, strode over, and punched him in the face.

First published by Lethe Press, Amherst, MA.

"Redneck Food"
(for Dorothy Allison and Erica Abrams Locklear)

Redneck food? Hillbilly vittles?
Call it what you will, sophisticate,
and screw you if your nose is in the air.

Vienna sausages, Lord yes, dipped in
a little yellow mustard, or rat-cheese-
and-fried-baloney sandwiches, mayo-

rich on white bread, or those legendary
forest-wild ramps that make you reek
for days (not true if cooked, but, hell,

anything that will keep the world
at a distance is a precious charm), or,
mmmm, driving back roads with a bag

of fried pork skins and a sweaty bottle
of sweet iced tea, or snapping up country-
ham cat's-head biscuits at the local farmer's

market (said biscuits smothered, on luckiest
Sundays, with sausage gravy spicy with
pepper and onion), or simmering pinto beans

with pork jowl on the back of the stove,
black sorghum atop a steaming slice of

buttered cornbread, collard bowls ham-rich,
dear God! Oh, rough-bearded, wood-musky
redneck brothers, weary-boned mountain
sisters, sit down, dig in, welcome home.

First published by Lethe Press, Amherst, MA.

Karen Salyer McElmurray

Conferencing

I'm somewhere on I-81, just past Christiansburg, my windows rolled down and Patti Griffin singing "Living with Ghosts," when I grow aware of it, that keen wish in my chest. *Mountains like home.* I've driven across the New River Valley many times—once for a fiddler's convention when I was in my thirties, and another time before that for a storyteller's festival—but the mountains always make me realize I'm holding my breath, releasing it, taking in new lungs full of air I've wanted and wanted without knowing just how much.

Karen Salyer McElmurray.

I'm traveling to Radford, Virginia, where I'll spend a week at the Highland Summer Writing Conference, doing a reading and teaching sessions in creative nonfiction. *Conference.* I always like that the oldest definition of that words means *coming together.* In Radford I'll meet up with people I like very much—Jim Minick, Theresa L. Burriss and, nearby in Pulaski, Jeff Mann and Donia S. Eley. There'll be a group of students each morning for a week for a class in memoir, and I've already memorized their names. I've also spent the time since my invitation to the Highlands getting prepared. I've planned discussions, scoured my shelves for the right essays and exercises. On the last night there will be a gathering where I'll read from my memoir and, if I can get up the nerve, from a new essay. I imagine myself talking books and writing and the writing life with others at the conference, and maybe with others who long for home as much as I do. *Coming together.* My hand coasts on the wind outside my car window, following the shapes of the mountains.

I don't know Radford very well, so I have to stop at a convenience store to ask about the place I'll be staying. The Inn on Grove. I pass the place twice before I decide I've got the right parking space near the big white house that is the inn. There's a small porch and I try the front door before I see that there's a mailbox with a note sticking out of it. The note tells me the Inn-keeper will be back, that there's a code to use, and that the room downstairs on the right is where I'll be staying. I wonder if I'm the first person to arrive for the conference, then try the push-button code that opens the door.

Later on, I'll remember the floorboards with an extra creak. I'll remember loose shutters that caught the night wind and sounds that give and take inside the walls. It's been several years now, so I'm not certain which sounds there were and which I imagined as I wandered kitchen and dining room, called upstairs to see if anyone answered. I carried in my suit-cases and backpack and a box of books, tried the number on the back of the Innkeeper note. A voice message promised she'd be back directly, or I remember it that way. I remember pacing in the long hall leading back to the kitchen, wondering when the other conference writers would arrive and whether there'd be wine at five.

There are ghosts in that place if you ask me. The checker at the store a few blocks from the Inn told me that, and I didn't doubt her at all. As it turned out, I was the only writer there that week, so I was the lone sleeper in a big old house with rooms and rooms, a ghost my own self. But neither my own ghostliness those nights alone in the Inn on Grove nor any tale of haints are the real hauntings from that summer. After all, I'd grown up around ghosts a'plenty. Shining at the back of the holler that might or might not have been fireflies. Spirits on the dark path down to the outhouse at my grandmother's place of a winter night. None of those are the ghosts that matter most.

The haints I'm talking about lived inside me on the level of blood, bone, and wishing. They raised Cain, on occasion. They filled my dreams with long-gone houses. My granny's house, gone to make way for a highway. The other grandmother's place, gone, too, for yet another road. The ghosts I'm talking about made their way into the sentences I wrote, wrapped their ghost-limbs around all the words and all the pages. Think you're getting us right yet? These ghosts knew me better than I knew my own self. They knew just how long I'd been gone and just how much I'd forgotten about the mountains, the home I'd left behind, all those years ago.

As it turns out, the conference covers two weeks, one writer per week-long session. Notes I find in my room tell me about the week before I arrived, with poet Joseph Bathanti, whose focus was on writing about place. My session is writing memoir, which I love, and I quickly grow really fond of the small class I have. Some of them are Radford students seeking a course credit for their degrees. Others are teachers, ones who have come to a summer conference like the Highlands to work on accreditations. My thoughts about memoir are challenging and we spend part of our mornings together just talking about what telling stories from your own life means. One day we do a prompt from something Dorothy Allison once said. *Until I dared to go to the darkest places, the places where terror hides, my writing wasn't worth a damn.* And we spend part of a morning watching a documentary by Gary Hawkins, about writer Harry Crews. *Ritual ways of doing things,* Crews said, *keep us safe.* One of the teachers in my class and I disagree strongly about what exactly ritual behavior is. A ritual, she says, is a thing we want to escape from. A thing that takes a toll. For me, I say, rituals can be a kind of dark comfort.

That night, at the Inn on Grove, I turn those words over and over in my mouth. *Rituals. Tolls. Dark comfort.* Somewhere on the second floor or up in the attic of the big white house, I imagine ghost-hands turning knobs. Doors open, close. I'm propped up in bed, eating cheese and crackers with my red wine and I'm willing the Inn ghosts to settle down for the night. I'm asking the ghosts inside my bones to tell me more about themselves like they try to do every time I come back to the mountains. On occasion, they tell me more about myself, and this time, I somehow know, I'll have to listen.

The twin ritual behaviors I grew up with were those of cleanliness and those of godliness. My mother, she of obsessions, she of vacuuming and bleach-water, was the cleanliness that made me. She bathed me until I was thirteen. And God? He'd washed me in his blood more than once. I'd been baptized at nine. I'd quit going to church at fourteen, but the Holy Ghost knew me well enough to follow me down every highway I'd taken ever since. Moving. That was my ritual behavior, one I'd adhered to like a sacred law. If I could move often enough, change towns, states, leave behind lovers and kin, then I could forget what I'd come from. I could forget what hurt and who and how. Safety meant distance, but every time I came back to them, the mountains and their long, cool shadows, longing kicked me in the gut. Remember us, the ghosts of childhood said. I wanted to forget and I wanted to remember and I was lost in the space between. That week in Radford, the mountains were all around me like arms, like two wide hands holding hold. Those nights in the Grove Inn, the ghosts were incessant. *Isn't it about time,* they said, *to be who you really are?*

On the night of my public reading at the Highland Summer Conference, I'm not sure what work I after all want to share. All week, I've urged the participants in my group to risk telling their stories. Writing, I tell them, has the power to heal us. But on this night, I'm gripped by uncertainty. The new essay I've been working on shows my mother as she is these last years. She is descending into Alzheimer's, that land of forgetting, and her story is none too sweet. These days, she wears diapers. She calls all things, from love to the heat of the summer sun, chocolate. I sit with her in the one-hundred-degree heat outside the nursing home, and she tells me that there's nothing for it, when its cold out like this, but to wear chocolate. Will my essay do her justice? Offer her kindness? How to portray someone who is teetering on a precipice, ready to fall into a forever of forgetting? I do not, in fact, know if I love her at all, and how to say that at a reading?

The reading is at a library, a place I always feel comforted. The library's windows are open to the cooler evening air, and the room for the reading is shadowed by shelves and magazines and books in the summer heat. I stand at the lectern, still uncertain, even then, about what I'll read. I let my hands find the pages, and I read some of my memoir, *Surrendered Child,* then take a deep breath and let the new essay begin to speak. "Sweetness," it's called, and I read parts of my mother's life, some of them sweet, some of them painful enough I find myself wrapping my arms around my own shoulders, chilled by the memories I'm summoning. *She has always been a purveyor of strange tongues, I read, a person of powerful languages. I think of all those nights I visited her, back when she was cognizant, back when she lived in the little house in Lancer, outside of Prestonsburg. It was the family home, after Dwale was bought up by the government to make room for a public highway. She lived there over thirty years, first with her mommy and daddy, then by herself, after my grandfather moved up the hill to live with my uncle and his family. He said it wasn't right for a man to be alone in a house with an unmarried woman like that. House. Her five dark rooms with the curtains drawn at all hours of the day. Rooms where she once daily put rouge on her mommy's cheeks, set her hair, clipped her nails, then for a long while decorated my dead grandmother's walker with plastic flowers. Rooms where she, I believe, lived with all kinds of ghosts.*

As I read, I meet the eyes of a woman in my morning class, the one who wrote a piece about her daddy, the one who hid his love behind nights of drinking. I find myself looking at the high school teacher who wrote about her great, unfulfilled wish to have a child. I feel my own words about loss, my words about ghosts of the past, meeting their words. Are they thinking, as am I, about the words from Dorothy Allison, with which we began this conference week? *Until I dared to go to the darkest places, the places where terror hides, my writing wasn't worth a damn.* Not just my writing, I think as I reach the last page, the final sentence of my reading. Not just writing, at all.

These several years after my time at the Highland Summer Writing Conference, memory sometimes fails me. The student names I made sure to memorize now escape me. I remember my room at the Grove Inn, though I have no memory of the number of that room, nor the hall or the stairway I took to get me there each night that week. And as I remember that last night, my reading in the big library room, I wonder, after all, if the windows were open to cooler air of a late summer night. Still, certain things from that time are truer than true. As I read that last night of the conference, my story was no longer just mine. My story became her story, the woman's in the first row of chairs. And her story was far more than her own. One story became another, one person's history met another's, one voice became the other's voice. I can almost imagine all our stories on that library night, stories taking on a life of their own. I imagine them like ghosts of the past, transformed, floating out, traveling through the night. Stories, riding the roads beyond Radford, reaching through the darkness until they came to the sweet shapes of mountains and settled there, a conference. *A bringing together.*

Linda Parsons

A Grateful Confluence

Before a land grant lured my Parsons ancestors to Tennessee, they had emigrated from England to Virginia in the early 1700s—so Virginia has long felt welcoming to me, like a cousin twice or thrice removed. Although Tennessee meets Virginia in the northeastern corner, with shared history and culture, I always notice a change when crossing the state line—in the homes and architecture, the increase of rolling hills, even the scent of air heightens amid unfamiliar trees. My third poetry collection, *Bound*, was published in 2011 (Wind Publications), and I was delighted to be invited to participate in Radford University's (RU) Highland Summer Conference that year. I was delighted

Linda Parsons.

to spend time on the campus, which I had visited previously, to see how fully and proudly RU embraces its southern Appalachian heritage—unlike the more urban and sprawling University of Tennessee campus where I worked in Knoxville. I was delighted to return homeward to both land and people.

The conference staff and English Department faculty, particularly Dr. Grace Edwards, were attentive to every detail during my stay. I was especially impressed with the interview by Dr. Theresa L. Burriss before dinner and the evening reading. She had done her homework in reading my new collection and in asking astute questions, noting the common threads in my work, the family ties that "bound" the poems together. I believe a collection of poems is most effective and moving as a united body, something I aspire to in my books. As I began creating the work, I realized I stood smack in the middle of five generations—from my grandparents to my granddaughters. The book, which reflects this lineage before and after my familial place, had arrived at the perfect time to share with the RU audience. A grateful confluence.

Of course, the superb dinner at Sal's was made even better by the stories and communion with the English faculty—Grace and Theresa, Jim Minick, Parks Lanier, Ricky Cox, JoAnn Asbury—all dedicated educators, fine souls to know, and writers in their own right. At the reading in the McConnell Library, surrounded by books, I was grateful my work touched the audience, several of whom spoke to me afterward to share their own stories. I try to make my work accessible to a wide range of listeners and readers and, though experiences vary, family concerns and struggles are universal.

I greatly appreciate not only the personal consideration by many helpers on campus and the attentive audience, but RU's commitment to document and archive the interviews and readings, thus preserving an invaluable storehouse of writers and others invited to share their artistic gifts and their own commitment to the southern Appalachian region. I am proud to be part of this ongoing family bound in history and words, proud to be in this compilation of conference participants which deepens those ties.

"Divine Rods"

You must believe, and I do, believe
in the blood of my cousin thrice removed
who takes up copper rods to unearth
Civil War dead of the Franklin Campaign
whose father and grandmother witched

wells. Believe in the bartered blood
of Jesus, the Baptist cracker in my teeth.
Believe in these coat-hanger rods, plain
as the grail, as the questioning lips
at Gethsemane's table. Believe in

the fairy ring of my backyard, the already
gangly tomatoes, Kinnebecks, chard sails
hoisted, the bed of lilies sounding brief

horns on Father's Day. Believe the rods
will bend to Earth's shaky mantle

and tremble as I approach the old cistern,
plugged with river rocks, buried in green
just as the tracks where he used to park
have grassed over. And they do, the rods,
nod inward, toward whatever depth

channeled April rains for whatever
generations removed from my dailiness
under the same roof, from my turning
days' deckled pages. Believe, and I do,
in watertables untapped, tremors unfelt,

in rods divining my move from this world's
slippery source to the next, realigned
as if breath never caught or turned
askew, as if gravity's field or faith
never held me dear.

First appeared in The Baltimore Review, 2017.

Dana Wildsmith

Teaching the Teachers

They're a tough crowd, a hard sell, some tough nuts to crack. Every August, they put on the armor of certitude before marching valiantly into public education's unforgiving battlefield, and they trudge home weary but basically intact the following May or June, thanks to their shield of authority, their breast plate of knowledge, their helmet of comforting certitude. For at least one more year, they have saved their students from drowning in a sea of social flux and technological tsunami, constantly waving them in to shore: *Over here! Swim to me! I have the answers.*

And they do.

Therein lies the rub, when it comes to teaching teachers. We—for I am one of you forever—have little patience with any CEU or Professional Development program which does not present us with a clear purpose for being there, the clearest of purposes being to provide us with something useful to take back to our classrooms. I've sat through way too many sessions myself where the only bright moments sprang from the brilliance of the snarky comments we teachers muttered to each other. At Radford's Highland Summer Conference, I was to be the one facing the snarkers.

So it was with uncharacteristic trepidation that I headed up 23/

Dana Wildsmith.

441 and then eastward on I-81 to Radford, Virginia, to teach at the Highland Summer Conference. I stopped in Dillsboro to stretch my legs and buy handmade cards at an artist's coop there (I send out an unlikely number of cards every month). My phone rang just as I turned the engine off.

"Hey, Snow, what's up?"

"Barry said I should call early because you might want to stop for a minute when you drive past us on I/77," my daughter answered, "but I told him, *Mom won't go that route.* He didn't believe me. *It's the only logical way to go! I know that,* I told him. *Mom won't go that route.*"

She knows me well, Snow does. Mom didn't go that route. I chose the slightly longer, but ever so much more interesting road that winds through Franklin and Weaverville and up through Sam's Gap before dumping me onto the paved hell of I/81. If I had spent that day of travel on interstate alone, I would have arrived in Radford bereft of whatever is left of my soul.

I needed not just the beauty of the mountain route, but also the sense of riding the spine of the Appalachians as a way of strengthening my own spine through the sort of transference from nature to need well known to hikers, before I had to deal with the spirit-sapping logic of the interstates. I body-Englished my way around curve after curve, as if the tilt and weight of my lean to the left or to the right might be integral to my car hugging those same curves securely. How eerily like the worst of state-mandated goals for educators this is, I thought: *just lean in the direction they recommend and all students will reach an equal stage of accomplishment.* Even if we believed such nonsense. we'd still not be interested in any approach so soullessly generic. Teachers live for single moments of unexpected brilliance, each one unique and individual.

By the time my students and I gathered in a second-floor seminar room in the Social Work section of Waldron Hall, just over the heads of toddlers and their moms in the clinic below, I knew all would be well. These were teachers, like me, who'd escaped the bonds of administration and testing for a week to tinker around with regional literature, figuring out what makes it stand and stay, like a Lego tower of right words.

"Okay," I began as I passed around a double-jointed persona poem exercise I'd gratefully borrowed from Frank X Walker. "We're going to walk through the structure of these poems step by step, so it won't seem quite so daunting when you work on your own poem for homework tonight."

To their credit, they pulled on their walking shoes and traced with me the multiple paths through a poem that can be read across the line, as with any regular poem, or down the left-hand column of words, or down the right-hand column of words, or down the middle column, And each path must form a separate and readable poetic line. Most people snort in derision when I present this poetic form. *Right. Like that's possible.* But not so, my students on that hot Virginia afternoon. I watched as slow smiles of challenge crept upward in their faces. *Neat.* One after the other nodded their heads, shaking burgeoning ideas into place. *This'll be fun.*

This is what we who teach love best: we figure out ways to connect the dots in comprehension's borderless puzzle, so that we can later help our students do the same.

As our week's journey wound along through the literary byways of Jim Wayne Miller and Lee Smith and James Still and Silas House, like a Country Music Highway of writers, I began to remember what great good sports teachers are, left to their best instincts.

"Okay, we have a couple of hours left," I told the group on the last afternoon. "We're going to write a novel."

They all laughed. I began to hand around the worksheets: Create a Character, Establish a Setting, etc.

"Oh!" Lindsey looked at the handouts and then back at me. "You're serious."

I was. I was serious about having fun with learning, which is the default mode of the best teachers. Not logical, perhaps, but teachers don't take the route of administrative logic, given a choice. They take the scenic route through the hearts of their students. I understand, because I am one of them, forever.

"One Light"

A single light can lead you home. One light
is all you need to break the back of night
when darkness seems to weigh more than it has
on all the nights before, and nothing's as
it was. Bit by bit, the lighter shades
of night you used to trust have faded as
you stopped believing in relief. The dark
goes on forever, and begins right where you are.

But when your eyes can't guide your steps, you learn
to trust your heart instead. You rise and turn
toward where you need to go, and in the dark
you think you see a glimmer like a star
that wasn't there until you headed home
through darkness, trusting that a light would come.

First appeared in *One Light*, Texas Review Press, 2018. Reprinted by permission from Texas Review Press, Huntsville, Texas.

"Emergency Room"

The neutral air has neutral hands that lift
and roll and—*on my count*—lay you down.
Fingers insinuate through mist to strip
and survey you. The hallways mumble and frown.
One man's eyes lack the grace to pretend; you wish
he had the grace to leave. Words priss around
your gurney, conferring. Machines sidle in
like auditors. Liquid sleep slides down
its tubular tributary. *Lullay, lully,*
it croons. This is not your concern. *Hush now.*

First appeared in *One Light*, Texas Review Press, 2018. Reprinted by permission from Texas Review Press, Huntsville, Texas.

"Pitched Past Grief"

This is my hymn to weariness
after another night
not sleepless, but sleeping in fits between
rising to help her rise
and rising again to lay her down
between clean sheets.
We leave the piano lamp on
all night and lift the cat
from her feet in and out of the light
as we change the sheets—
the tabby cat, our hands, her face
soft with forgetfulness
that is the gift of sleep. Tired
beyond words, beyond
the fix of one good night of rest,
these holes in our nights
drain us during our days, but we come
to love what is commonplace:
the jarring call to help her rise,
this stuporous routine,
the lessening weight of her
leaning in and out of the light.

First appeared in *One Light*, Texas Review Press, 2018. Reprinted by permission from Texas Review Press, Huntsville, Texas.

"Elegy"

Never to sing beside her again
is the gift and curse of her going.
Our altos clashed in life. Hers rang light
and pure, mine hangs low and dark as night.
We were the sun and moon of singing.
We always sang together facing
each other across a room, our sounds
blending on music's sweet horizon
of tonality where our voices
settled into sense, not discord. This
need to keep a distance for beauty's
sake died with her. Walking the woods with
my dogs, I sing wherever I please,
but her gone voice hums and haunts me.

First appeared in *One Light*, Texas Review Press, 2018. Reprinted by permission from Texas Review Press, Huntsville, Texas.

Frank X Walker

Contributions from Frank X Walker, a Kentucky Poet Laureate

Editors' Note: Over the years Frank X Walker has visited Radford University on various occasions for readings and lectures. In 2008 he came to lead a week of the Highland Summer Conference. Joining him that year were Darnell Arnoult, Dana Wildsmith, and Rick Van Noy. In other essays in this book students and fellow writers who sat in Frank's classes testify to the impact his teaching has had on their own thinking and writing. Some years later Kentuckians recognized the power of his poetry by naming him Poet Laureate of Kentucky in 2013. Known for his generosity, Frank has contributed the following six poems to be included in this book.

"Sweat Equity"
for Maurice Walker

You must have known
I needed to feel close to him,
so we dug holes, mixed
and poured wheelbarrows of cement,
and planted posts
Conversing with more sweat
than words,
until the evening sun called it quits.

For days I sweated through my clothes
carrying boards, sawing, hammering
marking and measuring,
then we paused,
pyramid builders
raising something grand

Frank X Walker.

147

out of the desert, out of the mud
in your backyard.

Of all the grandsons
you look most like my father,
especially with a cigarette
balanced on your lips
and a pencil behind your ear.

Earning these calluses,
performing an "honest day's work,"
Coaxing your new deck
out of the ground,
allowed me to imagine
I'm building a temple with him,
something broad and enduring,
that could be witnessed
for miles and miles

like his laughter,
like both of your smiles.

First appeared in *Last Will, Last Testament*, Accents Publishing, 2019.

"Ritual"
for Kumasi

We migrate to the front stoop
still in night clothes
to stretch and greet
an end of summer sun
that peeks over mountains
between tall trees
and across rooftops
to kiss his face,
to bathe my eyelids.

All the leaves, our flowers,
and almost every blade of grass
leans and reaches with us
towards the warmth.

He listens for morning sounds,
passing cars and buses,
cicadas, birds,
all already hard at work.

At sunset
we turn down all the lights

put on soft music
move much more slowly,
whisper,
re-open the blinds
and let sleep crawl in.

He closes his eyes
wrapped in the comfort of darkness
learning that life
is what happens in between
Son rise, and Son Set.

First appeared in *Last Will, Last Testament,* Accents Publishing, 2019.

"Rock Paper Scissors"

There is no scrum
in the treetops this morning.
The birds that have come
for the webworms all week
have been silenced
by the heavy rains.

My lil' caterpillar and I
peek through the blinds
and cock our heads
towards the sound
of the downpour
on the roof.
His eyes big up
when lightning flashes.

Fifty years of tobacco moths
laid eggs that hatched
as a many legged chimera.
It crawled around inside
my father for months transforming him
into a chrysalis.

But even alive, he was as stoic
as a rock.
while his son exercised his grief
on paper.
and a newborn cut
much of the bitterness away.

First appeared in *Last Will, Last Testament,* Accents Publishing, 2019.

"Hoofers"

Catching up with the three of us
Is less awkward than the slow dance
the two of us have done
for fifty years.
Maybe because the music was different.

Instead of the slow heart-aching
waiting for you to say "I love You" ballads
that always play
in the movie version of us,
the air is filled
with lyrics to children's songs,
that are much faster
than traditional lullabies.

You stare at my brand new son
with a wide grin,
perhaps looking
for your trademark eyes
and wry smile.
I stare at you and imagine
you're looking back at me,
across time,
barely two months old,
tiny hands still learning to grip,
choosing to smile at dance partners
by the amount of light in their eyes.

We drove a long way to make sure
this moment happened.
I waited even longer
to be sure I'd seen it before.

First appeared in *Last Will, Last Testament*, Accents Publishing, 2019.

"Wheeze"

The new one is full of mucous
and has not yet learned to breathe
through his mouth.

The old one is doing his best
with one lung
collapsed under the weight
of a mass of cancer.

In the wee hours on the hospital ward
and in our bedroom nursery
I listen at them struggle to live.

One needs saline drops
to cut through his blockage.
The other hacks and coughs
until something thick and wet
is hauled up the well of his throat.

A blue rubber bulb will reach deep
in the nasal cavity and perform
much needed excavation for one.
A breathing treatment and oxygen tube
can pretend to be a lung for the other.

Holding my own breath,
I lie or sit here listening to my guys
gasp and wheeze and wish
all my worry was air.

First appeared in *Last Will, Last Testament*, Accents Publishing, 2019.

"Eclipse"

This trioka
A sun, and a moon
and a planet.
Three Black Russian nesting dolls.
A Father. A Son, a man almost a ghost,
The beginning, middle and end
of a complicated drama
gathered here smiling

It is not something
necessarily spoken aloud,
but the way the entire room witnesses
us holding each other
with the same almond eyes,
and the same wringing
over-sized hands

It is clear that we all understand
this rare celestial alignment
will only happen once
in our life times.

First appeared in *Last Will, Last Testament*, Accents Publishing, 2019.

Rick Van Noy

Reading the River

I think it was my first reading. My book of narrative essays on children and nature came out that summer, and my slot at the Highland Summer Conference was among my first. I had given presentations before, readings of someone else's writing, but a reading reading, one where my job was not just to interpret words, in what I hoped would be some highly original and hereto-never-before-thought-of insight, but something different— sweep readers and listeners away, get them lost in the imagery and words and story.

Rick Van Noy.

I was grateful for the opportunity. Why not dip a toe in this water? One of the things I read was an essay on finding a swimming hole, in which I spent a summer traveling in about a 200-mile radius around our home to find, with kids, the best place to cool down on a hot summery day. Devil's Bathtub. Hippy Hole. The Cascades. But also our home waters, a little spot on the New River, right outside the window of the room we were all seated in, just beyond those trees it runs, clear and cool and inviting.

I had good models who came before me. All I had to do was ask Ricky Cox and he produced a list. Memory strains, but I'm pretty sure I saw Robert Morgan in 1999 because I reviewed his *Gap Creek* for the newspaper. I remember it as a book both rough and tender, about a young couple facing an uncertain yet hopeful future in their region, persevering through hard times. And I caught Wilma Dykeman too, because I was finishing up a book on the sense of place, and she had written something about the way maps "draw all the minor and major divisions by which we separate this green whirling planet to fit our human imagination." Vastness and variety, scenes and smells, "reduced to a dry, stiff bit of cardboard."

Ron Rash in 2006, Jim Minick too. Ron was also looking for saints and sprites in the river, and Jim helped us find a clear path, plant bushes in the clearing, pick berries, get our hands dirty. And Rita Riddle, ruddy-cheeked Rita with the sassy grin, who always made me feel warm and welcome, brought us out back behind her house, among the irises purple and pale, dancing naked in the rain.

Particular words, images, a vague figure standing at the podium come back, but what stays is a shared experience—people silent until a giggle lets out, a satisfying "ahh" at the end. It means I get it, I liked how you wrapped that up, that was just the right word, in the right place.

I can't recall if any of those sounds came out of my reading. To look back at what I read, I pull a faded copy of *A Natural Sense of Wonder* off a shelf. In it, I wrote a line with an arrow pointing down, "start here," another line, which meant skip some stuff, resume.

I'm not from this region but I have lived here for as long as I've lived anywhere. In addition to finding swimming holes, I hike and paddle and explore. Twenty years on, it feels like home. To become more placed, I read widely, another list Ricky gave me, learning more about the long layers of association and memory, the textures and rhythms that give us a sense of place. I don't know if I can be called Appalachian, perhaps "Adoppalachian," in that I've adopted (and adapted) to this place to make my home, or it has adopted me.

And I've had some good guides. One that I wrote about was Radford naturalist Clyde Kessler. As we walked through Wildwood Park, he kept calling out species, bringing an otherwise ordinary landscape to life. "You won't learn what Clyde knows in an afternoon," I wrote, "but you can catch on to the way he looks." My son said he wanted a "map," of the park, one that would include not only topography but the detail Kessler knows. Which led me to think about kids having maps like that, of not only where they are but what else inhabits where they are, and what if kids knew these things the way they know brand names, "if they knew mountains the way they know malls." *Malls* should be updated now to something else, *media* perhaps.

I've learned in living here that there is no one Appalachian culture, just as there is no one South. In coming to know the region's rivers and mountains, I've come also to learn of the struggle to halt environmental damage to them, to the demands for clean water, the preservation of not only place but culture.

When I swim in the New River near Bisset Park, I have to pass a sign that says "No Swimming." Why tubing seems to be encouraged but not swimming never made much sense, so I ignored the warning. But if you ask people you find a prevalent attitude that the river is dangerous, full of "holes," that it rises awful fast, though it seemed pretty placid to me.

The best of culture can teach us, lift us up, as the Highland Summer Conference certainly does. It can also give us prejudice, as any resident of Appalachia surely knows and has felt when they see themselves reflected in national media (or supposed elegies of hillbillies).

More recently, I caught my friend Thorpe Moeckel, finding food, every word carefully chosen, cutting to the bone. And Mark Powell, telling us about the paradox of attending both the Citadel and Yale Divinity School, a clash of cultures.

I continue to range and explore beyond my home. One thing that fascinates me on these forays are old gothic farmhouses, now vacant. I spy one from a frequent walk, and one spring day I hopped the fence to investigate. It was a clear, sunny, windswept day. The cows all watched me suspiciously, warily, as I made my way toward the weathered structure. At the top of a hill, some bones lay loosely in a pile. Cows roamed around and from one, I saw the red trail of the afterbirth, the new calf suckling. The wind rattled the tin roofing, as swallows flew out of the eaves. I crept closer to the grey clapboards, peering into an entry, the living room now loaded with bales of hay. The floor boards creaked under foot but held, and I gazed out through the bay window, frames but no glass, a view of a mountain above and a pond below—this place was situated for beauty. Window weights still hung in the sashes. Behind me was the stone hearth. It was built during a time when we were fascinated by detail, intricacies. And I wanted to know what stories it could tell.

There should be a list of such places (if there is I know who to ask). But why do I even mention it? Why do we tell any of our stories, obsessions, loves? Why fill them with detail, intricacy, beauty, birth and death? If that house did hold stories, there was no one around to say. If our own houses tended toward decay (and current trends have me worried), I am assured that organizers of the conference would have recordings of the stories told (including this book), of our human compulsion to say how it is or was.

In "Swimming Hole" I was writing about a culture-at-large that feared the river, and nature in general. Bass that bite. Crayfish that claw. Parents, I thought, could model something else. It didn't help that a section of the river was said to be called the "river of death." But I found other examples where people long ago in the Highlands, including past presidents, would once "take the waters," a remedy for a range of ailments. They took to these pools to escape the heat and humidity, soothe in curative baths.

On a hot summer night, a reading at the Highland Summer conference is a dip in the river. Refreshing, maybe a little bracing so it quickens the pulse, speeding up some in places, changing course unexpectedly, maybe a little bit forbidden, drifting too into eddies and pools to join with a larger body of thought and power—moving us, changing us, until that instant when it catches our breath and carries us away. It happens at the height of summer every year.

Donald Secreast

The Highland Summer Conference Could Have Added Ten Years to My Writing Life

To work with the Highland Summer Conference is to gain a deep appreciation for the remarkable changes in attitude toward Appalachian culture that have come about as a result of Appalachian Studies programs. Certainly, Appalachian writers have exerted a serious influence in bringing the region's unique culture to a broader audience with writers like Charles Frazier, Lee Smith, Robert Morgan, Barbara Kingsolver, Ron Rash, and Crystal Wilkinson reaching national and international audiences. When *Cold Mountain* made its debut, I was on a plane out of Charlotte, going to a conference in Puerto Rico. It turned out that the flight was semi-chartered by a Charlotte country-club group headed to the island for a two-week golf vacation. At least half the people on that flight, none of whom struck me as Civil War scholars, were carrying copies of *Cold Mountain*. But even at the risk of committing the logical fallacy of hypothesis contrary to fact, I can't help but speculate how much of the groundwork for Appalachian

Donald Secreast.

writers' success might be attributed to the work that has been done by Appalachian Studies.

I believe in large part that such programs have not only educated readers to more fully appreciate Appalachian literature but have, to a serious degree, helped direct and train writers to approach their subjects with more emotional and literary accuracy. The two times I participated in the Highland Summer Conference, I found myself charged up by the enthusiasm shared by all the participants in the program. In addition to the passion of the conference's students, during my twenty-five years at Radford University, I witnessed a steady rise in "regular" student interest in their Appalachian roots. By far, the best work turned in to my fiction writing classes came from students who explored the dramatic possibilities of their own families, towns, and region. One graduate student, Tempi Hale, won the Best Graduate Creative Thesis Award with a novel about a cousin who goes missing. Her novel was also a study in the rituals and psychology of an Appalachian family. Recently, another Radford University graduate Teresa Jewell has published a book steeped in Appalachian lore derived from her own family history. As much as I admired the wisdom that these two students manifested in knowing very early in their writing careers that they wanted to write about their Appalachian heritage, I was also jealous of how soon in their writing lives they had recognized the rich literary possibilities of their region. It took me roughly thirty-three years to discover my true region of literary inspiration. Even though Appalachian State University offered me several opportunities to encounter Appalachian literature and culture, I suffered from what I think was a widespread prejudice against it.

I first learned about the importance of place in my fiction when I took a creative writing class from John Foster West around 1970. Specifically, John wanted all of us to consider those "places" where we came from, where we grew up. Of course, the majority of us had come from the towns and counties around Appalachian State University. Regrettably, most of us had grown up believing our hometowns were places we either needed or wanted to get away from. So, at first, John's insistence to write about what we knew felt counterintuitive. Now, this was pre–Harry Potter, and Tolkien was known only to a few avant-garde students and medieval professors. Consequently, we didn't have students who wanted to write fantasy fiction. We did have students who wanted to write about being rock stars, hippies, and detectives. Anti-Vietnam War stories frequently found their way into class as well, but unless such stories were extremely well-written—and they usually weren't—John could be brutal in his responses. At the basis of all his critiques, once he got past grammar mistakes and factual errors, was his demand for plausibility. And plausibility came most reliably from working out of a definite sense of place.

Certainly, John emphasized the importance of characterization, but the most effective characters, the most plausible characters, had their roots in our experience more than in our imagination. Our fictional characters didn't have to be strictly drawn from friends and relatives. In fact, John encouraged us to simply take parts from the people we knew and stitch them together into our fictional population. Most importantly, John stressed, we needed to feel strongly about every character we created. "Love your characters or hate them, but never be indifferent to them." This sort of dramatic valence in our characters arose most naturally if we had, at some point, actually known a real person with those traits we gave our characters. Again, according to John Foster West, the people who probably held the most memorable places in our memories were those people with whom we had grown up.

For our final assignment in John Foster's class, we had to write a fully developed short story. Because it was an introductory fiction writing class, we'd been required only to write scenes or develop aspects of possible characters throughout the semester. For most of the class, I had been writing scenes that had taken their contents from movies or television shows I'd watched. But for this last assignment, I had the chance to go home and work on it. While catching me up on the local news, my mother mentioned that the derelict but historical train depot at the edge of town had been condemned by the town because it had become infested with rats. The citizen who had brought the infestation to the attention of the town council was one of the town characters who frequently caused slight traffic problems in town when he would stand in the middle of the road, trying to sell old newspapers to the motorists. During a city council meeting, our town character had walked in carrying two dead rats. Being handed such a clear climactic scene made it easy to construct a story whose dramatic trajectory led up to that city council meeting. With that first completed short story, I became a regional writer although at the time, I didn't fully realize it. Except for rat infestations, I still didn't see the potential for serious dramatic conflict in Caldwell County.

Part of my problem was that my concept of "regional" was still somewhat second hand. As a college undergraduate, I hadn't read enough of Faulkner to appreciate the artistic lens through which he viewed his little postage stamp of reality. Besides, Mississippi struck me as a region as alien to my experiences as Florida or California. The only book I had read about the Appalachian region was John Foster West's autobiographical novel *Time Was*. His setting was a place that I knew fairly well because my mother came from the same area in the Brushy Mountains of Wilkes County. One of my aunts had even attended the same elementary school with John Foster West. From the stories she told, I was left with the impression that she might have bullied him on occasion because even as a boy, John Foster might have been more bookish than my aunt thought was proper. And the Wilkes County that John Foster wrote about wasn't quite the same place that I knew.

To the detriment of my development as an Appalachian writer, I never quite felt comfortable when we visited my mother's family in Wilkes County. First of all, my aunt and uncle were farmers. They lived in a four-room shack, its wood weathered nearly black from age. They had one spigot at the back of the house and no indoor plumbing. I don't want to sound as if I'm judging my aunt and uncle for their lack of indoor plumbing. My father didn't add a bathroom to the house we rented until I was four or five. Even now, after some sixty years, I can't pretend, even through the veil of nostalgia, that I hold any sort of fondness for outdoor toilets. Modern porta-potties have certainly improved on the design of what still remains essentially an outdoor toilet, but even on their worst day, a modern porta-potty can't equal the olfactory belligerence of a semi-permanent outhouse. (I consider myself something of an expert on this subject for two reasons: [1] a large part of my childhood, winters and summers, was spent using my aunt and uncle's outhouse, and [2] I spent a very long summer as an adult cleaning porta-potties.) I think it's still a matter of debate about which is the worst season to use an outhouse. Obviously, winter temperatures provide unique challenges to a person's resolve and metabolism. But for me, summer provided a particularly disturbing outhouse experience: insects. Naturally, the flies were a nuisance, but wasps and hornets always seemed interested in the outhouse's possibilities as a nesting location. While flies could be ignored and wasps could be swatted away, the insect that really concerned me was spiders. Of course, a seasoned outhouse user knew to check the nearby nooks and crannies before settling down to business, but what tormented me was the possibility of having a spider lurking *under* the seat.

Another element of surprise common to my aunt and uncle's outhouse was the diversity of toilet paper I encountered. Both my aunt and uncle were avid readers. So quite often, their outdated reading material became the outhouse toilet paper: newspapers, *Readers' Digest, Life, Look, Farmer's Almanac*, and my favorite, *True Detective*. On some visits to their outhouse, I was startled to find not reading material stored in the magazine rack but a row of corncobs. I didn't appreciate the literary nature of this sort of toilet paper until I took a course in Renaissance literature and read *Gargantua and Pantagruel*.

Although John Foster West first inspired me to write about my region, I was still reluctant, on a deep level, to embrace not only my matriarchal connections to the Brushy Mountains but also to my more immediate region of Lenoir, North Carolina. What blinded me to Lenoir's literary potential was its abundance of furniture factories. Both of my parents worked at various furniture factories for a big part of their lives. My first summer job was in a veneer plant where I worked as a "tail-boy," which meant that I sat at the "tail-end" of a veneer splicer and pulled out the freshly, hotly glued veneer panels as they were extruded from the machine. After just a couple of hours, I learned seven important lessons that would guide me through several more furniture factory jobs. First, don't grab the freshly glued veneer panels in the middle, where they've been spliced, if you want to keep the skin on your fingertips. Second, never sit down on the job. Third, even if you don't have anything to do, look like you're doing something. Fourth, stack veneer or any sort of processed wood neatly; don't just throw it on the hand truck. Fifth, you must get permission to use the bathroom if you're a tail-boy. Sixth, someone is keeping track of how long you stay in the bathroom. Seventh, a factory bathroom is a public place.

Before leaving Lenoir for college, I worked another summer in another furniture factory, again as a tail-boy, in a plant that made beds, dressers, and chests. I didn't have to worry about hot glue. However, I did worry, in various degrees, about saw blades, drills, lathes, router heads, and static electrical shock from drum sanders and belt sanders. (I always marveled at my mother who worked in the cabinet room of a furniture factory. For many years, her job was to staple the backs on dressers and chests. Occasionally, she would staple her hand to the back of a dresser, usually through the web of skin between her thumb and index finger. She never reported her accidents to the plant nurse after she pried the staple out of her hand, while walking beside the dresser clanking along on the conveyor belt, with a borrowed screwdriver. When I asked her once why she didn't get treatment from the nurse, she replied, "Because it's one of the best jobs in the cabinet room, and I don't want her taking me off of it.")

In a furniture factory, the actual amount of manual labor can vary, according to which part of the production process one works in. For example, the rip saw requires a high degree of dexterity and movement for both the man "feeding the saw" and the tail-boy. Watching these two men feed and tail their machine when the conveyor belt is cranked up to full speed is like watching some frantic ballet coupled with a juggling act where the two men are sliding a constant flow of ten-pound wood cores at each other with a whizzing saw blade at the center of their choreography. However, even in the less demanding jobs, simply standing on a concrete floor for eight or ten hours a day becomes in itself a form of labor. One of the happiest moments of my life came at the end of that summer in 1967 when I ended my stint in that factory with all my fingers intact. But if I thought summer factory work alienated me from my Lenoir roots, the winter I spent as a tail-boy in another factory after I dropped out of college really motivated me to disconnect myself from my hometown.

For twelve or thirteen more years, I wrote stories without much heart. I did reread *Time Was* and *Appalachian Dawn* with a growing sense of nostalgia, but I still knew that John Foster's Appalachia wasn't my Appalachia. Then, on a long bus ride from Huaras to Lima in the summer of 1982, in a serious fit of nostalgia in a landscape of mountains that were nothing like the Appalachians, I found myself bombarded by ideas for short stories that centered around the furniture factories of Lenoir. During that eight-hour trip, I outlined ten ideas for factory stories which eventually became my first published book, *The Rat Becomes Light*. Here was my first serious encounter with myself as an Appalachian writer, but the literary product was conceived in Peru and written in Iowa. I think what I needed to overcome my prejudices against my hometown, my roots, was the perspective provided by time and distance. What I most appreciated about my association with the Highland Summer Conference was how its instructors and its participants shared their enthusiasm for the places in the Appalachian region. There's a remarkable dynamic that characterizes all the writing activities that go on during those two weeks. Teachers inspire students, students inspire teachers, writers inspire audiences, audiences inspire readers—I'm certain if I had been exposed to the conference's instructional and creative energies when I first fled Lenoir, I might have found my regional voice at least ten years earlier than I did.

PART III

The Inspired

B. Chelsea Adams

The Truth We Share

A handmade quilt was hung at the front of the room where the Highland Summer Conference readings were held each year. The quilt greeted us and set the stage for the many readers and attendees who had grown-up wrapped in quilts made by their mothers, aunts, and grandmothers.

I started attending the summer conference readings in 1986, when I began teaching at Radford University. Each time, I was impressed by the journeys the fiction, poetry, and essay writers took us on, the stories they told, the experiences they shared.

B. Chelsea Adams.

In 2000, I attended the two-week writing workshop as a student. I had graduated from Hollins University's graduate creative writing program and had taken part in many writing groups and conferences over the years, so I was comfortable when I walked into the first class.

This workshop was taught by David Huddle the first week and Joyce Dyer the second week. That first day in class, David Huddle announced we would be working on autobiographical writing. I was totally shaken, wanted to run out of the classroom, find the elevator and descend.

Autobiographical writing was something I had never liked and had always avoided. And my situation was complicated. If I stayed and wrote fiction and tried to pass it off as truth, I'd be caught in a falsehood, for not only were many of my friends in the class, but my daughter, Cori, was in it as well.

But I had a plan. At the first break, I took Cori aside and said, "I can't write truth. Don't let them know I'm faking it." I said the same thing to my friend, JoAnn Asbury. This calmed me down.

Yet, as David Huddle challenged me, I found myself widening my definition of my comfort zone, as well as the scope of what I could and would write. Up to that point, I wrote only fiction in both my stories and poetry. Writing truth was something I avoided, feeling I could never get it right, never be fair to all its aspects, all the people it touched.

Somehow my attempts at personal essays had never seemed completely true to what had really happened, or I would feel I needed to add long histories to make it fair to each person I wrote about.

But something in me makes me at least try the assignments given to me. David Huddle let us choose from subjects like our first memories, early childhood stories, and places we've lived. Those subjects from childhood were so far back in the past, I felt freer exploring them. I would be describing my memories as a young child, and I rationalized that young children couldn't be expected to present their memories absolutely correctly.

The first piece I handed in was entitled "53 Edgewood Place" and described my grandparents' home where my mother and I lived from my birth until my father came home after serving in World War II. My Aunt Barbara and my grandfather's brother Vincent also lived there.

Not only did I surprise myself and enjoy writing this truth, it brought me back to my grandparents' house, a place I was very attached to.

I skip up the sidewalk, between the yew bushes that are taller than I am, holding a cup filled with bright red berries. Mounting the big gray steps that lead to the porch, I am careful not to spill my raspberries.

Grandpa swings back and forth on the glider reading the newspaper article about the war. I knew about the war. My daddy was a Marine and drove a tank. As Grandpa reads, he scratches the eyelid he tapes up with scotch tape because it closes even when he isn't sleepy.

I have gone outside before finishing my pancakes, so I am still wearing my big pink bib. I bring my cup of berries into the kitchen and pour them over the pancakes, smelling lilac and flour and hearing my grandmother humming. She leans over the table rolling out pie dough, her housedress unbuttoned at the neck.

She puts down her rolling pin and picks me up. When she pulls me close to her, I sink my head down against her breasts, breathe in the lilac smell, and rub my hand over the warm, wrinkly skin on her neck and chest.

I realized as I wrote this memory how much I liked remembering, but there were memories I wrote about during those two weeks that were more disturbing and painful to recall.

My grandmother and I returned from the store to that same kitchen weeks later to find my Great Uncle Vincent with his head lying on the open oven door. His face looked blue.

I was whisked away, taken to a neighbor's house. It was years before anyone spoke to me about what I'd seen. That day they just told me he had died, but my great uncle had committed suicide. He'd been gassed in World War I, recently lost his wife, and had come to live with us because he was having trouble taking care of himself.

But writing about that moment when I saw him with his head on the oven door, somehow helped to bring back other memories, helped me face something that everyone had tried to protect me from and let me bring back my memories of the days before he died.

All at once I was on my great uncle's lap and he was reading stories to me; I was holding his hand as we walked down the street to the playground where I could climb on the jungle gym and zoom down the slide; he was laughing as I climbed up on the piano stool and played the piano by pressing down random notes with my toes.

I had begun to write poems during the two weeks that expressed "true" feelings about my past. This first poem was written only a little while after my grandfather died and the house was for sale.

"The Part Gone"

You think about those years,
as if you could pick them up,
hold them in your hands,

as if each scene had been shut in
the picture album, leather bound,
a black and white photo,

and now the triangular corners
that held it
are coming unglued,

as if you could step
into those glossy scenes,
skip in full color

up the walk between green hedges,
plucking off slick red berries,
and find yourself in front of

the lemon colored house, swinging
in the porch glider, its burgundy cover
cracked and peeling, and know

she is inside, know you
can sink your head into her lilac
scented breasts, if you need to.

"The Part Gone" was first published by Sow's Ear Press in the chapbook, *"Looking for a Landing"* in 2000.

The following poem about my father and me going to his favorite pub was also written during those two weeks. Until my twin sisters were born, it was almost okay that I wasn't a boy. After all, there was still hope my father would have a son. When they came along and were both girls, it became less certain he would ever have someone he could teach to play ball, someone to carry on his name.

"The Nineteenth Hole"

smoky, dark
and the bartender knows
to put out a bowl of peanuts
and to drop two cherries
in your Ginger Ale
as he shouts, "Hi Larry!"
to your father and pours
a Budweiser in a tall glass.

As usual, you sit on the end stool
and men come out of the shadows
to say things like,
"You've really grown" and
"You're becoming quite a looker."

These men love your father
and want to talk about Willie Mays'
most recent catch, even though
this is the place where you learned
not everyone is a New York Giants fan:
Dodgers, Cubs, and even Yankees fans
are foolish enough to bet against them.

Your dad winks when he puts down
a fifty dollar bill.
And you feel special
that he trusts you not to tell
your mother. You almost think
you are a child to be proud of

and forget how disappointed
your dad looked when the boys
in the neighborhood said
they no longer wanted a girl on their team.

As I thought back to those two weeks, I decided to call my daughter Cori and ask her what she remembered from the workshop. Reflecting on her experience, she said, "I remember the first week when David Huddle said to write fifteen pages. I was overwhelmed and thought I couldn't do it. I thought here I am working most evenings waiting on tables and he's asking for fifteen pages. But when he gave us those two pages of writing prompts, they inspired me.

I wrote about the restaurant and how I felt like I wasn't going to be able to hold my temper with the customers and about how I couldn't take the way they talked down to me. I still remember starting the first page with, 'I almost got fired again today.'"

She also remarked, "I liked being in class with you and my professor, Dr. Rita Riddle, I felt encouraged by both of you and by the writers who taught the workshop. I was surprised by how much I enjoyed the writing. I remember getting comments back from the teachers and others in class and being impressed with myself."

As we talked, I felt pleased that each of us from different generations had enjoyed the two weeks and learned from them, built confidence from them. My friend JoAnn and her son Roger had also been of two generations, and each had spoken positively of their experiences.

That day, I realized that what I had appreciated most about those two weeks of writing autobiography, or memoir as Joyce Dyer introduced it, is that I'd learned ways to add my past to my writing; it had always been percolating behind the scenes. Now, I could allow it to surface, to accept and embrace that we all write from our own perspectives, that we all get some things wrong. And the truth we are sharing is our own truth.

Charles A. Swanson

You Made Me One of Your Own

One summer day as my wife, Gail, and I were driving to Radford to attend a session of the Highland Summer Conference, she was telling me about the essay she had written. I still love the title: "Leaving Appalachia to Study Appalachia." Although we were driving from a pocket-sized farm in Pittsylvania County, Virginia, down in the Piedmont and to a much more mountainous location in Radford, she felt she was Appalachian to the bone. Along the road between home and Rocky Mount, she pointed out house after house where a kin person or a close family friend lived (or had lived), and she told me of tragedy after tragedy. Murderers, suicides, drunks, moonshiners, ancestors, kinfolk, and ghosts seem to people Appalachian lore, and she felt that, she knew that first-hand.

Charles A. Swanson.

I have never considered myself an outsider either, but I knew my own family had as much of piedmont as we did mountain running in our veins. Our home sits where the east to west migration met the north to south migration patterns. We have as much of Jamestown in us as we do of the German and Scot folks who came down from Pennsylvania. What makes us the most Appalachian, however, are our living patterns—how close our ties are to the land. We know what homeplace and home-house mean. We know what it is to live off the road. I grew up on dried apple pies and cracklings. Hunting and fishing and farming were not sport to us as much as a way of providing for the table through all seasons. Nevertheless, I did not know what kind of reception I would find in the mountains of Southwest Virginia, studying at the feet of well-known writers and teachers.

I first learned of Radford University's Highland Summer Conference through classes I took at Central Virginia Community College with Professor Phil Leonard. Professor Leonard taught classes in Appalachian Literature and Appalachian Folklore, and he not only took his students on field trips, but he invited guest lecturers. Two lecturers I had the privilege to hear were Dr. Grace Toney Edwards and Professor Ricky Cox of Radford University. Ricky read one of the most interesting pieces of nonfiction I have heard that took me into the heart of Floyd County and helped me visualize the people and the customs of the area. If I remember correctly, either emus or llamas crossed the public highway in his essay. The idea of an exotic animal lazing down an Appalachian highway, how incongruous and how delightful! Later I heard a tale of an elephant walking down the twisting two lane Route 40 west of Ferrum, Virginia. These are the kinds of things one hears about in Appalachian writing classes. The strange seems to constantly crash heads with the familiar.

Dr. Edwards came armed with pamphlets about organizations such as ALCA (Assembly on the Culture and Literature of Appalachia) and the Highland Summer Conference. I had some doubts—as well as ambitions—at that time about pursuing a master's degree in English, but I had no doubts about wanting to sign up for the Highland Summer Conference. The very idea that I could study under professional writers, writers from Appalachia and who made Appalachia their heartbeat, thrilled me.

That first summer conference, studying under Jeff Daniel Marion and Kathryn Stripling Byer, was all that I could hope or wish for. I absolutely loved the design of the program. To have a whole week with one published author, morning and afternoon, to share my writing and to hear what other students were producing, was inspirational. Then the second week followed with another professional writer. In addition, we took trips to Selu—Radford's farm and conference center, ate dinner together before the evening readings, and heard two additional writers read from their work during the two-week intensive course. An added bonus, and one that became absolutely essential to me, was the team of Grace Edwards, Ricky Cox, and JoAnn Asbury, all professors at Radford, who sat at the side of the room, always engaged in the teaching session themselves, and ready to help with necessary arrangements. I had never experienced a class with four professors, all totally committed to the class, and all inspired by the work at hand. I could tell that they were moved by writing and by writers. The sessions were as well-targeted as the one-on-one lessons I had experienced with piano and voice teachers, and yet I was in a community of writers.

I enrolled in Radford's Master of English program, and I took the Highland Summer Conference for credit every summer that I was a student. Dr. Edwards even went to the Registrar's Office for me and had the course renumbered so that I could take it a third time for credit. During my degree program, I studied with six different authors from the Appalachian region in the Highland Summer Conference program, writers who were guest teachers and who visited the campus for the express purpose of teaching in the conference. I attended the Summer Conference even after I graduated for the same reason—the reason that my writing blossomed as I had the opportunity to see, hear, read, study, and converse with gifted, talented, and inspirational writers. Truly, writing in community is better than writing alone.

At Radford, I was nurtured and included. At Radford, I became more than a student but a member of a family. At Radford, I felt like an equal even though I was just a fledgling.

To go forward, I must name names, because there were so many writers that were helpful to me. I name them out of respect and love, not because I want to sound like somebody. However, I do include many of those names in my cover letter whenever I send out a batch of poems to a magazine, for they are names that are recognizable. This is, of course, another benefit of such a strong program. Submissions are more likely to be read by an editor of a publication if he or she recognizes a familiar name. We stand stronger when we stand together.

One of the writers who influenced me greatly is Cathy Smith Bowers, who became my thesis advisor in later years when I entered Queens University's MFA program. I learned that Cathy's father loved a song I had long treasured, "Fraulein," a song I had learned from an album by Hank Locklin. I often sang "Fraulein" as I drove along the interstate, and I thought few others knew the song. Cathy and I also bonded over the Emmy Lou Harris song, "Boulder to Birmingham," and we sang the song together at the start of one of the Highland Summer classes. I can still hear her sweet, strong, yet fragile soprano in my head. Singing happened often at Radford, especially when Ricky Cox picked up his guitar, and especially when we made the trip out to Selu.

Another fond memory is of Robert J. Higgs, Jack, who could take a person on a journey about sports' mythology, and lecture about deep structures, but who also was an old soul who loved nothing more than a good chat about any Appalachian topic. My wife took the class with me during that particular summer session. Dr. Higgs told us he would read anything we had to give him, and my wife and I took him seriously. We loaded him down with pages and pages we had written. That very night, he read them all and came back the next day with comments and encouragements. Due to Jack Higgs' generosity in reading our work, my first piece was published in *Appalachian Heritage*.

Through meeting George and Connie Brosi at the evening readings, I became attached to a couple who treated me almost as if I were one of their children. I always thought of them as the stereotypical blend of a mountain couple crossed with social activists of the hippie generation. George could say anything to me, and it didn't have to be nice, because good will was at the heart of it. Connie dwelled in quiet affirmation. She didn't speak loudly, but her kindness carried weight. When Connie passed away, I felt as if a mother figure had passed out of my life.

Several of these dear people are no longer with us. I heard Wilma Dykeman read, and not only did I admire her talent and her political savvy, but she could have stepped right out of my mother's family. The speech patterns, the intonation, the way she carried herself were so much like my mother's oldest sister. Jack Higgs is no longer here, nor is Kathryn Byer. JoAnn Asbury is gone. I cannot believe how fortunate I was to have met these dedicated and inspirational writers and leaders, and blessed connections came through the Highland Summer Conference.

Even now, Ricky Cox and I meet at least once a summer. We talk and talk, and we talk some more. Whenever I teach a unit on ballads, I think of him and his singing of "Naomi Wise," or his rendition of "Three Nights Drunk" (the Cabbage Head song), or I think about how he distinguished between the English ballad and the American ballad. The American ballad often has an ending stanza that moralizes. A great example is "The Wreck of the Old 97" that ends with "Now ladies, you must take warning...." The English/Scottish ballad ends more openly. The sense of wrong and tragedy doesn't have a resolution. I think of "Edward, Edward" and its bitter closing stanza:

> "And what will ye leave to your own mother dear,
> Edward, Edward?
> And what will ye leave to your own mother dear?
> My dear son, now tell me, O."
> "The curse of hell from me shall you bear,
> Mother, mother:
> The curse of hell from me shall you bear,
> Such counsels you gave to me, O."

Ricky plays and makes the Appalachian limberjack dance at the same time. He attaches the limberjack to his guitar, and the wooden toy jerks in a snappy jig while Ricky plays and sings.

The poem which follows represents one of my wonderful experiences from the Highland Summer Conference. I wrote it in Cathy Smith Bowers' honor. Cathy is a master of the poem form called the minute, a 60-syllable pattern of 12 lines written in three stanzas. The syllable count for each stanza is 8 4 4 4, with a rhyme scheme of AABB. One of Cathy's books of verse is titled *A Book of Minutes*. This poem is based on memories Cathy shared at a Highland Summer Conference.

"Fraulein"
for Cathy Smith Bowers

How does a body count distance?
Only a stance,
open or closed.
With your small nose
pressed in a book, you are Crusoe
on Tobago
in your backyard.
Your father's hard

war duty makes him still remote,
and yet you know
heart, tune, and lines—
his song "Fraulein."

What makes a good program? Good people make a good program. As grateful as I am for the inspirational leadership, for the wonderful writing, and for the great design of the Highland Summer Conference, what I am most happy about is the people I have met. I am Appalachian, despite the fact that I live in the foothills. I am Appalachian because of the values I share with other Appalachians, but I am mostly Appalachian because good-hearted Appalachian people took me in.

"Old Work Shirt: Let Me Praise the Pansies"

I've heard you tell, you yearned for Mama's praise.
Tell me I'm pretty, like Mary, you'd say.
Just do as good as you look, she'd say back.
Such wrong-handed words stung you like a slap.
Your sister had the breasts, the curls, the beaus.
At quilting bees, your mama scorned your work.
She said your stitches would snag your husband's toes.
She sent you out with papa to do his work.
But she did admit, you had at least one gift.
Your embroidery was as neat on back as front.
I look now at my threadbare, tattered shirt.

Through years of sweat and labor, stitches hold.
Two ribbons knot bright pansies in a row.
The satin stitches blossom still with gold.

"Old Work Shirt, the Hand-Stitched Swans Most Gone"

What brings to mind your body, this shirt of mine
so worn that I can hold it and see through
to sunshine, with two dwindling swans in blue
of dim embroidery pattern, transfer lines
that tell the stitches, the lost design,
as lost as the lake where the marshes grew,
where the white and purple flowers bloomed,
where once whole swans swam back in time—
such was the time of youth, a time I've saved
despite the dingy fraying of this shirt,
despite your growing old and lying there,
a time I've saved, eternal in my heart,
two swans swimming together on a lake,
two bowed and graceful necks, two swans in prayer.

"Forward: Row-ing for O-hi-O"

Let this be recorded for a generation to come,
so that a people yet unborn may praise the Lord:
that he looked down from his holy height...
to hear the groans of the prisoners....
                                    Psalm 102:18–20, RSV

The owl says, *Who, Who,* distant O's
rolling over wide water like waves;
the blade answers, *hush, hush,* dipping
softly; the prow pushes bravely on.

The moon says, *Who, Who,* too-bright glow
accusing from a starlit sky;
black water answers, *low, low,* hugging
discreet black forms plying north.

The hounds say, *You, You,* distinct echoes,
urgent pulsing from the river's edge;
no one answers, *me, me,* clutching
breath, but for the water's gurgles.

The law says, *You, You,* shall not go—
chains of slavery, unremitting;
five hearts say, *O, O,* within the boat,
praying wide-eyed, not uttering a sound.

"Homeplace"

*...The homeplace is a safe world of manageable scale,
distinct boundaries, and clear of arbitrary rules.*

—Ricky Cox

1. Oh, for Childhood
*Singers and dancers alike say,
"All my springs are in you."*

Psalm 87:7, RSV

Does memory green-over like copper? Age
adds accretions, dirt and oxidation.
The burnish of pink-orange gold, a potion
of pixie powders tossed in fire to engage
spirits to combine—colors like no pages
ever wore, not even jesters, such is the notion
of copper sprites. This is newness, invention.
Copper is youth's color. It's all the rage.
But greens that creep like embossed weeds,
do they choke true color deeper down,
down below a vegetative surface?
Is nostalgia wakened when abrasions bleed
a throbbing copper through an outer wound?
Homesick, I pull the green canker off of place.

2. Sighing
*The Lord records as he registers the peoples,
"This one was born there."*

Psalm 87:6, RSV

The creeks meet below the barn
Ferrum College wanted to buy—
1800s log stable—bank style
with double thick threshing floor—
the wind whips though the slats
and dances stray bits of old hay.

Frogs peep in the bottoms, narrow,
sinuous, where an uncle still runs
cows. The unwanted woods keep
their place behind rusting barbwire—
but pines in tree farm formation
have been deployed across old fields.

The old English boxwoods
have lost their etiquette. Tips
of two posted on either side the walk
lap each other. On a wet morning
the scent of a damp dog rustles
in their overgrown branches.

The dirt daubers know the way
in and out of the home house.
Busted panes, broken glass, litter
the upstairs floors, mix with
birds' nests, feathers, droppings.
The wind sings here too.
From the lower porch, long legs
range on the rail, sock toes angled
toward the tree line or the Dog Star.
No. That was yesterday, when
six boys worked the farm, picked
the banjo after darkness settled down.

Faraway, I hear those voices
sometimes singing, sometimes
no louder than whisper of grasses,
of small frogs making noises,
of stars that have not forgotten
their places in the night sky.
Or is that a street lamp humming?

Termites undershore the walls,
concrete crumbles, rooms echo
to the curious foot, for all goods,
serviceable, sentimental, have found
a place in someone else's home.
The house looks an outpost

but claims an inside space.
We return to look, think, listen.

Is that Mama, Papa? She pats biscuits
in the kitchen, he lights the wood stove.
Back and forth, they have worn a path
across this hillside that will not heal.

3. What is This That I'm A'borning?
Glorious things are spoken of you,
O city of God.

Psalm 87:3, RSV

The hospital on Fairy Street
where I was born
is now an old folks' home—
and I can direct you
to the brick house my daddy built—
but no longer owns.

Time takes shape like wind
rattling the roof.
A banging noise lets me know
the world is restless.
I say, *Come in. I'm ready to go.*
Though I look back longing.
My bones crave the rotten rock,
of my native soil,
but my spirit craves, I tell you,
the white stone,
the hidden manna, the new name,
that the Father waits to give.

First appeared as part of an entry by Ricky Cox titled "Homeplace" in *Encyclopedia of Appalachia*. Eds. Rudy Abramson and Jean Haskell. Knoxville: U of Tennessee P, 2006. 219–20.

Donia S. Eley

From Long Dusty Roads and Tobacco Rows to a Selfie with Gurney

As co-editor of this volume I have read the HSC manuscript numerous times, and I don't think it's my bias that draws me back, but rather seeing something new each time I read the reflections and creative writing. Often I've thought, I wish I'd written that, especially words penned by my fellow Inspired section contributors. Tim Thornton wrote that he was a writer for two weeks. Bonnie Erickson celebrated a journey into the heart. Ruth B. Derrick experienced fun, terror, and gratification. All those sentiments applied to me in the three times I enrolled for credit, and another time or two for non-credit. Since learning about the HSC, I have rarely missed the visiting authors' readings in McConnell Library. What better way to spend an evening than hanging onto words by David Huddle, Robert Morgan, Jeff Mann, Wilma Dykeman, and so many more.

I am a self-described project developer, not a writer. I put things together. The legends and celebrities writing here could have so easily intimidated my feeble classroom attempts, me and others like me, with a few short words or sentences, but they have not ever done so in my HSC experiences. When I look through my files of Appalachian Studies course work over the years, including written research projects, unpublished fiction and nonfiction, short poems, I'm embarrassed. But all I ever received from HSC leaders was positive reinforcement. Somewhere along the way these accomplished writers learned the art of making a student's day, young or middle aged such as I, passing on inspiration, claiming that we are all writers and making us believe it! All it took from these celebrated teachers was a mark in the margins of a student's bad poem or story indicating the fledgling writer had written at least one good sentence, one eye-catching detail, one active scene. I wonder what Bill Brown, Danny Marion, Ron Rash, George Ella Lyon, Silas House, Kay Byer, Frank X Walker, Cathy Smith Bowers, Darnell Arnoult, and others REALLY thought!

Donia S. Eley and Gurney Norman.

Yes, I've published two books, both labors of love such as this one you're browsing, about a beloved Appalachian pencil artist, but I would be delighted to rewrite the first one, knowing what I do now about how to make it better. The story of the talented pencil artist was not difficult to put together once all his drawings and subjects were rounded up across the country. They speak for themselves and required little writing.

I've come a long way from the dusty roads and tobacco rows of my childhood to days of standing close enough to Gurney Norman at an ASA Conference to ask him to take a selfie with me (he agreed). And to be greeted by George Brosi's wide welcoming smile and twinkling eyes, one's day turns brighter.

Personal relationships form the framework on which to build a community, and the HSC has provided that framework year after year for over forty years. It is most certainly a reason to celebrate. Appalachian literature is not an oxymoron, as one author's editor once implied. Though I missed sitting at the feet of Jim Wayne Miller, Mr. Still, Cratis Williams, Jo Carson, I have their works lining the shelves that cover the walls of my home. Their words, their books, and those of their numerous Appalachian fellow authors are essential because they illuminate and celebrate this region I am so passionate about.

"I Am From"
For George Ella

Long dusty roads and tobacco rows
Handing leaves

Riding in the slide
And on tobacco stick horses

Molasses and churned butter on hoecakes
Fresh warm cow's milk
Luzianne chicory coffee
Creek trout

Snapping beans, shelling peas
Blackberry picking
Watching for snakes
And the bull in the field

Peeling peaches under the oaks
Sweet cantaloupe and red watermelon with salt
A swallowed seed
Making a melon grow inside

Homemade ice cream cranked forever
When raw eggs didn't matter

No television, a radio
And the Saturday night Victrola
Mother strumming, singing
Dreaming of being a Carter

Dinner on the Baptist grounds
Deacon Daddy and all his brothers
Dancing was a sin
Leading to who knew what?

A place of prejudice
An outdated culture
Education only for town kids
With blue concrete swimming holes and tennis courts.

"The Captain"
(For Hunter)

"When you're at sea and the sails are up, you don't ask where you're going. You're already there."

The sting of the wind and salt is sandpaper against his face. Sea swells, climbing just so close, test every muscle, challenge every hard-earned skill, slam his yellow slickered body and boat backwards. Let's do that again, the sea seems to laugh. He laughs. He loves it. He's ready.

The Captain knows what lies ahead of this storm. He's seen plenty. At day's end the sun will set over a calm blue sea, a time to draw down the sails and lower the anchor. He will pull from the wine cellar, create a feast from his provisioned galley, and relish that day's glory under the moon glow.

Tomorrow he will set the sails again and glide through calm seas to a place where shapes on the horizon turn into small colorful buildings painted shades of pink, blue, and yellow. Chattering dark skinned children will scamper across the cream colored sand to dive and cavort in the water around him, like little dolphins. Greetings from the dock master will be friendly and foreign, the island culture relaxed and different. Provisions gleaned for the next odyssey will be a new explosion of tastes and textures.

The commonality the children, the dock master, and the Captain share is their love of the sails, the sea, the wind, and the challenges. "Can't Wait."

"Sputnik"
In Memory of Lefty

An athlete in cleats, aspiring scientist, a boy 12,
You were struck out by imagination.
School day done, ballgame won, Daddy's lawnmower shed beckoned.
Matches, gasoline fuel, dreams looking to space.

Then, singed grass, bubbled back porch linoleum, white sundried sheets.
They said the outdoor faucet stopped your shrouded flaming run and melting skin.

Clad like a mummy on a ferris wheel bed,
You took twenty-seven vacations to the surgical ward that summer.
My vacation, to the tiny cot by your bed to turn the wheel,
I earned an honorary nurse's award.

Ferris wheel turns once an hour, 24 times,
And coaxing down life-sustaining formula.

Therapists, teachers, others moved on after a time,
And you did for a while.
Then Daddy died and the doctor said,
Because he worried himself to death over you.

Sputnik and your dreams of space ignited the accident.
Setting up failures, an obstacle course for life.
We didn't burn on the outside like you,
But we scarred on the inside suffering with you.

While your life went on in a pain-filled amputated way,
We wished back your limbs and childhood dreams.
Our scars might have healed,
If we could have watched yours disappear.

"Evening Light"
In Memory of Pa Pa

He came in from the fields and wet heat that hung over the earth weary and worn, but never too tired for me. Removing his ragged straw hat uncovered a brow where tender white skin lay alongside skin made rough and dark from long hours tending the land. His brow looked as though he wore a flesh-colored headband around his flattened hair.

Warm eyes and always a kind word, an invitation. "Let's go find us a watermelon" denied the fatigue he showed, and so grabbing his calloused hand I struggled to match his stride as we headed for the patch. My cool sandals and brightly colored clothing contrasted with the heavy overalls he wore over a worn plaid shirt washed so many times there was only a blur of color remaining. I skipped to the heavy stride of his worn leather high top work boots.

Returning after our treat to the wide porch of unpainted boards at his feet, he settled into an upright split oak chair, his back to the zinnias, the snowball bushes, and climbing pink roses. Only time gave me to understand why the tall large-boned man turned his back on the color and beauty of the yard, but eventually I realized he turned to capture the day's waning light, to see the fine print of his newspaper.

Today I, too, turn to the light to read.

Kevin Stewart

From a Montana Vantage Point

I first learned of the Highland Summer Conference in 1991 while interviewing with Grace Edwards and the late Scott Christianson for entrance into the MA in English program at Radford University. Unknown to them, I was suffering from bulging discs in my lower back and sat there answering questions while painkiller and muscle-relaxant addled. I must've fared okay.

During this interview, Grace also invited me to the HSC. A big reason (hardly my undergrad transcripts!) I'd achieved the above honors was that my writing sample impressed her. It was a short story about an arsonist in Southern West Virginia. She admired the grittiness, the Appalachian setting,

Kevin Stewart.

and the attention to detail, which was, then, more precise than my attention to plot. She explained the HSC's two-week program, the Appalachian theme, and the academic credit. Moreover, she informed me of the visiting writers we'd be working with, one whose work I knew and admired, Denise Giardina, and another whose work I didn't know but would come to greatly appreciate: David Huddle. What I saw in David's work and had already seen in Denise's (and Breece Pancake's) were characters who were much like people I'd grown up with. These folks were plausible subject matter for literature!

But working with Denise and David, and the other conference members, provided so much more. Honest critiques and close-readings. Interesting writing prompts and approaches. Introductions to new writers and refreshing reflections on familiar ones. The conference, as I recall, presented a theme of autobiographical fiction. Denise offered one of the more liberating exercises for me by having us write about a life event in first-person and then rewrite the same event from the POV of another person who was present during the event. Emotional distance. The hardest thing to achieve and to teach. Nonetheless, it's lessons such as those that I still carry with me as a writer and teacher.

My second appearance at the HSC, however, is probably more notable to me. After the 2001 release of my novella, *Margot*, Grace invited me to read at the conference. At the time, I was teaching at LSU and made the drive up from Baton Rouge. Before the reading, Scott Christianson and Tim Poland barged into the room like Trapper John and Hawkeye from M*A*S*H and, after the reading, hauled me to a bar, probably BT's, before dumping me off at the campus motel. Though that was fun, it didn't overshadow what reading at the conference meant for me.

The HSC is important to Radford, the region, and to greater Appalachia, as it showcases the Appalachian writers, storytellers and other cultural warriors. It educates its conference-goers on the importance of maintaining an Appalachian identity, which I still try to do even out here in Montana! Ultimately, it celebrates Appalachia in ways I haven't really seen or been involved with outside of Hindman. I'm proud to have been a part of it and hope to return someday in some fashion.

Silenced

On US 19, I look at things, take in the scenery. I try to get a feel for each part of the road. Wait for a vibe. I'm looking for our role in this. I need to know our role.

I can't do it in a car. I must walk and feel the road under my shoes. I must sniff the air and simultaneously smell, say, ragweed or mowed ramps or bean trees. I must study the crushed bones of a flattened possum. I must think about this, about what it means. The right song must be in my head, "Mansion on the Hill" or "Lost Highway" or possibly the earliest recorded version of "Blue Eyes Crying in the Rain."

You see, Hank Williams may have died on this road. On December 31, 1952, he was driven through here, on the way to a concert in Canton, Ohio, by a college student named Charles Carr. Around Blaine, Tennessee, they'd been stopped for almost sideswiping a passing cop car. The cop u-turned and pulled them over for driving left of center, joking that the man in the back looked dead. Carr thought he'd noticed Hank was breathing, and he'd heard him hiccup a few times. He followed the cop to the magistrate's office in Rutledge, paid his ticket and drove on. He was worried about Hank, though.

Back in Knoxville, in the dark, Hank had to be carried from the Andrew Johnson Hotel to the car and shoved inside. Carr didn't know that Hank was so wasted he'd forgotten about a WROL radio show he missed earlier that day. Once, somewhere along the dark rise and falls of US 11 in east Tennessee—or before they'd even left Knoxville?—just to check whether Hank was okay, Carr asked him to sing a song. Hank asked what he wanted to hear. Anything, Carr said. Hank laughed and said they'd sing one for "Old Red," and they sang a Red Foley song together. Ironic. He knew Hank didn't like "Old Red" much, said he was too slick. Carr felt a little better after they sang, and soon they arrived in Bristol and hit US 19, which, along with US 11, served as the state line between Tennessee and Virginia. On the Tennessee side, Carr stopped at a cab/bus station to piss and get coffee. He heard a man asking the dispatcher was he sure no busses were going to West Virginia until later tomorrow. Carr checked his watch, 9:22, and said, "We're headed to West Virginia."

"We?"

Carr paused a moment. "My passenger and myself." The man considered this and peered through the grimy cab-stand window.

"That your Cadillac?"

"My passenger's." The back door on the driver's side opened, Hank emerged, swayed, his back to them. Hank stood in Tennessee and pissed on Virginia. The man in the cab stand asked, "Mind if I ride in the front seat?"

"You do any driving?"

"You offering me a job or a ride?"

Carr shrugged. "Whichever."

They left. The man was Donald Surface.

I walk on, trying to feel something along the road under my steps, but I am exasperated at not feeling anything and for wanting, really wanting, to feel something, to learn something. To be sure. I need for it to have happened here. I go maybe a hundred yards, searching, the sun slipping behind the ridges, the sky streaked with pink, Venus on the rise, the first light of night.

* * *

Hank was inspired to write "I Saw the Light." Drunk, he woke up in a back seat of his rolling Cadillac in north Alabama. A bright light flashed on his face. He wondered if they'd wrecked and died, and he faced the lights of heaven. The light passed, and he saw an airport in the valley. He was a little pissed, but he took out his notepad and wrote, "I saw the light."

That's one version of the story, of how the song came about. The best one. I always choose the best version, even if it isn't true.

> I saw the light, I saw the light
> No more darkness, no more night
> Now I'm so happy, no sorrow in sight
> Praise the Lord, I saw the light.

No matter how optimistic it might sound, you must figure he still somehow meant it to be sad. After all, God created light out of darkness, and not vice-versa. The dark came first.

East of Summit, West Virginia, several hours after leaving Bristol, Carr pulled up to Nebakanezer's, a long, squat Quonset-hut of a roadhouse run by a Lebanese man named Wheby Jabour. The bar was still open, but the Pabst clock over the liquor shelves was pushing 3:00 a.m. Carr parked and asked Surface whether he was going in or wanted anything. Surface said, no, that he was all right. Inside, three men in flannel coats hunched over the bar, the sorry remnants of a depressing New Year's Eve, no doubt. Jimmie Rodger's "A Drunkard's Child" scratched away on the jukebox. Carr bought himself a cup of coffee and Hank a fifth of bourbon from the gracious Middle Eastern man, who kept repeating, "Thank you. Thank you," nodding with each "Thank you." Carr answered, "You're welcome," each time, growing weary of it after the second. He was tired, having driven from Alabama to Knoxville, and now up these curvy mountain roads in snowy Bumfuck, Virginia, and, God, he'd just gotten to West Virginia, the worst yet to come. He wanted to let Surface drive now, but when he got back to the car, Surface was gone. He looked both ways up and down US 19, a rare straightaway that lay along Oak Mountain River like a length of bone at the base of a deep gash. Carr didn't see his new passenger in either direction, so he climbed back in the Cadillac, tried to hand the fifth to Hank, who was still asleep, slumping but sitting up. He dropped the bottle into the singer's lap, cranked the car and drove on, through Triple Oaks, the tires singing across the steel-grated bridges as US 19 snaked Bluestone Valley before climbing Flat Top Mountain.

I love the mountains when they're green and they look like broccoli bunches. The trees will soon be afire, though, the leaves red, yellow, orange—the kind of thing people take Sunday afternoons to drive the backroads and gawk at. Once winter arrives, the mountains look like they need a shave.

Gravel crunches under my shoes. I kick a partially flattened Rolling Rock can into the dried weeds, the aluminum pinging, and the stalks whispering after it. On Flat Top Mountain to the north, the folds of the hollows begin near the top and flare toward the base. Shadows paint the western slopes.

I prefer to start with the tops of hills, take in as much as I can view. Overhead, steel towers carry sagging, staticky power lines from Glen Lyn, Virginia, down through the valley below me and then up and over Flat Top. A swath cut through the trees beneath the lines has regrown with chest-high pines, laurels, locusts, and blackberry brambles around the rock outcroppings. The swath looks like a scar. It is a scar. It wasn't here when Hank passed through, so it is of no concern. Nor are the mines to the west, surface or deep, the gouged-out Walmart lots north and south.

The senses I feel are hard to explain. They're not just your five senses. I've felt things before, here and there. Not enough to make me think I was on the spot, but enough for me to realize something happened there. It's like a divining rod. Something pulls at me. It's as if there are spots where gravity gets stronger and tugs at my guts. I think these are significant places, like where Hank wrote his last lyrics. But the pull on these spots doesn't seem strong enough to be *the* place. That spot will grip, and when it lets go, my insides will buzz like an amp.

I spy something in the gravel and pick it up, hefting a cool penny in my hand, Abraham Lincoln's profile staring toward home. I turn it over. A wheatie, 1949. It might've lain here since that night, or someone might've lost it only yesterday.

In Oak Hill, West Virginia, well into that new year, Carr pulled into a gas station. He glanced over his shoulder at Hank. He said, "Mr. Williams?" When Hank didn't answer, Carr got out of the Cadillac and opened the rear driver-side door. Hank was slumped against the passenger-side. As if reaching for a coiled copperhead, Carr eased his hand forward and touched Hank on the elbow. Hank Williams was still. Dead, Carr knew. He noticed a piece of paper clutched in Hank's dead hand and pulled it from the cooling fingers. The wind whipped snow all around him and into the open car door, the flakes not even melting on Hank. Carr read the note:

> We met, we lived and dear we loved
> Then comes that fatal day
> The love that felt so dear fades far away

He jerked back out of the car and slammed the door, breathing hard, his throat tightening, his hands and feet numbing.

Whether Carr, at that moment, pondered the significance of holding the most influential country-music songwriter and singer's last written words, I don't know. He was likely mostly scared. A dead man slouched in the back seat of his own Cadillac, and Carr was driving it. A friend of Hank's, Carr was eighteen, a college student alone on Christmas break before being hired. A couple more weeks stood between him and the start of spring semester, so Carr thought, "Sure. Easy money. Free concerts. Why not?"

Now, his emaciated boss was dead. Carr wanted to run, but he was stuck smack dab in the middle of West Virginia. He didn't know anyone. He considered driving back to Knoxville, just park the car in the hotel parking lot and leave this dead drunk in the backseat. Goddamned Hank Williams, and his I-am-bound-to-die depressing hillbilly shit.

Yes, Carr could just leave Hank to be found in the Andrew Johnson's parking lot and go back to his Montgomery apartment and read his history books and continue with his dream of being a history teacher. He wanted to teach it, not necessarily be a part of it, but now he was, he realized. He was forever.

In the months and years to come, when Carr'd turn on the radio, Hank came on and Carr changed the station. A little while later, Hank came on there. Carr tuned in to the black station. Surely, Hank couldn't come on there. But even in those old blues and R&B songs, Carr heard chords and notes and phrasings that echoed Hank or that Hank echoed. He'd have to turn off the radio. Maybe even break it.

In Oak Hill, West Virginia, though, Carr decided to call the police and found a phone booth nearby. A short time later, a patrol car pulled alongside the Cadillac and the cops got out. One cop opened the rear driver-side door and craned his neck inside and said, yep, it was Hank Williams, all right. The other cop said that he wasn't no bigger than nothing. He shook his head.

Carr wasn't sure, but he thought he saw the first cop slip something into his coat pocket. While they waited on the ambulance, Carr peeked inside one last time and saw Hank's watch and fifth were gone, but what could he say? At the hospital, several doctors examined Hank and pronounced him dead on arrival.

Hank's Cadillac remained at the gas station, where, once word got out that Hank died right there in Oak Hill, it was stripped of anything that might be valuable or make a good souvenir. Maybe this is our legacy in the death of Hank Williams. We weren't thieves, per se, but his songs weren't enough. Nothing is that can't be held in our hands. We took his shit and gave nothing back until the 1980s, when the old truss, steel-grated bridges were replaced on US 19. The one closest to Frenchburg, West Virginia, in Oak County, was named the Hank Williams, Sr. Memorial Bridge. Some replacement: a sleek non-descript, Department of Highways bridge.

The next morning after Hank died, Carr took a bus back to Knoxville. At the Tennessee line in Bristol, he cried. When he reached home in Montgomery, he stared at the radio. Hank Williams loomed in there. If not right now, he would be soon. Hank Williams would be everywhere on the radio. "I'll never get out of this world alive." The dead son of a bitch would never leave him alone. Carr opened his window and threw the radio out and watched it burst on the pavement of the alley two stories below. He couldn't do the same with cars, though. The rest of his life, every time he drove, Carr frequently checked the rearview for a slumped, hunched-over body, cold in the backseat.

The autopsy showed Hank Williams died of alcoholic cardiomyopathy, but he lived a life of pain from a birth disorder, Spina Bifida Occulta, that gnarled his back. Hank suffered continual chronic back pain, and the morphine he ingested to ease it mixed with the booze had killed him after he'd written those lines. Add that to the internal injuries from a fight down in Montgomery, two days before he'd hit Knoxville, ending up in the backseat of that Cadillac, a bottle between his legs.

He wrote those first two lines, felt the pain in his back and in his gut. He put the pen and paper down on the seat, unscrewed the lid from the bottle and took a long pull. He closed the bottle, picked up the pen and paper and wrote the last line. He squeezed the pen in one hand and crumbled the paper in the other. He gritted his teeth and grimaced, the pain raging in his spine before moving to his chest. He thought about his last performance. The Montgomery, Alabama, chapter of the American Federation of Musicians. Mostly jazz musicians. It was said that Hank blew them away. One guy even claimed the musicians listened as though Hank were Billy Holiday.

After the show, he ended up in his own element, some old honkytonk. A fight ensued. Over why, only a dead man knew. But for part of the night, Hank took that unfamiliar audience of kick-ass jazz musicians, people who may have ventured into that show thinking they wouldn't like him or hadn't even paid attention to who the hell he even was, and Hank made them pay attention, all right. He made them his.

In the backseat somewhere in West Virginia, Hank's left arm grew numb. His alcohol-marinated heart failed. He died. The pen and bottle fell to the floorboard, whiskey sloshing inside for some unknown miles until Carr stopped in Oak Hill and found him dead.

* * *

On US 19 in Oak County, I've walked all the way through Barrel, over Barrel Mountain and Black Oak Mountain to Triple Oaks. I've walked almost to Tent Creek, to the top of Cornpone Ridge. The road is exactly the same as it was when Hank Williams died on it, and I've studied it like a jeweler as I've traversed it. I've explicated it, searching for something, anything that might hold a clue to the exact spot where he died. Thinking that maybe

Charles Carr knew when Hank Williams died and wanted to somehow memorialize the spot, I've looked for markers on trees, on the old white guard posts, on rock outcroppings. I have found nothing.

But now, standing on the Hank Williams, Sr., Memorial Bridge, I feel it. Not the bridge. It. This is the spot. Hank's hit when he died was "I'll Never Get Out of this World Alive." These old hollows have trapped a lot of living people, much less dead ones. Maybe Hank felt at home here, or like he'd finally made it home. I mean, it was dark. He was drunk, aching from his back and his insides from that fight in Montgomery. Pumped full of morphine, chloral hydrate and vitamin B-12, he never saw the scenery that night. I'm sure he'd traveled through here before and seen it, and I'm sure it appealed to him—towns and farms cut off by steep mountains, or perched on them. "Mansion on the Hill" might be literal here. Standing on this bridge, I realize the state got it right, for once, and marked the spot, but it still screwed things up.

Let me explain.

Hank had lost control of his body to disability, disease, drugs and booze. He'd lost control of his career to his wife, Audrey, and to his mother, to the record companies, to the fucking Grand Ol' Opry. I read once he was asked what his next record would be; he answered that he didn't know, that he hadn't been told yet, that everyone else always knew before he did. I imagine he said this with more than a bitterness in his voice as sour as whiskey, and I imagine he knew what it was like to have the one thing that kept him going taken from him. During that time, he merely moved around, a zombie, to that next show. He passed through these mountains, which demanded nothing of him, mountains that allowed a man to live however he wanted to as long as he left them alone. Maybe Hank decided that if he'd been offered one last chance to spring free, this was it. There was only one way out, though. He couldn't do it alive. He'd never get out alive.

As his Cadillac's wheels wailed across that steel-grated bridge near Frenchburg, Hank Williams wailed, too, hoping that, if there were such things as spirits and ghosts, he would slip from this Cadillac and wander these hills, a place that is about as wild as a man could find back in those days, and these.

Hank then grimaced one last time, seeing the light, as if the brightest dome light ever inside a Cadillac flashed on. It radiated from the windows. He saw the mountains through spitting snow, trees, ridges, and hollows, and he emanated out with the light. Where it gave way to darkness, he slipped away. The light vanished. The Cadillac's tires hushed on asphalt swirling with snow. Hank Williams was gone from his body, imbued in the hills.

For a long time, he roamed these hills. I know for a fact he did. For years, tires on that old truss bridge, on the steel grating, would absolutely wail. A whippoorwill, a train, a voice. The concrete surface of the new bridge is quiet. Hank Williams has now been silenced, replaced by a green, flimsy galvanized sign bearing his name in white.

First appeared in *Appalachian Heritage*, Fall 2007. Winner of the Plattner Award for Fiction.

Becky Dellinger Hancock

APPALKIDS at HSC

Having heard that many share the same experience, I've come to believe that all things related to Appalachian Studies—college and university departments, storytelling and musical careers, courses, conferences, and festivals—evolved because of the perfect timing of a calling to the study of this unique, complex, and rich mountain culture.

Some have received their calling from outside Appalachia, adopting her causes and appreciating the traditions and values of her people. Others, natives steeped in the traditions of and love for their mountain home, had their calling instilled in them by heredity or perhaps cultural osmosis. Then there are those who, despite being born and reared in Appalachia, grew up ignorant of their heritage. Lastly, there are those who are either ashamed of or see nothing special in their culture and long only to see these mountains in their rearview mirror.

Becky Dellinger Hancock.

I was one of those ignorant of her heritage. Though I was born in coal country, lived in a holler, picked out my few toys at the company store, and waited each evening for Daddy, caked with coal dust, to come home from the mines, that was my life. It was all I knew, and I would become no wiser throughout high school, college, and several years of teaching.

Then in 1983, I began graduate work in English education at Radford University and there received my calling to learn about my roots. An astute professor, noting my background and interests, guided me to the Appalachian Studies program as an education concentration. My first class was Appalachian Folklore taught by Dr. Grace Toney Edwards, and it was during the first hour of class that both my view of self and my educational philosophy shifted. As soon as Dr. Edwards began to share her course "opportunities," I saw in them a reflection of my family, our values, our traditions, and more. I saw my heritage appreciated, valued, and validated. My story was important, and I wanted to teach others that their stories were important too.

The following summer of 1984, I participated in the Highland Summer Conference under the direction of Cherokee-Appalachian poet Marilou Awiakta. Through the poems in *Abiding Appalachia: Where Mountain and Atom Meet*, she told her story, blending her mountain upbringing in Oak Ridge, Tennessee, with the history, legends, and myths of her Cherokee people. Her passionate story, told in the context of celebrating her dual heritage, reinforced what had inspired me in Dr. Edwards's class. That fall I created an Appalachian Studies class which was added to Pulaski County High School's English Department curriculum. The students excelled in collecting oral histories and delighted in storytelling. Soon they asked to form a club so they could tell Jack Tales on club day, continuing an activity they had enjoyed with their middle school Language Arts teacher Carolyn Mathews. For the uninitiated, these are folktales about a boy named Jack who undergoes various trials and tribulations, but through his wits and occasionally a helper or two, he always comes out a hero. These stories circulated widely through the mountains in the early 1900s and were collected and published by author Richard Chase.

While the club met throughout that year, a group focused on more structured storytelling and musical performance had been evolving. In March of 1985, the APPALKIDS (American People Presenting Appalachian Life through Kids in Dramatic Skits) was formed and in May answered their calling in their first public performance. Over the next nine years the group wove music, folktales, oral histories, and original dialogue into performances created to promote a positive image of the Appalachian region, its people, history, and culture. In 1989, Teresa Wheeling, an HSC alumnus who had received her calling through traditional music in Radford University's Appalachian Studies program, joined the group as musical director. Under her guidance, untapped talent emerged and performances were enriched by musical interpretation. From the group's formation in 1985 to its retirement in 1994, the APPALKIDS traveled over 13,000 miles throughout six states and Washington, D.C., presenting 203 performances for audiences totaling over 28,000.

Many requests for performances would come over the years, but it was in 1989 and 1990, that the APPALKIDS received an invitation from the Highland Summer Conference. Two may seem an insignificant number in a list of 203 performances, but we have always considered these two of special significance, and all because of the timing.

The APPALKIDS' performances were written in the summers and performed during the following school years. *Living Memories*, created in the summer of 1988, and performed throughout the 1988–89 school term, was inspired by Jim Wayne Miller's "Brier Sermon: You Must Be Born Again." Though this poem is multi-themed, the APPALKIDS, just beginning to create life experiences themselves, had one audience goal in mind: To inspire each person, no matter the age, to savor experiences so that years later those experiences could be "born again" through their memories. To be invited to perform by HSC in the summer of 1989, and to learn that Miller, the HSC guest writer, would be in the audience was a delightful surprise. Though he had read the script and given us permission to quote his work the summer before, we never imagined that he would ever attend a performance, the very one performance inspired by his writing. Reflecting now on a long list of performances, this invitation from the HSC provided a unique and unprecedented experience for the APPALKIDS.

The following summer of 1990, the Highland Summer Conference again invited the APPALKIDS to perform. That year's script was filled with music played on guitar, autoharp, mandolin, and upright bass by students who, only a year before, had never held musical instruments. *Celebrating Appalachia* was inspired by Marilou Awiakta's passionate celebration of mountain values while at the same time dispelling the negative stereotypes of Appalachia and all ethnic and cultural groups. The APPALKIDS, having learned a valuable proverb from her in 1987: *"The tree that has deep roots need not fear the wind,"* hoped their audiences would celebrate their own heritages and, as the APPALKIDS had, take the advice to heart: *Celebrating Appalachia*, written the previous summer without knowledge that Awiakta would be the 1990 HSC guest writer, became yet another opportunity for the APPALKIDS to perform in the presence of their inspiration.

Throughout their years of performing, the APPALKIDS entertained many different audiences. Each performance was an honor, but the Highland Summer Conference provided this dedicated group of students a unique opportunity. By embracing the writings of Appalachian authors and practicing the craft themselves, the APPALKIDS continued their calling—celebrating their Appalachian heritage in hopes that others might receive a calling of their own.

Rick Mulkey

Homecoming

When I was twenty-three years old, I wrote my first honest story. By honest, I mean it was the first piece of writing I had ever produced that dealt with real emotion, real fear, real confusion, real attempts at understanding. I wrote the story for a workshop David Huddle led at the Highland Summer Conference. Before that story, I'd never written a word that I hadn't expected to write. I had never surprised myself. And as the wonderful writer Eudora Welty once wrote, "if you haven't surprised yourself, you haven't written."

This was the summer of 1987, and I was a graduate student at Radford University completing my final courses for my Master of Arts

Rick Mulkey.

degree in English. I had been a devoted reader since I was little more than a toddler. But as a writer, I was very much a novice. I wanted, however, to know more and so I read as widely as I could and I wrote daily in journals, and on scraps of paper. Most of this was at best poor imitations of other writers. Without guidance, I wasn't sure how to proceed. Then Grace Edwards, Director of Appalachian Studies at Radford, encouraged me to participate in the Highland Summer Conference held on the Radford campus. Growing up in rural Southwest Virginia, I'd never been exposed to living writers. I didn't know anything about writers as a group: talking and working among them, the habits and processes of literary communities. I knew I would be more naïve than many of my fellow workshop participants because I had never taken a writing class or been in a workshop. In college I had studied literature because I loved reading, but I didn't understand books as living art. When I decided to embark on writing, it was mostly by myself in a room full of novels and poetry collections, or with my notebook in a diner or bar.

What would a writing workshop offer me, I wondered? How, if at all, would I be different after?

Of course, I had a few expectations about possible advantages: a group of new writing acquaintances, a few new pieces of writing, some insight about the writing life and about art, the basic items for a more useful writer's toolbox. I was also a bit worried. Responses to my academic writing in college and school had mostly been unhelpful at best, and intimidating at worst. What I couldn't imagine, however, before entering David Huddle's wonderful workshop that summer was how those hours and days would change the direction of my life.

I remember I was sitting in my office the morning after I turned in a new story for David's workshop. A quietly intense, yet supportive presence in the workshop, David had grown up in Virginia only a few miles from my own hometown. I was amazed that someone originally from our area could have the kind of writing success he'd already had. That morning I could hear him in his running shoes making his way down the hall long before he came to the door of my office. I'm sure he knew I was concerned about the group critique the story would undergo in a few minutes. It was my first time providing a workshop with any piece of writing. He leaned into the office, smiled and said, "Congratulations. This is a powerful story." Later that morning he and the workshop group were kind, supportive, and constructive. After that summer, I kept in touch with David Huddle and he encouraged me to continue writing and to apply to MFA programs. So did Grace Edwards.

It was through this early experience, and others like it, that I learned what kind of poet I wanted to be and what kind of writing teacher. I've learned over the years that poetry, at least for me, matters the way home itself matters. Without we're lost. The support of my work and the constructive feedback I received during that workshop gave me, in many ways, the literary home I had always wanted. Those two weeks mark the moment I discovered for the first time I could actually become a writer. Then in 2004, I was honored to return to the Highland Summer Conference, but this time as a visiting writer and visiting speaker. It was, for me, an important literary homecoming. Now, five books and 30 plus years after my original conference participation, I owe a debt to Grace Edwards, David Huddle, and all those who participated in the workshop that summer of 1987. It is a privilege to have participated in and benefited from the Highland Summer Writers Conference.

"Concerning Whisky"

Potent, peaty, brine-filled dram
like the salt-washed rocks of sheltered bays;
like the turf fires beneath thatched roofs; like rain
falling hard and soot blackening the stone hearth;
like the venerable who curl into themselves
and wait for spring, old women, grown diaphanous,
who flutter like moths embalmed in their silver-haired cocoons,
aged, at last, into their ghostlier selves; like their men
no longer storming pastures as fierce scouring winds,
but, lost in their suffering, now gnaw remorse
and grasp at guilt as they once did pipe and pint.
This is the alchemy of fire and air, the chemistry of creek and valley.
The distillate of place and time. Distillate of memory.
Soft, sugary, amber-clouded elixir like the lure
of meadowsweet and chicory, like October smoke
hanging over maple and oak; like the sophistry of sex
on sunlit mornings in late December,
cold hands along the flushed length of spine and breast,
breath passing across the altar of tongue, frosting bedroom windows;
like the dulcet notes of mandolin, the sorrowful soaring of fiddle;
the primal groan of Cash's *Ring of Fire*,
or Elvis's moaning call to *Love Me Tender*.
This is the push and pull, the liquid mystery train
of peril and possibility we can't explain
though it carries a little of everything: the bog, the raisin,
the raison d'etre, the pie safe and gun safe, the morning promises
and midnight faults, the scars forgotten and reclaimed,
the ice, in expectation, clanging in a glass.

"Concerning Whisky" first appeared in *MacQueen's Quinterly*, Issue 1.

"Cured"
for Albert Goldbarth

Albert, I'm here to tell you
Bluefield, Virginia, has the best bacon
in the Eastern U.S. I know
you've never been there, but it's the kind
of place you might visit on a Sunday,
clear blue sky and mountain ridges frosted,
when all the evangelicals in their aging
chapels and strip mall sanctuaries are off to pray
that folks like you and me won't turn
their fruitful lands into a salty waste,
and you'd be left alone
or nearly so, in the only diner
open on a Sunday morning. Just like me
you'd be lured in by the satisfying
aromas of peppered pork belly, the sensation
of eating the blistered fat of swine.
We wouldn't care that it was spiritually unclean,
or that all it touched was unclean,
the unclean plate, the unclean scrambled eggs,
the filthy toast and jam, the way our fingers
lathered in its fatty sweetness
were unclean, or our mouths unclean,
or the BLT we'd order to take
with us, piled high in bacon, unclean.
And later, as we walked the empty streets
before the local parishioners labored out
to find their way home to sanctified roasts
they'd ravage from pristine platters,
you and I and our friends would grow hungrier
and hungrier as we'd compare the subtle flavors
of acorn and truffle, the sugary-salty depth of pig.
Then you'd quote from Su Shi, Martial,
or Matthews' sensuous song of swine,
"Sooey Generous," and we'd agree that eventually
we'll all be offered up on one altar or another,
salted with fire and smoke, salted with age, salted
in baths, entering a covenant of salt, cured,
if you will, of any worries about what might
come to pass tomorrow. And knowing this life

is the one life and wanting to make the most of it,
we'd pick up a glass of very cold, very sweet tea
at the Dairy Queen, and we'd unwrap our sandwiches,
drink deeply from the cup, and eat of the crispy flesh,
satisfied celebrants of this porcine priesthood.

First appeared in *Southeast Review,* issue 37:1 and received the Gearhart Poetry Prize.

"An Explanation"

I know nothing of the way
a comet sings its melancholy song to the ether,
or how it scores its cold path repeatedly.
The sun and moon are as alien to me
as the colony of ants busily foraging, or the herd
of buffalo swaying in the prairie's tall grass.
I've little understanding of farm subsidies
or urban blight, of how a town called Prosperity
is little more than an abandoned Rite Aid store
boarded and smothered in kudzu,
all of it ditch weed scented, a breath the wind
trapped and forgot to exhale.
I know nothing of Wall Street bandits
or political priests in their great marbled halls.
There is little I can say about the rich
or the poor or women and children.
Or men either. And while I'm told
there are many gods and many prophets:
Jaweh, HaShem, Bhudda, Vishnu, Shiva, Breged,
Allah, and Mohommed, I fear there is
no god, no prophet, no shaman,
only profiteers and con men.
While there may exist an afterlife,
the cradling void is all we've discovered.
And though I want to understand
the intricacies of time, light and the everlasting now,
the ways in which retrocausality suggests
in the quantum world the future shapes the past,
this, and more, eludes me. Instead, I sweep coal dust
from the floors of my mother's house
because I know that's what she'd do
if still alive. And she did it because it needed doing,
simple as that, a moment of grace.

How else to understand the comfort
this repetition offers, how else to explain
the rhythm of blood navigating veins,
wind surfing corn stalks, planets orbiting,
galaxies expanding. The raspy whisper
of broom straw across linoleum
calls me to the only prayer I know.

First appeared in *Still: The Journal*, Fall 2016, and received the Judge's Choice Award.

Matt Prater

Looking Back

In thinking back on the two Highland Summer Conferences I attended, I think about the ideas about writing that I still bring into my own classrooms, and that still inform the way I think about my work, both creative and academic; and I really am struck by just how much of those two weeks' ideas have stayed with me, ten years on.

From Frank X Walker, I learned the idea of writers as living in certain, deliberate ways that are conducive to their work. Also the importance of close reading in the life of the writer, of taking poems on their own terms and learning from them and staying with them and in them—that poems contain theory and idea enough

Matt Prater.

on their own. Also, that writing is a holistic activity, which to do at your best requires attending to your health in many ways: taking care of your body, taking care of your mental and emotional life, and—something that is often overlooked when we consider writers and writing from a stereotypical mindset—*taking care of other people.*

From Darnell Arnoult, I learned the idea of writing as a "quilting" process, and the fact that neither writing nor life are linear activities. We build up our work at a pace and in an order that can't be forced; the best path forward is to be ready for what comes, in the order it comes, and accept it and work with it rather than to try and force it. We can really only look for and see the patterns after we have enough materials; planning it all out ahead of time rarely works.

From Crystal Wilkinson, I learned the idea of writing as an act of listening closely to others. This means both being attentive to other people in the "real" world and being attentive to the people in our stories—that if we don't know their intimacies, what they would have for breakfast, how they would react to a given situation—we don't know them, and certainly don't know them well enough to write their stories.

From David Huddle, I learned the idea of writing as a life work and a professional discipline. It is something that is returned to, over and over, daily, with the practice and attention one gives to any serious work. And it is serious work, if taken as such. Also that specializing as a writer, in genre or idea or mode, is unnecessary. The discipline of writing is a paradox: we come back to the same activity, over and over, but we do different things each time. The rigor of practice and the repetition of the work is what gives us the freedom to do and be many things.

"Trieste"

For writing as he did, James Joyce preached
silence, exile, cunning, & tried to fly to Mars
with stranger prose; though the higher he flew,
the more the ghosts of Irish folk crawled out,
until in the end he was nothing but
a conduit of voices, a smatter and echo
making little sense at all but in its saying
& sound of song. Still, there was sun in Trieste,
& his guitar carried airs, & enough language
that away from his nation forever,
he could write of his nation forever.
But I cannot go James Joyce's exile way.
Carter Woodson & Woodrow Wilson
are both my fathers. That will not change.
I have opened a door I do not want to open,
though there is sun, and the sound of airs,
on the other side. & perhaps a good life.
Let the dead bury their own dead, I imagine
Jesus telling me. But I imagine Him also
telling me of the life in these bones. I am torn.
The sun is growing higher in the day of my life.
I have no pretty words left, and hard choices.

I've never seen James Joyce's country, this is true.
As true as that I've never seen my own.
Except in myth & hymn & poem has either
ever had a home. *There is no Appalachia.*
Find the border, if you doubt me. Trace it down.
Whatever your map is, your map's not mine.
Or the US government's, whose map is...fine,
but no one trusts the government in Appalachia,
left or right. Which makes us something like
a quantum country, charmed & strange,
made by observation from all sides. Meaning:
I have never been there. Meaning: I can never go
away. Meaning: I am free. & meaning: anywhere
I do go, being from there, I am there—forever.

Sam L. Linkous

Remembering Jim Wayne Miller—and More

The Highland Summer Conference definitely became a life experience for me. I was a "non-traditional" student who had started college as a 40-year-old freshman and after about three or four years I discovered that I liked putting my thoughts into written form. The caveat was that no one was interested in what I was writing because it wasn't very good, just ramblings. I finally figured out that I just needed to write for myself and not worry about how anyone else felt about my writing. I also realized that I like ramblings. But I have to admit that if someone likes what I write, that does make it a lot more fun.

Sam L. Linkous (photograph by Ricky Cox).

I had discovered Jim Wayne Miller's writing, and to me, he was just a legendary person out there writing these amazing poems and stories. I never expected to have the honor of meeting him. Then came the Highland Summer Conference with Jim Wayne Miller. I was actually going to meet JWM, and even more incredible, he might even see something that I had written. He oozed wisdom. From his old white station wagon filled completely with boxes of folders of reference material, writings, and who knows what else, to his slightly relaxed appearance, he was a wise and amazing presence. When he picked one of my poems to read and comment on in the class, I thought that

I had arrived. If I never wrote again, I had reached that pinnacle in my writing. At least that's what I thought at the time. I actually sent him a copy of that edited poem with a humorous comment and he responded with a nice note of appreciation. I'll always remember his parting words to us at the conference, "May the metaphors be with you." If you're a certain age, I do not need to explain that.

Most of my writing from that point on was, and is, influenced by those days. Jim Wayne Miller, Anndrena Belcher and others, showed me that I need to write for myself and write about what I know and love.

"Catching Supper"

On cold November mornings
heavy frost remembers my footsteps.

Clover, Orchard Grass, Timothy,
crackle beneath leather-soled boots.

From the ridge, I can see
a rusty hoe,
leaning against slack American wire,
waiting
for spring's mild days,
moist tilled earth,
green sprouts,

Mama's Rhode Island Reds
clucking, scratching for their morning fare,
wood smoke hovering in hollows.
Slate creek,
nearly dry.

Box traps checked every day.

Fat rabbits for supper,

rolled in flour and

fried like chicken.

"Sacred Ground"

Richard brought Dan and Buck to turn our ground.
I love walking barefoot in cool, damp,
new-plowed earth.

Pickin' up night crawlers,
fishin' for Red Eyes in Slate Creek,

in that same hole where they
broke ice, baptized
Charlie Lawson in 1939.

"They done things like that back then.
People was tough." Daddy said.
He should know.
He helped bring Percy Henry out
when the mine exploded—
helped put him in the ground too.
"Percy's own mother didn't recognize him."

This ground knows:
where Granny walked,
Uncle Walt dug Ginseng,
where there's water,
where Grandpa knelt to pray, and
when my footsteps cross theirs.

Found some Indian stuff: arrow heads, pottery, tools.
Found'em where Grandpa had a brush arbor meeting once.

Man from the college says
this could be sacred ground.

I could have told him that.

Reflections

Sammy

Gypsy women don't wear any underwear. At least that's what I believed when I was seven years old. Irma, Uncle Malean's wife, was teaching us kids how to do somersaults in the front yard when we all made the discovery that led me to that belief. Irma was not really Uncle Malean's wife; she came back with him from some of his travels one time and stayed. I think he met her in Louisiana. People referred to her as his wife for the sake of appearances.

Irma wore colorful scarves around her neck and sometimes tied around her head holding down her very black hair, and usually had lots of rouge on her cheeks. She also wore big loose floral-print skirts and brightly-colored blouses. Since I had never seen a real gypsy, I took Daddy's word for it that she was a real gypsy. He had seen gypsies before and said that Irma was certainly one.

Uncle Malean was not really our uncle either, but lots of people called him Uncle. I think he may have been kin to some of Daddy's cousins and Daddy got in the habit of calling him Uncle because they did. Uncle Malean would sometimes go on his trips and not come back for weeks, or months. Malean was a tall leathery man who most always wore khaki-colored shirts and matching pants and a grey felt fedora with sweat rings and a satiny ribbon band with a little feather. He had the aroma of Old Spice and hand-rolled cigarette tobacco. I thought that was a rather pleasant smell. He taught me how to whistle and showed me how to make a sound like crows calling with a blade of grass and a split stick, and to sound like a train whistle when blowing between my thumbs into my cupped hands.

Malean

I have traveled most of my life doing everything from carpenter work to rigging to working on a fishing boat in Louisiana. That's where I met Irma; she was really something I'll tell you. I found her working in this little-ole shop on the street selling jewelry, scarves, and trinkets. I just went right up to her and pretended that I was interested in buying something and we hit it off right away. I met her when she got off work that day and we went to get something to eat and, after that, I made a point to stop by that little shop every time I was in the village. Sometimes we'd walk and talk and sometimes we'd eat. I'd been working on that fishing boat for quite a while and was very happy to have some female companionship. I liked that she always wore them bright colors and big swirly skirts. She was right pretty and dark skinned too and not much younger than me. When I got ready to go back to Virginia, I asked her if she wanted to go. I did not have much to offer, just a little four-room house in the holler, but I had running water and a pretty-new outhouse. She said she'd go and we got bus tickets for Virginia the next day.

Irma

I grew up traveling from place-to-place because my family never seemed to settle anywhere for very long and that habit continued even after I grew up and got away from my family. I had been in Louisiana for several months only because my old man, that son-of-a-bitch, found someone he'd rather be with and left me sitting in that run-down motel room with no money or any way to get around.

I did what I had to do to get by, including some things I'm not very proud of. The motel owner let me clean rooms to make enough to pay for my room and get a little something to eat most days. I finally got a job in a little street market selling souvenirs—scarves, knick-knacks, jewelry, and what-nots. Most of it was junk from Japan. I met Malean when he stopped by to look around but I knew that, by looking at him, he wasn't interested in any of the stuff that we was selling. He was a little older than me, probably by about 10 years, and a little rough, but seemed nice enough. Finally, one day after stopping by three or four times, he asked me if I wanted to go with him to get a bite when I got off from work. I jumped at that because I could not afford much, especially eating in a restaurant. He did say that he had to leave to go back to Virginia soon so I figured that I'd never see him again. Some days he'd come by and we'd talk, or go to eat, or go to his boarding house room.

One day he stopped by to tell me he was leaving in a couple days and asked me if I wanted to go with him. I thought, what the hell, and said, Yeah, I'll go. I ain't been to Virginia before. I had my little bag ready and we got on the bus and headed out. We had to walk the last couple miles from where the bus dropped us off.

His place was a little four-room house in a holler that needed painting, but was livable and was better than a cheap motel room. He had friends and relatives near-by and we walked to visit them pretty often and occasionally they'd ask us to eat supper with them. I liked playing in the yard with the kids and teaching them tricks like turning somersaults and spinning until we got dizzy.

Sammy

We lived in the old brown brick-sided company house on the corner across from Mr. Jimmy's blacksmith shop. Uncle Malean lived about a half mile down the hollow from us and walked up to visit pretty often. Many times, he'd show up about supper time and Mama would have to figure out how to stretch the meal out to feed one more, and after Irma came, two more. Sometimes she'd say that she wasn't real hungry and not take very much for herself.

Mr. Jimmy had his blacksmith shop across the road from our house where he made shoes for his two big grey workhorses, Dan and Buck. Once a strange fox wandered into our yard and Mama made us kids come inside. She said that the fox was "acting funny" so she hollered across the road to Jimmy and he came with his pistol; his bibbed overalls and blue chambray shirt were reminders of several days of working in the shop and garden. Another thing he used his shop for was to sneak a drink from a bottle of Old Crow he kept in the big wooden tool box. This was one of those times, except that this time he had snuck more than one drink and was having a little trouble walking a straight line. He missed the fox at point-blank range two or three times before finally killing it.

"Probably had rabies." Daddy said when he got home from work. "Lucky it didn't bite one of you."

Mr. Jimmy

All I had ever done was farm and do a little blacksmithing for people when they needed something made or fixed. Usually it was something like door hinges, pokers, or the occasional hook to hang a flower pot on. Of course, we always kept a milk cow and chickens. Dossie sold butter and eggs, and milk when we had extra. I loved that homemade cottage cheese and buttermilk. I liked to sneak away from Dossie to my shop every now and then to have a little nip; she was raised Pentecostal and was sure that people would go to hell for drinking so I found it easier to just not let her know. Besides, I did not do it much. Some days a sip or two of whiskey helped me get my work done. I tried to be careful that the kids across the road didn't see me. I don't think they even knew I kept a bottle hidden in my shop. The one boy, especially, liked to come down and watch me when I's blacksmithing. I let him hit the hot metal with the hammer every now and then. I always took Dan and Buck up and plowed their garden for them, as well as a couple other gardens around here close. All of mine and Dossie's young'uns was growed up and gone away from home so I kinda liked having the boy come around.

Sammy

When my younger brother, who is three years younger than me, was born, Mama had Stella Mae come in for a few days to help with the baby and the housework. In those days, most families did that because the common belief was that, after giving birth, women should not get up and walk around much for several days. Daddy would go and pick her up before he went to work and take her home when he got home. I can still hear the old Ford rattling out of the driveway before daylight and our dog, Whitey, barking. Stella Mae was a big woman. Looking back, I think she must have been well over six feet tall and probably 300 pounds. I remember seeing her dust the walls and ceiling. She didn't even have to stand on anything to reach the cobwebs. I noticed this especially because my mother was about five feet one inch. Stella Mae was married to Lester, who was her opposite in most every way. Stella Mae was a strict Christian who did not believe in the four deadly sins—cussing, drinking, gambling, and smoking, all things that Lester enjoyed quite frequently. Sometimes she'd go and take him out of poker games and lead him home by the arm, all while he told her how sorry he was and how much he loved her. She always forgave him and they always made up.

Stella Mae was helping with refreshments at the VFW dance when Lester asked her to dance. That was quite a sight, my daddy said, because Lester was about five feet five while Stella was well over six feet. Stella was impressed that Lester was friends with Shady Melvin and the Drifters, the regular Saturday night band at the VFW. Slow dancing was a little awkward because Lester was not sure where to put his head without offending Stella, but they worked it out and that was not a problem for very long. That night, they ate their hot dogs without onions and Lester walked Stella home.

Stella Mae

Most all of my life I had been doing housework and taking care of younguns. I helped Mama take care of my younger brothers and sisters as soon as I got old enough, since Daddy wasn't interested or around very much, and then took care of Mama when she got older until she died. I had to start hiring out to make enough to live on. I helped the Linkouses when their middle boy was born. Two or three days a week, Mr. Linkous used to come and get me at six o'clock before he went to work and then take me home in the evening. I'd spend most of the day washing clothes, cooking, and cleaning. Them old houses had to be dusted every day and cob webs knocked down. Mrs. Linkous pretty much took care of the little one except I'd help her with bathing and such when I was there. I'd make sure the other two young'uns got something to eat and had clean clothes to put on. I always had supper ready when Mr. Linkous got home from work and sometimes they'd get me to stay and eat before he took me home. I worked there for about a month or two until Mrs. Linkous got her strength back. They was nice people and I enjoyed helping 'em. They always gave me my money right on time every week too.

One Saturday night my friend, Mabel, talked me into going to the dance down at the VFW hall to help her serve the punch. I usually did not go to such places but she talked me into it and said that a lot of respectable people came. I used to dance some when I was younger but usually just fooling around at home with my brothers or uncles. By the time I was about 14 years I was taller than all the boys and that made it harder. I had noticed Lester across the room; he was hard not to notice because he was the sort that talked to everybody and was always laughing and joking, plus his head was slick and shiny as a bowling ball. He was short, much shorter than most. Lester seemed to know everyone there, even the band. He went up and talked to them when they were taking a break and walked outside with them and stayed about the whole time until it was time for them to play again. I saw him walking toward me and was trying to decide what to say if he asked me to dance when he just took hold of my hand and said,

"Let's dance." I can't say it wasn't a little awkward at first because I was several inches taller than him and it was a slow dance.

Lester

I had seen Stella around the community a couple times and liked what I saw. She was a big woman—no doubt, but I didn't mind. I had heard that she was religious and was surprised to see her at the dance. Most of the people around here went to the Holiness church and thought you'd go to hell for sure for such things as dancing, drinking, and playing cards, things that I have to admit I enjoyed from time-to-time. I didn't see no harm in a friendly game of cards or a tasting of good whiskey on special occasions. I usually took a little bottle to the VFW dance but hid it out back in case I needed it. Shady Melvin and the Drifters was the regular band at the VFW most every month and Melvin and the boys usually liked to sneak out back for a nip when they took a break to go "get some air."

I finally decided to see if Stella would dance and just went right up to her and asked. Neither of us were very good dancers but we managed with my head right up against her big bosoms, since I was a good bit shorter than her. She didn't seem to mind and I didn't either.

After we had danced a couple times, I asked her if she wanted a hot dog and punch. Louise Jones from the VFW auxiliary always made the best hot dog chili. I pretty much waited to eat my supper at the dance every time. I went and got them and made sure to tell the ladies not to put any onions on them in case we danced again or I got to walk Stella home later.

I knew the last dance was coming up so I asked Stella to dance and she said okay. After the dance was over, I asked her if I could walk her home; we both lived in the community and it was not far for either of us to walk. She agreed but said Mabel would be walking with us. By the time we got to Stella's, Mabel was walking in front so I reached over and got hold of Stella's hand and she didn't mind. I knew that night that I'd be back another time sitting in her porch swing and holding her hand some more. We always had to leave the light on for sake of appearances to maintain Stella's good name.

Stella

That night after the dance, Lester said he'd like to walk me home and I said it'd be okay but my friend, Mabel, would be going too because she lived close to me and was scared to walk home by herself in the dark. Lester didn't think much of that idea, I could tell, but he agreed and down the road we went. I let him hold my hand right at the last and agreed to let him come by for a visit the following night. We sat on the front porch and talked mostly and ate some cookies I had made—molasses cookies with powdered sugar sprinkled on them like my mama used to make. Lester didn't like it much that I left the porch light on, but I know how people will talk even if they don't have something to talk about.

We courted for about a year, going to the dance or church, but mostly with me cooking supper and him coming over, or we'd take his old Chevrolet to town sometimes, before he asked me to marry him. I told him I would but he'd have to stop that drinking and playing cards and go to church with me. Even though he wouldn't drink when I was around, I knew he did it and wouldn't tolerate it. One time he came to the house smelling like liquor and I shut the door right in his face. About two months after we got married by Preacher Green at the parsonage, Lester was late coming in and I suspected that he may be down at his buddy Claiborne's trailer playing cards. I had heard that he did that sometimes. I went right down there and beat on that door and said, "Lester, you come outta there right now!" They all tried to stay real quiet so I would not know they were there, but I knew it and beat on the door some more. Finally the little latch let loose and the door popped open. There was Lester sitting there with cards in his hand and a bottle on the table next to him. I grabbed him by the arm and led him right up the road toward home. All the way home he pleaded and begged for me not to be mad. He told me how much he loved me over and over and promised to never do it again. I told him I forgave him like I had the other times.

Sammy

"Got some real nice Elbutta peaches," the man at the door said as my mama looked through the screen door at him. We snickered as kids do sometimes at things that should not be funny. The man couldn't talk plain and had trouble pronouncing Alberta. "I'll take a couple bushels," my mama said after she walked out to the truck to inspect them. We knew that this meant we'd have plenty of good peach preserves for the winter, and if we were lucky, maybe a peach cobbler for supper. A cobbler made with a cup of flour, a cup of sugar, a cup of milk, and a quarter pound of melted butter with the cut-up peaches put right in on top of the batter in a big old hot cast iron skillet.

The man carried the peaches and put them on the back porch for Mama and she paid him his four dollars.

Mama

I grew up down in the Shenandoah Valley but Daddy was a preacher who tried a little of everything to make some sort of living, including moving from place-to-place. He did some barbering and had a little street car diner once, but mostly we survived off of the goodness of his little country congregations. They did not have any money themselves but they held "poundings" for the preacher. That's when they bring food to help feed the preacher and his family. We got country ham, live chickens, eggs, and, in the summer, lots of fresh tomatoes, green beans, squash, and onions; in the fall, someone always brought some apples and pears. So we did okay in spite of not having much money.

I first came to the little community of Coalton with Daddy when he decided to pastor the Holiness church there. At that time, we lived about 30–40 miles away in Narrows, where he had been preaching at a little church near the town, and he drove back and forwards on Wednesday evening and Sunday. We'd usually get invited to someone's house for Sunday dinner so we'd end up spending the day there and driving home after Sunday night prayer meeting. One Sunday the widow who lived up on the hill from the church invited us to eat with her and her children. That's where I first met her handsome oldest son, Harrison. I was 19 then and he was two years older than me. If I have to say so myself, I was right pretty in those days—short and slender with blonde hair. Me and him met eyes and I knew then that something would come of this meeting. Daddy was dead-set against me meeting up with boys, let-a-lone getting serious with anyone. I was the oldest still at home and he counted on me to help Mama with the four younger ones. Mama was a little woman who did all she could but was not always in the best of health and Daddy did not always understand that she couldn't work as hard as he thought she ought to. In spite of Daddy's objections, I started dating Harrison when we came over and sometimes on Saturday he'd drive over to Narrows in his uncle's Chevrolet.

Pretty soon he asked me if I'd marry him, but I knew Daddy would never agree to it. I talked to Mama and she cried when I told her but said she'd talk to Daddy for me. She did, but he was a stubborn man and said he'd never agree to me marrying this "wild boy" from Coalton. I admit that Harrison had a little reputation of running around and drinking some and going with lots of girls, but he was settling down and we loved each other. He had taken care of his mama and younger brother and sister since his daddy died real young.

It was a hot August day and they were having a church conference meeting at the Coalton church where preachers and congregations from the whole area come together for a service and to talk about business, elect officers, and assign preachers to churches that had lost their pastors. Harrison's uncle had a general store across the road from the church and me and Harrison had decided that we was getting married no matter what. Harrison was waiting with his uncle's Chevrolet and when Daddy was leading the congregation in prayer, I ran out the back doors and across the street. People said that when Harrison hit the gas on the car the only thing they saw was a cloud of dust. We went to a Justice of the Peace in the next town over and he married us that Sunday afternoon. Daddy was fit to be tied when we came back that evening, mostly because I disobeyed him. We lived with Harrison's mama for several years and our first baby, a girl, was born there. Harrison's mama died a few years after we got married and we moved into a little house, not far away, that had been a company house when the mines were going full blast. That's where our two boys were born.

Daddy

I grew up in the little community of Coalton. My daddy died when I was 11 years old so I had to take care of my mama and younger brother and sister. My Uncle Thomas helped us a lot because he had a big general store in the community; he used to let me work in the store unloading trucks, putting up stock, sweeping up, and anything else that came up. Uncle Thomas was married to my mother's sister and was from Ceria, coming over as a young boy as an indentured servant. Everyone in the community owed him one way or the other. He had a family, but they just took off of him and never helped. After he died, they were so wasteful that they eventually lost the store.

When I got to be about 13, he let me start driving his old truck picking up coal down at the mine and delivering it, sometimes even going all the way to Roanoke. He did not have a license to sell in the city so I had to go at night and unload the coal into people's bins; they'd leave the money in an envelope just inside the bin so I could get it before unloading the coal. Lots of times Uncle Thomas would give me some food to take home for Mama. When I was 16, I started working in the coal mines at Coalton. Sometimes I worked the low seams because I was small and sometimes I drove the mules pulling the coal out. 'Bout all I ever knew was hard work but I got used to it 'cause that's about all I ever knew.

When I was 21 years old, Mama invited the preacher and his family to eat Sunday dinner with us. One of the preacher's daughters was really pretty and close to my age. I knew right away that I had to get to know her better but her daddy wouldn't take his eyes off her when I was in the room. I did give her a little wink a couple times and she grinned at me. I think her mama saw me but she didn't say anything. I saw that I was going to have to go to church to get to know her, so I did. Her daddy did not say much when we started sitting together, but we had to set where he could see us even though she was old enough to do what she wanted, but in those days young folks had to always worry about the sake of appearances. I think maybe that the parents worried about that more than the young'uns.

Sammy

In those days, traffic on our little country road was mainly in the mornings and evenings when the men went to and from work; kids played kick-the-can, Daddy smoked cigars on the Fourth of July to light the firecrackers, and we saw Hopalong Cassidy at the drive-in. Mama went on the Greyhound to visit her sister in Baltimore once and that was the first time she had ever been away over-night since I was borned. I cried that night, but no one knew.

Elizabeth McCommon

You Asked, and I Came

The first time you asked and I came, I was the grateful beneficiary of Gurney Norman's workshop leadership. I participated in the Highland Summer Conference hoping to find a way into prose, having written a repertoire of over 100 songs where ideas came to mind complete with rhythm and rhyme. I was finding it hard to escape the genre, and was striving to find other ways of telling stories. I don't recall the exercises he used to get me there, but I vividly recall the results. That summer I began one of many memoirs that I continue to work on to this day. Bits and pieces have found their way into live performances as I have taken them to the stage, sharing the enlightenment that came from that master storyteller, Gurney Norman. That summer taught me, also, that editing is the heart, if not the soul, of any writing.

Elizabeth McCommon.

The second time I came when you asked, I was still searching for a way into written prose. Fiction had been a weak link for me, with inspiration continuing to come from personal memories. Leader Darnell Arnoult's magic worked like a miracle. She came with a collection of photographs that we were encouraged to choose from to motivate a fictionalized account of the people's lives. I can still see the photo I chose in my mind's eye of a grandfatherly figure in work clothes who introduced himself to

216

my imagination as Letcher Brandscome. I knew his story right away; the hard, dangerous work he had done for years at the Radford Arsenal, and the sweet grandson who was his heart, the difficulty of being retired. I continue to work on Letcher's story, not a bit sure that fiction might be my forte, but Darnell's wonderful encouragement has kept me at it.

The third time I came was because former Floyd County neighbor, Jim Minick was leading. My reading of his work demonstrated that he balanced himself well with one foot in memoir and the other in fiction. I hoped to find a similar meeting place for my own work. I know that writing can be done anywhere. I've done some in fast food places, but to experience that work at Selu must surely have enriched everything. Any direction one looked, there was the calming beauty and the quiet of nature at her best. These glorious images come to mind whenever I continue work on what I started there. Among the stimulating exercises Jim brought to us, writing our own version of "Where I'm From" seemed to be the solidifying action. That was the summer that led me to gather a group of writing friends to work on "prompt" exercises that helped keep the mental wheels greased. Jim's "Where I'm From" exercise was especially enjoyed.

My three encounters with HSC have resulted in the on-going stage performances of my life stories. They have also inspired me to lead memoir writing workshops, and to serve as a journalist for the *Roanoke Times*, where writing essays has strengthened all my other writing. I have had poems and stories published to my delight, and all with the heart-felt thanks of RU's Appalachian Studies Program. The HSC is always filled with a rich diversity of writers from schoolteachers to students to hopefuls like myself. Being in their company as well as the company of the richly talented leaders that are brought to us has been a splendid gift. Thank you for "asking" so that we could "come."

Up On Locust Hill

She was pregnant, again. Would this have been Miriam, the last born, the one who was never "quite right," the last of the nine, the embarrassment to the whole family, but, especially eldest daughter, Elsie, returning home from the teacher's training school to this humiliation? I choose to imagine it was Miriam, the one who had not lived out her first year, and the loss of which my grandmother had grieved and wept tears of sorrow for, even into her seventy-fifth year.

The Upper King and Queen Baptist Church, where she played the piano to accompany the singing, stands as stately and as beautiful now in its rural isolation as it did when buggy traffic would have choked the roads leading to it on any Sunday morning. Her failure to be there to play would have been her only announcement of her condition. Words would have been insufficient to deal with the occurrence of original sin from which would have been born a child that must be born yet again, washed in the blood, dipped in the water, cleansed of the means by which he or she had been conceived.

As the story was told to me, my grandfather Tom appeared that Sunday without her, accompanied by any number of their children, and is known to have said, "Dessie won't be coming to church for a while," the ambiguous but loaded response to someone's inquiry about her absence or the condition of her health. His words would get back to her, and, of course her friends and neighbors, if not the entire congregation, would understand the veiled allusion to the carnal act. Of course she was humiliated. Had she asked him to say even a word? Had she asked him to explain her absence? It would all have been understood if nothing at all had been said.

Was it on that Sunday or days later that she acted? Perhaps a delighted neighbor had reined her buggy into the sandy approach to the hill on her way home from services to express her happiness, or to gloat. Who could welcome the news of a ninth pregnancy? Perhaps it was this neighbor who came that very day to quote her husband and inquire, with veiled satisfaction as to Miss Dessie's health that provoked her anger, her embarrassment and her decision to lock the chamber door against the very man responsible, not only for her condition, but for her humiliation as well.

There must have been knocking and questioning, loud enough to be heard throughout the old dwelling, the very place where George Washington is thought to have stopped on his way to Williamsburg. Their children must have been mystified, horrified, even, at this inexplicable behavior. Had they all been shooed out into the yard? Were they there as witnesses when Granddaddy Tom tried another approach, leaving the house, going outside, looking for the open window of the bedroom? At least their eldest daughter, Elsie, was there watching him begging and pleading, trampling the bed of daffodils beneath the window, because she is the one who tells me the story so many years later. If there had been one witness to this drama, perhaps there was another, my father, barefoot and sparkling clean from his Sunday reverence, hiding behind one of the massive locust trees for which the farm was named, listening, wondering what was to become of his father, his mother, and his life.

Teresa Stutso Jewell

From Hairdresser to Writer

I was a hairdresser for thirty-five years and basically thought my life was set in stone. But, something clicked, and I wanted more; I wanted an education. I started taking night classes at Southwest Virginia Community College and ended up graduating with honors. Every one of my friends and family was shocked when I told them I was going on to Radford University.

I was a storyteller years ago when I had my beauty salon, mostly to make the little children hold still while I cut their hair. I didn't know that I was just doing what Appalachian people did ... they told stories that were handed down from one group to another. When I closed my salon to go to

Teresa Stutso Jewell.

Radford, the stories stopped, but they were still rolling around in the back of my brain, sort of in hyperspace. I still had that unsatisfied mind and the yearning for something I just couldn't put my finger on.

My little simple, unchanging and sheltered life made a complete 360 when I put my foot on Radford University's soil. While taking a class, I heard all the chatter about the Highland Summer Writing Conference; it was Grace Toney Edwards and Ricky Cox who told me how much fun it was. Grace urged me to attend. I knew, of course, I was Appalachian, as I was born and sheltered in the heart of the coal fields of West Virginia, but there was something missing in my soul, and I wasn't sure why or what was burning. Yes, I was from the mountains, but I had no idea how beautiful my life was after all, and how much I had to say about it!

The teachers in the Appalachian Studies Department stoked the fire that was needed to make the flame grow. My first semester, which was in the summer, I was encouraged to attend the Highland Writing Conference, and it was there that the smoldering fire in my soul became an open flame. I listened to Bill Brown, a famous poet, who was the guest and teacher. His earthy, personal poems of his life and experiences opened my eyes, and I saw as if I had been blind for years. I was hungry for more and was being fed from every class I took from Grace Toney Edwards and Ricky Cox.

The university invited Maya Angelou to come for a symposium, and I saw yet another side of thinking, writing, and understanding. Just when I started getting hungrier, I met Marilou Awiakta. Ms. Awiakta was one of the wisest women I have ever met, and I was enthralled listening to the story of Mother Selu and the Cherokee Creation Story, and of course, her "stump sitting"(which I now do every chance I get). I sat in awe listening to her approximately four separate times and was so encouraged to write. I was just as inspired when author Crystal Wilkinson came for the Highland Summer Conference; I learned so much from her. I had some student/teacher time with her while she talked about her experience living her life in Appalachia and having her bookstore in Kentucky. When she read from her works, she just blew me away. Because of my Italian heritage, Crystal gave me a nickname, "Itali-achian," as we shared similar stories about growing up in the Appalachian Mountains. We still write to each other from time to time.

It was Lou Gallo, a creative writing professor at Radford University, who taught me how to "step out of the box" and write freely. He said not to worry about whether someone didn't know what you meant with your verse; just let go and write. I did just that. I had great professors at Radford, and every one of them helped me to "step out" and think differently. It was a thrill for me to learn new things, but it was also a challenge as well. I was what is labeled as a "non-traditional" student. I was fifty years old when I started at R.U. I was always the oldest person in my class, but I wasn't the cow's tail. I graduated with honors and got my Master's Degree in the year, 2000. I am the only one of my family to have graduated from college. It wasn't the beautiful buildings of Radford University but the brilliant people who teach there that I will never forget and will always be grateful for their sharing of their precious knowledge.

I started writing my first book in the year 2000, the year my first grandson was born. When I started writing, I heard every one of the voices from every one of the Highland Summer Conferences I attended. I would change things and try to remember all I had heard. It took me until January of 2018, to finish it up, doing all the artwork on the cover and inside. I finally decided to let a publisher have it. I felt I was giving over my child, but I figured a child living in the house for eighteen years needs to "grow up" and try it without me. So, I did it, giving my book to a publisher. *My Bucket's Got a Hole in It* was delivered by a guy in brown shorts and shirt from UPS to my house on the first of June 2018, in seven big boxes. It took a few trips to finish delivering my new life in those boxes. I've emptied most of them quickly. Now, I am doing book signings and readings all over the southwest Virginia area. I've been on television being interviewed! Twice! It's been so exciting talking and watching the faces of my audience. I have received mail from total strangers telling me I should write more. I even had a woman from Washington D. C., write me and tell me she believed that she was related to my characters in the book and knew exactly where they lived. I wrote back and told her that my book was fiction and came from my imagination; I made up the characters and even made up the name of the mountain where the story took place. She wrote back and said I was probably protecting those innocent people and my secret was safe with her. I didn't write her again. I've got enough to deal with, so I just had to let that one go. My husband and I had a good laugh!

In 2013, I joined my husband in his bluegrass band, which he and his brother started in 1972. When his brother retired, there was a void, so I filled the spot. I do not play an instrument; I sing, and I write some music. We play all over the place, and I love doing that. One could say I am somewhat busy, as I teach three classes four days a week, have band practice and shows, and am currently writing a sequel to *My Bucket's Got a Hole in It*. I have named it *My Bucket Runneth Over*. I am going to publish my first poetry book, *My Mountain Laurels*, and I have a bunch of stories I want to put together into a book of short stories soon. I haven't named that one yet. The wonderful people I met while attending the Highland Summer Writing Conference set me going at breakneck speed, and I can't stop writing. Now I know how most of those people feel, and man, it feels great. I think I have the same mindset as Grace Toney Edwards, as I don't want to slow down because I believe it would be boring not having something to do every five minutes. I want to return to Radford and attend the Highland Summer Writing Conference again, and perhaps one day, if it is in the stars, I will be asked to come and share my work.

My main goal? Well, I guess I want to be known as a good writer, a great teacher, a talented musician, an inspiring artist, a good friend, a good mother, a good mother-in-law, a loyal and loving wife, and a devoted daughter to my mother, as well as being a cool grandmother. I don't think that is too much to ask. Will I add something to that list? No doubt! Stay tuned!

"The Plea of Brother Mountain"

I Am a Mountain
I have lived through many years alongside my other brothers
I was here to watch the first two-legged red children roam through
my hills and valleys
They were the first beings who honored me
I spoke to them and they listened and learned
They walked softly upon my back
Every step taken was careful not to bruise
I fed them and sheltered them
I guided the waters that fell upon my head
Down to where they drank
They did not take anything that was not given with love
The red children lived many years within my shadow in peace
Sadly, as I have watched the eons come and go
So did my red children
They have been replaced by others who are takers
They have plowed my valleys
Burned and scorched me
Took my ancient timber
Tunneled inside into my black rich veins
Even now there are some of them buried inside me
They seek the riches that make me poor
They care not for the sacred reason I am here
They have carved a highway deep into my sides
I cannot see my brothers
Where are they?
Where are my red children?
Please come back to save me.

Luther Kirk

Impacts

Although I don't remember the year I enrolled in the Highland Summer Writing Conference (perhaps 2005 or 2006), I certainly do remember its impact on my writing pursuits. Grace Toney Edwards was a member of my Ph.D. committee at Virginia Tech, so I knew her before HSC. She was one of the many strong women who encouraged my writing; when offered an opportunity to work with her again, I signed up for the summer class. HSC set in motion a series of events that impacted my writing life in deeper ways than I could ever imagine.

Luther Kirk.

On a visit to the Selu Retreat Center to hear writers read from their work, Grace mentioned the Appalachian Writers' Conference at Hindman, Kentucky, and suggested that I apply. Thinking that I would never be selected, I applied anyway and was accepted. It was at Hindman that I met Darnell Arnoult who became my writing mentor. Not only did Darnell encourage me to attend other writers' retreats over the years, she guided me through the completion of a novel. *Cry of the Nightjars* has not found a publisher yet, but it is currently under review by several publishers and various excerpts have come from the novel. A short story, "The Bastard Child of My Oldest Vivian," adapted from *Cry of the Nightjars*, won first place at the 2011 Tennessee Mountain Writer's Conference, "Pearly Gates," another short story from the novel, won honorable mention at the 2014 Appalachian

Heritage Literary Festival, and an excerpt from the novel appeared in *Still: The Journal.*

As well, my poetry has appeared in *Anthology of Appalachian Writers: Charles Frazier, Volume IX,* Shepherd University Foundation and the West Virginia Center for the Book, and *In God's Hands: Inspiration from Top Regional Writers,* Oak Ridge, Tennessee.

Woodhaven Press published two of my poetry chapbooks: *Appalachian Woman* (2017), and *Child of Appalachia* (2018). Both are available through Woodhaven Press or on line at *Amazon.com. Postcards, Poems, and Prose Magazine,* an online publication, recently published "Murmuration," one of my poems (November 2018).

As you can see, the Highland Summer Writing Conference—and especially Grace Toney Edwards—had a profound influence on my life as well as my writing endeavors. They will forever be in my gratitude.

Opal Jean

Elbert pulls off the road and parks nigh to a spring that spouts from the bank. "Callie," he says. "I reckon this looks like a right good place to camp."

"I reckon so," I say, "for I'm wore out and Eva Rose and Izzy is, too. We've been on the road since dawn with nary a bite to eat."

Before it gets too dark, Elbert gathers up some wood and builds a fire. I fetch my skillet, some spoons, cups, and bowls from the back of the truck and warm some beans, cornbread, and fatback. Then, Elbert scrubs the skillet and dishes with sand and rinses them with water from the spring. I take the girls into the woods to pee.

Elbert crawls into the truck's cab to sleep. I climb on the back, shove Momma's kettle aside, and push Pearly's rocker to the front. The girls climb up, and we scoot under a pile of quilts nigh Momma's hump back trunk with Lela's journals and the Clabber Girl Baking Powder tin Pearly give to Eva Rose all them years ago hid inside. I pull the young'uns close and we snuggle amongst each other's warmth.

A bitter chill seeps into our bed during the night. I rouse to stare at the heavens. Stars glitter like broke glass strewed across a ash heap. Nearby, a screech owl whinnies on a tree limb. Over a hill to the east, a coonhound bays into the hushed land. Far off, a train engine moans low and lonesome.

At daybreak, Elbert builds a fire, and I hurry into the bushes with the girls. He's perked a pot of coffee by the time we get back. I render some fatback and fry eggs in the grease. After I scrub the skillet and dishes and stow them back on the truck, I fill a Mason jar with water from the spring, and we set off.

Rosy-gray streaks cut across the western sky by the time Jeter, the man that got Elbert a job working with him drilling wells in Fauquier County, meets us at a country store and leads us to a two-track path jutting off the main road. We follow it along a weedy fencerow and end up at an L-shaped, double-storied, chalky colored house that sets by a straight stretch of railroad tracks. It leans south, and for all the world looks like it's listening for the whistle of a northbound train. After Jeter stops under a windblown mulberry tree in the side yard, Elbert pulls up beside him.

"Mr. John Botts, the man that owns this farm, will let you live here for free if you help him tend to the milking and other farm chores," Jeter says. "You and me will work together drilling wells, but you can help him in the mornings and evenings and on Saturday and Sunday. His woman passed on a few years back. He ain't got nobody but a colored housekeeper. Her name's Miss Lettie. She helps birth babies around here."

Straightaway, I think, *I'll be paying a visit on Miss Lettie.*

Dark has settled upon us by the time we get the truck unloaded and move in. I ain't got no light nor no way to cook, so Elbert builds a fire in the yard, and I warm the last of the beans and cornbread then lay out some quilts on the floor. Long trains roll by the house all night, their iron wheels rattling the doors and windows. Ain't none of us slept much.

"You girls don't never go on them tracks. I'll switch you if you do," I tell Izzy and Eva Rose the next day when the trains keep on rumbling past. Ever now and again, a passenger train slips by and I can see people watching us from its windows.

Nigh noon a week later, I set off to find Miss Lettie, telling the girls, "I don't know how far it is and it's too cold for y'all to go, so stay in the house. I'll be back after not too long."

I step from tie to tie. A cold wind cools the sunshine around me and pesters the weeds along the tracks. I hear the rumble and squall of a train and step into a clinkered ditch. The cold air stirred up by the train swirls about me.

I reckon I'm nigh on to two miles from home when I tramp through a pasture to the front of a two-storied, green-shuttered white farmhouse. Penned inside a white picket fence, it appears to be hiding under some maple trees that must be a hundred years old. A stone path lined with round squat bushes leads up to a wide porch where fat posts along its front stretch way up high. The squawk of the gate wakes up a dog around back of the house. It sets up a woof till somebody bawls, "Hesh, Jack!"

I ain't never seen a dark-skinned person before, so I can't help but gawk at the tiny, stooped-shouldered old woman who pops around the corner. She hurries across the yard and stops a foot or so in front of me. Her black skin is leathery and lined, and her brown eyes look like they swim in thimblefuls of cream. Her head is wound tight with a flannel rag knotted at the front, and her ankle-length dress is covered with a red-spattered apron. She don't give me a chance to say who I am.

"I know who you is," she says. "You be Mr. Fogelsong's woman, ain't you? He say you be coming round. Axe me if I help. I say, course I help. What yo name?"

"Callie."

"Call me Miss Lettie. Everbody do. I can see yo chile be growing real nice. Come round back to da kitchen. I jus' put a cherry pie in da oven. You can set with me whilst it bakes. We talk about yo baby and drink some coffee."

"No! No! I left my girls at home by their selves. I can't."

"I come see you when we gets mo time, then. I be over in a day or two."

"Thank you, Miss Lettie." She watches me from a patch of sunlight, waves, and then disappears around the corner of the house.

Miss Lettie comes the next morning, yoo-hooing the house from across the yard. She makes a big to-do over the young'uns. Fingering Eva Rose's hair, she says, "Law me, I ain't never seen hair this red on a chile." Eva Rose and Izzy gawk at her like I done, for they ain't never seen a black person before.

After a while I knowed I liked her and me and her gets to be real close like me and Nona was down home. She starts to drop by for a set-down at least once or twice a week. We talk, drink coffee, and sew. "Yo baby going to be girl chile," she tells me.

One Sunday afternoon, me and Elbert's setting on the porch after a visit from Miss Lettie. We watch her trudge back along the railroad tracks, her thinness dwindling to a black dot. Eva Rose and Izzy chase one another back and forth across the yard.

"Callie," Elbert says, "folks might think it a bit quare for a black woman and a white woman to visit with one another pert nigh as much as y'all do."

"Well, I don't reckon it's none of nobody's business. Miss Lettie's one of the finest women I ever did know. She reminds me a lot of Momma."

Elbert laughs. "I don't reckon your momma's the same color Miss Lettie is."

"Miss Lettie might be as dark as a burned biscuit, but I'm as white as dough and look like I ain't never been put in the oven and that's about the only difference. She's got the same wants and needs as I do, and puts her drawers on the same way as I do, too."

"You ever listen to her talk?" Elbert says.

"Yes, and I ain't never not knowed what she's saying. Did you ever listen to how people talks hereabouts or from down in the mountains where we come from? Ever body's peculiar, but they want the same things. She knows a lot more than birthing babies. She's welcome here anytime."

Elbert grows quiet.

"Miss Lettie told me her momma and poppa was borned into bondage on a farm down in a place called the Tidewater. It's somewhere east of Richmond. After the war was over, her daddy and his brother raked enough money together to build a house, a barn, and some outbuildings on a piece of land give to them by the government. When she was ten years old, some men come one night, set a cross ablaze in their yard, and burned the place down. They hung her uncle and shot her poppa in the back. Her and her momma run into the woods, hid out in the day, and followed the stars at night. When they got here, they was so wore out they couldn't go on, so they hid in Mr. Botts' dairy barn to rest and he found them there. Mr. Botts was a honorable man, and him and his wife took them in. That's where she's been ever since. You ever seen that little patch of land all them flowers grows on in back of Mr. Botts' house?"

"I've seen it."

"Well, that's where Miss Lettie laid her momma to rest after she passed on."

Elbert flips his cigarette into the yard and calls to Eva Rose and Izzy, "Y'all girls need to come on in out of that heat."

It's pert nigh six o'clock on a Monday morning early in December when I sense the baby's downward turn. I get up, check on Eva Rose and Izzy, and then rouse Elbert. "The young'uns is still asleep, so you best go get Miss Lettie. My pains is about to start. The girls ought to be all right till you get back. You got to hurry, though."

By the time Elbert gets back to the house with Miss Lettie, Eva Rose and Izzy is peeping at me from the doorway. They know I can't get up to make them go back to bed. Elbert and Miss Lettie come up behind them. "My, my, you chil'rens ought not to be here," Miss Lettie says. "Yo daddy take you to da kitchen. I tends to yo momma."

"I knowed they ought not to be here," I say, "but..."

"They be jus' fine and you be fine too. Yo baby girl be borned any time now."

It ain't no more than half a hour before Opal Jean slips out and starts to whimper.

* * *

It's our second hot breezeless summer in Fauquier County and in all my borned days, I ain't never sweated and felt as gummy. I'm wore out from canning tomatoes late into the night. I wash and put away the breakfast dishes and tell Eva Rose and Izzy, "You girls is to tend to Opal Jean. I want to work the garden patch before it gets too hot." I grab the hoe that leans against the back porch post and set off for the spot of green along the railroad tracks. "I'll watch y'all from the garden. Keep Opal Jean in the shade of the mulberry tree, and don't let her go out of the yard."

Before I start to hoe, I look up to see about the young'uns. Opal Jean toddles about on the purplish berries that dot the ground. She plops down, squeezes them in her fingers, stuffs them into her mouth, and smacks her lips. Juice dribbles down her chin and stains her belly. *It's a messy place for them to play*, I think, *but they ain't no where else that's cooler. I reckon they can be washed.*

My hoe pings against clods and rocks. I smell the pink roses growing wild along the railroad tracks. The trains seem to be napping somewhere in this flat land that bakes like a mud pie on a fence post. I listen for Eva Rose and Izzy's giggles and glance ever now and again toward the mulberry tree.

Before I work my way to the end of the second row, my mind wanders back to Big Tumbling Creek. *It's been a while, Lela. I surely would like to set and talk with you some, but I don't reckon it'll be any time soon. I hope it ain't forever. I still got all your journals. Maybe sometime I'll read them. After you died, it was real hard for me to even open them. Seems like you was always looking over my shoulder. I won't never forget that day the floodwaters took you, Lela, no matter how far I go away from Big Tumbling Creek. I'm with child again, Lela. I reckon this next baby will get here when it's as cold as all get-out like Izzy and Opal Jean done. Seems like Opal Jean was borned but yesterday. I knowed I was with child again back in June. Sick ever day. I reckon Elbert was right, one ever year. Seems like he can't keep that thing in his britches, but I reckon I don't want him to neither. Law, Lela, I ought not to speak about such man and woman things to you. You was so young when you died. You won't never know about it. I'm sorry, Lela. I couldn't grab your hand that day on that slick rock.*

Halfway back on the fourth row of beans, I hear the rumble and then the wail of a train. Straight away, I feel uneasy, for I don't hear Eva Rose and Izzy. I shade my eyes and peer toward the mulberry tree. *Opal Jean! Izzy! Eva Rose! Gone!*

I sling my hoe into the balk and fly across the garden. *Two more crossings before the train goes by the house! Eva Rose! Izzy! Opal Jean! Where are they?* The rumble gets louder. The moan grows closer.

I run around the corner of the house. Eva Rose and Izzy set on the porch, a play breakfast laid out before them. They jump to their feet. Yellow-eyed daisy eggs fall to the floor, mulberry fatback strips slip from their hands, and wood-chip plates and acorn-cap cups clatter across the porch boards. "Eva Rose! Izzy! Where's Opal Jean?"

The train's horn wails. I charge through the house screaming, "Opal Jean! Opal Jean! Where are you?" I let the back door slam shut. "Opal Jean! Where are you?" I storm toward the railroad tracks and scramble up the cindered bank. My arms flail. "Stop! Stop! My baby! You've got to stop!" The train's racket smothers my pleas. Hot air rushes around me and sets my dress tail to flapping. When the train is gone, I stumble onto the tracks and follow in its wake. "Opal Jean? Where are you, baby? Cry so momma will know you're all right."

I hunt up and down the tracks. Eva Rose and Izzy watch me from the porch, their legs dangling over the edge. Eva Rose's right arm is around Izzy's waist. Their faces is ashy, their eyes wide. I know I need to go to them and say, "Ever thing will be all right," but I sense it's not, so all they hear is me sobbing and calling over and over, "Opal Jean, Opal Jean. Where are you baby?" I can't tear myself away from the railroad tracks.

The July sun burns away the haze, singes the top of my head, my shoulders, my arms, and stickiness hugs me like a wet blanket. When a train bears down upon me, I stagger into the grass, wait for it to thunder on, and then stumble back between the rails to plead, "God, let me find my baby. Please let Opal Jean be all right."

I'm still wandering up and down the tracks and calling out, my throat hoarse and dry, when Elbert gets home nigh sunset. I see him round the side of the house and go to Eva Rose and Izzy. His voice echoes slow and hollow, when I hear him say, "You girls look scared to death. Is they anything wrong?"

They bust into tears.

"Opal Jean! Where are you baby?"

Elbert hears my call, turns, and runs across the yard.

"Callie? What's wrong? Why are you out here?"

"Opal Jean! She's gone!" I manage to croak.

"Gone! What do you mean, gone!"

"Gone!" I point down the tracks.

"She's most likely in the house," he says. "Have you checked?"

"She ain't in the house, Elbert. I looked in all the rooms. She's gone, runned over by a train. I didn't watch her good and now she's gone." I crumple against him sobbing. He lifts my face to his. "How long's she been gone, Callie?"

"Since this morning when I was hoeing the garden. I left her with Eva Rose and Izzy. I fell into thinking about Lela and home and now she's gone."

He leads me through the house and to the bedroom. "You need to rest, Callie," he says. Eva Rose and Izzy watch us from the doorway. I know they need me but they ain't nothing I can do.

"You girls get in the truck," Elbert says. "I got to go find help."

I lay like a corpse on the bed, my arms crossed on my bosom, my eyes fixed on the ceiling. Outside, I hear a chuck-will's-widow's cry. Crickets chirrup. My arms fall to my sides; my fingers fidget with the tie-off threads of the crazy quilt. I get up and make my way back to the tracks. Cinders crunch. They sound much too loud.

Something tells me to pause in my climb up the slope. A tuft of dry grass at my dress tail stirs. I look down. The purple-stained finger lays under a clump of weeds. I fall to my knees, pluck it from the clinkers, cradle it in my palm, and bring it to my lips. "My Opal Jean."

Back in the house, I claw through Momma's trunk and find the linen hankie tatted with lace she give me from Lela's things. I pull the finger from my pocket and bunch the hankie around it. I lay it on the dresser and take from the trunk the Clabber Girl Baking Powder tin. I pry off the lid, push the hankie inside, and then drop the tin back inside the trunk with Lela's journals. I crawl under the covers to stare into the shadows.

* * *

They ain't nothing that eases my despair but sleep. I make myself get up to use the toilet and then I go back to bed wanting to rest but hoping I'll die. Elbert begs, "You've got to get up and eat, Callie. You're wasting away." So, I get up, but it's against my will. Miss Lettie watches over me and makes me eat; Elbert takes me for walks along the fencerow to the road and back.

Ever time I hear the wail of a train whistle, I feel my face go pale, I mutter Opal Jean's name, wring my hands, and pace. At other times, I can't bear it, and before Elbert or Miss Lettie can stop me, I bolt for the railroad tracks, claw up the bank and stand so close to the cars that their breezes yank at my tangled hair and dirty dress tail. Elbert or Miss Lettie run up and pull me back. After the last car rumbles past, I jerk away and step between the rails to look up and down the tracks. They take my hand and lead me back into the house.

In the nighttime, I unburden to Lela, *Opal Jean's gone, Lela. She's with you. Take care of my baby.* When I cry out, Elbert holds me close. "I'm here, Callie. I'm here."

It's a shoved foot here, a pointy elbow there, or a balled fist against the inside of my ribs that stirs me from my stupor. I jerk awake and blink at Eva Rose and Izzy. They study me from the foot of the bed. Tears fill my eyes and spill down my cheeks. "Your Momma's been gone a long time," I say. "Come here." I open my arms wide, and they climb up next to me.

Elbert's bulk fills the doorway. "I'm sorry, Elbert," I say.

He crosses to me, combs his fingers through my dirty, knotted hair, and kisses my greasy forehead. "We've missed you, Callie."

In the weeks that follow, days of sorrow and days of joy mix, but as the next baby's due date draws nigh, I begin to have more good days than bad. Miss Lettie comes pert nigh ever day. I know it's to help keep my mind busy.

We commence quilting again, and we pick and can what little we gather from my weedy garden. Elbert goes back to milking for Mr. Botts and drilling wells with Jeter.

Some nights when I can't sleep and need to know more, Elbert tells me how Mr. Botts and Miss Lettie come that night and how Miss Lettie kept on coming to cook and clean. He tells me the sheriff come too and tried to talk to me, but all I done was rock to and fro and stare. Elbert speaks of his own bouts of crying, his rambles along the tracks looking for his dead baby's body parts, his fear of losing me. We talk of going home.

One day in early December over coffee, buttered biscuits, and blackberry jam, I say to Miss Lettie, "We'll be leaving here real soon. The trains yank me out of sorts too much, and Elbert has fixed his mind on driving us back down home to the mountains."

Miss Lettie takes a sip of coffee, nibbles her biscuit, and stares at the table for a few minutes. She sets her cup in its saucer, the half-eat bread back on the plate, and then raises her head, her eyes shiny with tears. "I knowed in my bones you was going, and I needs to tell you something before you go."

"What is it, Miss Lettie? What do you need to tell me?"

She wipes her eyes, takes a deep breath, and hardly above a whisper says, "Whilst you was so sad and Mr. Fogelsong was tending to you, I gathered up your baby's body parts and put them in a little cedar chest my momma give me. I buried them with her. Your Opal Jean sleeps with Momma now."

I stare at her. Tears roll down my cheeks. "Oh, Miss Lettie!" I stumble around the table, fall on my knees at her feet, and lay my head in her lap. She says no more just pats my hair and lets me sob. After a while, I pull myself up and move back to my chair.

"I didn't say nothing 'cause white folks is odd sometimes," she says "and you was filled with such misery. I ain't wanted nobody to be mad at me."

"I ain't mad at you, Miss Lettie. I'll forever be beholden." I blow my nose and wipe my eyes. "I need to go see my baby."

"When you ready. We go together."

"I can't go till Elbert gets home. It's too cold for Eva Rose and Izzy, and I ain't leaving them by their selves."

Blustery snowflakes swirl around me, as I walk along the railroad tracks to the Botts's farm. Icy winds whip my coat, headscarf, and dress tail. Miss Lettie meets me at the front gate and leads me around to the back of the house. A mound of brown dirt with a simple stick cross at its head lays atop her Momma's grave. I huddle over the spot. Miss Lettie lays her hand on my shuddering shoulders.

"Ain't Never Went to the Ocean"

Ain't never went to the ocean, tasted salted sea spray flung with force into my face.
Yet, I've tasted fresh dewdrops, cold rain, and honeysuckle sap.

Ain't never went to the ocean, heard green oceans rolling mincing seashells into sand. Yet, I've heard rushing creeks smoothing stones within their beds.

Ain't never went to the ocean, smelled the rancid seaweed, brackish air, stinging damp. Yet, I've smelled oft-tilled soil, pasture grass, and fresh dug ramp.

Ain't never went to the ocean, felt fine grains of sand shift, sink, rise beneath my feet. Yet, I've felt plush forest footpaths lined with ferns, and moss, and leaves.

Ain't never went to the ocean, saw it swell up, heard it crash, then dash, along the shore. Yet, I've saw wild waters cascade over rocks and heard it thunder down the gorge.

First appeared in *Appalachian Woman*, Woodhaven Press, 2017.

"Witching Hour"

From her front porch rocker, she witnesses
crimson bathe western skies, deepening
shadows stalk along steep slopes, fill
yawning hollows, invade dense
woodlands, girdle fat trunks,
sojourn midst timbers
conceal thickets,
dominate
pastures,
spread
round
her yard,
surround her
house, slip up her
steps, ease athwart her
porch, laze about her feet,
encircle her, slip through her
doorway to darken each corner
of every room ere the stroke of twelve,
that spectral witching hour bout midnight.

First appeared in *Appalachian Woman*, Woodhaven Press, 2017.

"She Left"

can't bide here no more
she said, then left
her dress hanging on her wall
her shoes parked under her chair
her pocketbook hidden in her dresser
her bedspread flung cross her bed
her Bible spread open on her table
her curtains lifeless at her windows
her pictures dusty on her walls
her coal scuttle resting by her heater
her skillets waiting on her stove
her dishes stacked in her cupboards
her salt and pepper shakers scattered among
her jam and jelly jars on her table
nigh on to sixty years after her man died
can't bide here no more
she said, then left

First appeared in *Appalachian Woman*, Woodhaven Press, 2017.

"Child of Appalachia"

I am a child of Appalachia, born in
the fells of western Virginia where
gray-whites segue to minty-yellows,
minty-yellows shift to forest greens,
forest greens fuse to smoky blues,
orange-reds, golden-browns blend,
gray-whites meld, deepen, benumb
frozen ridges elbow up, hole-pokers
in the underbelly of God slumped,
aloof, leaden, o'er these mountains
dwelling place of my soul.

First appeared in *A Child of Appalachia*, Woodhaven Press, 2018.

"My Soul"

My soul lies down along Comer's Creek where my brother and me fished,
sharing a Luzianne coffee can of worms dug from the manure pile in back
of the barn, a rusty hook (plus knotted twine) found tangled in the bur-
docks burring up along the creek, and a hickory pole cut from the woods.

My soul lies down along the South Fork of the Holston River where my brother and me skimmed just above its ripples on a log chain dangling from a sycamore limb, let slip our grip to clutch our tender nuts against the foreseen sting of the pitiless waters, and then crawled upon its mud-slick bank to wheeze in the sun.

My soul lies upon a white hillside where my brother and me trudged up, up, up to slice down, down, down to tumble into drifts only to trudge up, up, up to slice down, down, down to tumble into drifts again, again, and again on a sled sculpted from a piece of curled up tin wind-ripped from the roof of the barn.

My soul lies in the kitchen where Mom baked biscuits warm, flaky and golden brown and my brother and me ate them oozing with fresh-churned, sweet creamy butter and spread with huckleberry jam—and elbowed each other for extra space along the hard bench in back of the table till Mom yelled, "You boys stop that!"

My soul lies in the back room where my brother and me wrestled over the covers, winter winds chattering the clinging oak leaves on the trees outside our window, moaning under the eaves, and leaching snow between the cracks to sprinkle into the wrinkles of our quilts, and trail across frozen linoleum nosegays of faded red roses, blue ribbons, and pink peonies.

First appeared in *A Child of Appalachia*, Woodhaven Press, 2018.

"Went to the Ocean"

I went to the ocean, Mom—I thought of you

heard wild winds roar 'cross wide unsettled seas
smelled fishy crests tumble back into the deep
watched ebbing neap tides rake footprints from the sand
saw brown pelicans skim in strings just above whitecaps
heard herring seagulls squabble all along the sea oats shore
tasted salted sea spray flung with force into my face
heard green waves rolling, mincing seashells into sand
smelled rancid seaweed, brackish air, stinging damp
felt fine grains of silicon shift, sink, rise beneath my feet
saw the ocean swell up, heard it crash, then dash along the shore
watched my orange-knit-capped, half clad grandson leap
then fling sand into the February surf

I went to the ocean, Mom—I thought of you

First appeared in *A Child of Appalachia*, Woodhaven Press, 2018.

Tim Thornton

For Those Two Weeks in That One Summer ... I Was a Writer

One reason I went to the Highland Summer Conference was I'd been there before. I wasn't a student the first time, I was a reporter. Sharyn McCrumb was there and I was writing something about her most recent book. I'd never heard McCrumb talk before. I'd never seen her hold up her necklace with its piece of serpentine and explain that stone runs in a vein all the way up the Appalachian Mountains and emerges on the other side of the ocean on the islands that sent so many settlers into those mountains. I'd never heard her talk about people inspired by her ballad series books to visit those mountains, people who wrote to her for advice about traveling among the pecu-

Tim Thornton.

liar mountain people they'd find there. How could the travelers ensure the locals wouldn't mistake them for revenuers? Would they need to bring enough drinking water for the whole trip? I'd never heard McCrumb compare saying "apple-lay-sha" in the southern mountains to saying "Londonderry" in Northern Ireland. Both were political and social statements, she said. Both put the speaker on the side of the occupiers.

Almost a decade passed before I got to legitimately attend a Highland Summer Conference. To give you some idea of how much impact those two weeks had on me, I spent about an hour this evening rummaging through upstairs cabinets and basement shelves looking for notes and papers from my second legitimate Highland Summer Conference before I realized I didn't attend a second Highland Summer Conference. All that stuff I remember—the reading, the discussions, the writing, the writers, the camaraderie—all that happened at one conference.

We had a week of fiction writing led by Crystal Wilkinson and a week of poetry writing led by Cathy Smith Bowers. Jim Minick was there to do a reading, just before his *The Blueberry Years* was published. Oh, and Sharyn McCrumb was back for another reading. There were four readings that year. The readings, the writing, the teachers, the students, it was all great.

I wrote for a living then. I'd started writing for pay when I was 16. I committed journalism, but I did not create literature. I met deadlines and stretched deadlines and fed the beast that is a daily newspaper. There wasn't much time for reflection. There was hardly time for proofreading. But for those two summer weeks, I could write. I could think about writing. I could talk with writers about writing. I didn't feel completely out of my depth that first week. Crystal Wilkinson was teaching us about writing fiction. It's storytelling on paper, which was not that much different from what I did every day—except my day job required facts, and fiction strove for truth. I felt OK. I felt good about some of the writing. The second week was a whole different thing. Like nearly every literate teenager, I'd written bad poetry and bad songs and then moved on. I tried hard that second week. I worked. I marveled at my classmates' aptitude and alacrity. Eventually, during a break, I confessed and apologized to Cathy Smith Bowers, who was leading us through the poetry part of the conference. I didn't want her to think I was mailing it in, so I told her how unnatural it was for me to try to write poetry, how I hadn't written even an imitation of a poem for more than 20 years. "I couldn't tell," she told me.

An encouraging lie may be a handy tool for a clever teacher, and it certainly is a tactic essential to some social situations. But she said it with such sincerity I chose to believe she might mean it. I was—if not truly inspired—at least a little elevated. I am not a poet, but I have written two poems that someone saw fit to publish. I wrote them both that week.

Now I spend a lot of my time trying to teach college freshmen how to think and write their way through an essay. Along the way, I teach them about Blair Mountain and Buffalo Creek and Appalachian writers and I flat-out steal George Ella Lyon's poem and writing lesson "Where I'm From" (which I first encountered at the Highland Summer Conference). And all the while I hope and pray I help my students find just half of the confidence and joy in writing I had at that Highland Summer Conference. That would be a lot.

Another decade has passed since my Highland Summer Conference. Some of my classmates from that summer went on to Ph.D.s and published novels and celebrated poetry collections. I went on to teach at a community college and write for not-quite-national publications. I even did a little radio. It's all storytelling, after all.

Between the freshman English classes, I still write stories about software engineers and barrel makers and people who ride buses. I am, still, an ink-stained hack.

But for those two weeks in that one summer in Radford, I was a writer.

"Mom and Dad, 1958"

In the fading gray photo
she poses like a pageant queen,
one foot poised before the other.
The lanky farm boy sailor leans down
in his gleaming Navy whites
to reach an arm around her waist.
Even standing uphill, even in those heels,
her head barely brushes his chin.

They are younger than their granddaughter,
all hope and careless confidence.

They have

no
idea.

Bonnie Roberts Erickson

A Journey into the Heart

There are two things in life sure to breathe new fire in my soul—a good tell-it-like-it-is church service and writing something that makes me quiver when I read it back to myself. In my world, spirituality and writing go hand-in-hand. I am convinced you can't really be happy in paradise until you've written the ultimate personal essay about the journey. In a multi-sidetracked pursuit of a degree, I had taken a total of seven classes most of them English, by the time I was 40. More than anything, I wanted to take the Highland Summer Conference, a two-week, credit-based writing workshop focusing on Appalachian culture and literature. It takes place in an upstairs classroom of RU's Young Hall and in the heart.

Though English 490 was whispering my name, other voices were calling. My church denomination's camp meeting—where services keep me pumped and ready to conquer the world from June to June—always begins the same week as the conference. I called up my friend and mentor JoAnn Asbury, a key grinder of the wheels in Radford's Appalachian Regional Studies Center. "What am I going to do? I'll have to skip camp meeting," I moaned. JoAnn replied, "Take the class. You won't be sorry." Perhaps it was part of my creator's grander

Bonnie Roberts Erickson.

scheme in planning my life. Perhaps it was coincidence. Camp meeting—or at least most of it—would be put on hold that year. I went out and bought a shiny blue three-ring binder. Life was good.

That was two years ago. The decision to take the conference changed my life. When I walked out of class on the final Friday afternoon, there was not only a renewed sense of pride in the Appalachia I love so dearly, but there was more spirituality and personal conviction seeping from my pores than I knew what to do with.

Experiencing the Highland Summer Conference has changed hundreds of lives since its inception over two decades ago. Celebrating its 21st year this past June, the conference is in a league all its own.

Grace Edwards, director of the Appalachian Regional Studies Center, is not shy about telling the world she is truly reaping the harvest from the seeds planted for the first conference. "It started with a man named Cratis Williams, who taught English at Appalachian State University. He was Mr. Appalachia to all who knew him."

Williams, whose first name alone emits a stirring aroma of Appalachia, joined forces with RU English professor Parks Lanier and two former RU professors, Michael Sewell and the late Deborah Dew. "It all started as three two-week classes divided into poetry, fiction and folklore. The National Endowment for the Arts gave us funding," Lanier recalls. "In 1977, if the word 'Appalachian' was mentioned when applying for a grant, they most likely gave it to you. 'Appalachian' meant 'dirt poor.' That's not the way it really was, of course," he says. The seed grant provided by the NEA fed the conference at its beginning. Soon, it flourished into a creative writing workshop pruned back to one class for two weeks. "Everyone wanted to take the Appalachian folklore class; it always was filled. We decided to just go with that theme. Looking back, I don't think any of us would change that decision or anything else about the conference," says Edwards. Today, as it has been for well over three-fourths of its life, the conference is self-sustaining. Lanier adds, "Right from the start, RU was behind us. They said they would support us any way they could. They've been wonderful."

All the people who have been visiting lecturers with the conference—including Marilou Awiakta, the late Jim Wayne Miller, Jeff Daniel Marion, Denise Giardina, Anndrena Belcher and George Ella Lyon—have made repeated trips to RU and all agree RU is truly blessed to be situated where it is. Edwards says each one leaves asking to be invited back. "They love it here," she says. "You know it's good when even the leaders leave rejuvenated. It's a wonderful feeling to know the conference has made such an impact."

People in the local communities get excited about the conference, too. Edwards comments, "Local folks like the idea that their way of living is being uplifted. To most, this is home." When Edwards talks about Appalachia, she confesses it sometimes can get very emotional for her. "This is a subject close to my heart. It's a way of life we are talking about."

The topic of Appalachia must be special indeed because the Highland Summer Conference has become the longest-running credit-based writing workshop in the east. The class fills quickly each year and participants are as diverse as the characters found in their writings.

In this class you write about life—your life. You write about those who have become a part of that life, whether intentionally or unintentionally. You write about the things life has done to and for you. Some write about happiness but just as many write about pain. Many write of success and some write of failure. Many come in wounded. Hundreds leave healed. I was among the latter.

Bill Brown, a nationally known Appalachian author and teacher from Tennessee, and RU's own treasure, English professor and accomplished author Donald Secreast, led the conference the year I attended. This year the classes were led by Barbara Smith, a writer and teacher from West Virginia, and much celebrated author and director Gurney Norman. (If you look through the pages of the *Last Whole Earth Catalog*, you'll find Norman's novel *Divine Rights Trip*.)

Four evenings of the conference are set aside for public readings by conference teachers and special guests. This June, two local favorites came as guests to share their stories. Sharyn McCrumb who repeatedly climbs to the top of the *New York Times* Bestseller List, and Virginia Tech professor Nikki Giovanni, former RU visiting professor and nationally acclaimed poet, enthralled their audiences with readings and tips of the trade. McCrumb instructed students: "If you want good lines for a story, listen to waitresses."

Norman prompted students to think back on their childhoods. Gazing around the class, he asked, "Where do your memories go when you don't think of them anymore?" Barbara Smith stressed the importance of writing to help others. "Service writing is gratifying and rewarding. Volunteer your skills for a nonprofit agency. Somebody needs what you write."

As I observed Norman and Smith's students, my mind drifted back to the time I spent studying under Brown and Secreast. Brown set up scenarios and we took it from there. He told us to mentally stand at a window in our home place, pause a moment, and write. What transpired for me was a three-page story about waiting impatiently for a dad who worked out of town to come home. Many times the writing hurt but it hurt good. It reopened sores and mended them back. Norman said, "There are so many stories on our bodies. We all have scars. Some we can see, some we can't."

Each time I rehash my own experience, I marvel at how much fun I had learning. I think about the many folks whose lives have been touched by a class that pulls everything out of you emotionally but fills you back up with all that is good. At the same time, there is an empty, aching feeling for those who have not had an opportunity to be part of this wonderful drama that unfolds each summer right under our noses. Lanier also aches.

He shared, "My vision is to one day have a conference similar to this at Selu Conservancy for rising high school seniors. I want them to have the opportunity to see what Appalachia is and how fortunate we are. With the funding, it could happen."

First appeared in *The Magazine of Radford University*, November 1998.

Jim Minick

Writing Community: Celebrating the Highland Summer Conference's 40th Anniversary and More

In the summer of 2017 at the fortieth anniversary celebration of the Highland Summer Conference, my friend and mentor and one of the founding mothers of Appalachian Studies, Grace Toney Edwards, spotlighted my work as an example of the great success of HSC students. I was honored but also overwhelmed and unable to articulate a great discomfort I suddenly felt. For as I stood in front of that crowd of kind folk, and as the slides of my book jackets covered the wall behind me, I couldn't find the words for what I really wanted to say, which is this: writing is a community art; the community of the Highland Summer Conference has been and continues to be one of the most nurturing I've ever experienced; and my success is meaningless without this community, without you.

Yes, in many ways, writing is an individual art—we all know the image, a stereotype, of the writer alone at her poorly-lit desk, pounding away on her keyboard. But that required solitude is nurtured and supported by others in many ways. Like, for example, when a writer is just starting out, a healthy community opens doors. For me, this happened in 1990, when as a graduate student at Radford University, I took my first HSC with Peter Stillman and Marilou Awiakta. For Awiakta, we danced to a heartbeat pounding loudly out of a boombox, all of us awkwardly moving in a circle in a square room. Later, we had a chance to do it again at the newly-christened Selu Conservancy; this time our feet shuffled a little less stiffly on the bare dirt under ancient oaks. *Listen*, Awiakta was teaching us. *The world is rich if we only open ourselves.*

I took the HSC again the next year with Denise Giardina and David Huddle. And years later in 2000, I took it alongside Sarah, my wife, where we studied under David Huddle and Joyce Dyer. In each of these classes, I was gently pushed by teachers and fellow students to produce writing better than I ever had before. Poems I wrote for Awiakta and Stillman eventually found homes in journals and then in my poetry collection, *Burning Heaven*. Essays written for Giardina and Huddle did the same, landing in magazines and then in my book, *Finding a Clear Path*. And with Dyer and Huddle, I began the years-long process of working through family stories connected by fire, faith, and healing, learning to ask difficult questions and shape narratives into art. That work eventually became my

Jim Minick.

first novel, *Fire Is Your Water,* published in 2017. But more important than the books, these writers instilled in me an understanding of the discipline and practice required of any art, and the patience required of any community.

As I became more published, the Highland Summer Conference community continued to nurture, giving me the chance to be one of the guest readers and teachers, first in 2006, then in 2009, and again in 2017. All three times celebrated the releases of new books that included work started in earlier HSC classes and finally shared here with the community.

And all of this story illustrates what a community can do, because not only does a healthy community nurture its new writers, but it also *reads* and celebrates these writers' growth and accomplishments. We borrow or buy books, we read and discuss and review them. With others, we share these physical objects that speak to us, that enlarge us, that we helped create, because both the writer and the reader *compose*, and without this joint composition, no art exists.

So thanks to Parks Lanier and Grace Toney Edwards, JoAnn Asbury and Ricky Cox, Theresa L. Burriss and Ruth B. Derrick, the founders and sustaining leaders of this HSC community. Thanks to all the writers, teachers, and students. And thanks to you, fellow reader and composer, for helping make a vital community through art.

"When You Realize the Future"

Pollen, like baby's breath,
clouds the air, a fine dust
of pine, chestnut, and oak.

At dusk, the same air swells
with quiet blinking
as lightning bugs
fire the dark.

Later a whippoorwill—
its beating song
a whisper
of a far away
heart.

None answer
in reply.

The quiet
of the country woods
suddenly turns
empty and

Afterword

Theresa L. Burriss

After almost thirty years of serving as the author interviewer for the Highland Summer Conference, Dr. Parks Lanier entrusted me to continue his legacy of interviewing the guest authors. Although I never participated in the HSC as a student, I understood the deep responsibility that came with interviewing Appalachia's best, most accomplished writers. After all, I had utilized Parks's recorded interviews in my own literature classes at Radford University, for example, pairing Wilma Dykeman's interview with my teaching of *The Tall Woman*. Not only did my students gain different, informed insights into the authors behind the novels, poetry,

Theresa L. Burriss.

or short stories, so did I, which aided my teaching of the texts. Thus, in 2008 when Parks handed me the interview mic, I strove to capture authors' commentary about their writing that perhaps would enlighten viewing audiences and inspire scholars, creative writers, and students alike. In the beginning, I did not anticipate the byproduct of these interviews, namely gifts of deep, lasting friendships. And in many ways, my existing relationships with some of the writers I already knew became stronger. Indeed, the opportunities to read and study the authors' works and engage with the writers on their craft have rewarded me both professionally and personally.

Since becoming Chair of Appalachian Studies in 2010, succeeding my mentor, Dr. Grace Toney Edwards, I have sat side-by-side with conference participants as a student again, learning various innovative techniques and artistic strategies from the guest writers. Although almost all of my writing these days is for nonfiction scholarly publication, I find myself employing some of the creative insights I have acquired at the HSC. Eventually, I will find the time and energy to write creative nonfiction pieces that writers like Darnell Arnoult and Jim Minick have encouraged me to commit to paper. In the process, I will be fortunate to draw from the tools derived from listening to master writers at the HSC.

Additionally over the past years, my colleagues and I have made various changes to the conference format. We reduced the number of weeks from two to one, began offering both course credit and not-for credit options at different price points, and eventually changed the venue for the entire week to the Selu Retreat Center. Selu is a fitting site to hold the Highland Summer Conference because Marilou Awiakta, who has served as HSC facilitator and reader numerous times, named this land gift from John Bowles to Radford University in the 1990s. Participants may spend the night at the Retreat Center for the entire week and enjoy occasions to hike, canoe, or simply sit on the deck to observe the beauty of Southwest Virginia. Participants also eat more meals together, thereby enhancing the bonds they create during the formal workshop sessions.

As I write this, we are in the midst of final preparations for the 42nd Annual Highland Summer Conference, where Affrilachian Crystal Wilkinson will once again serve as author facilitator and Radford University's own Tim Poland, retired English faculty member, will be our guest reader. Looking ahead to the 2021 conference, we have secured HSC veteran Diane Gilliam as our author facilitator and selected poet Leatha Kendrick as our guest reader. With such a long, rich history, the Highland Summer Conference serves as one of Radford University's premier programs. Equally important, the conference cultivates both seasoned and budding writers, necessary voices in the telling of Appalachian stories, while the videoed author interviews and public readings showcase the wealth of talent in our region. I maintain a deep sense of obligation to ensure not only that the HSC continue but that it also thrive and flourish. Without a doubt, the Highland Summer Conference is necessary for future generations of Appalachian writers, readers, and residents.

Appendix: List of HSC Leaders, Readers and Performers

1978
Cratis Williams
Sylvia Wilkinson
James Seay

1979
Parks Lanier, Jr.
Michael Sewell (Mick)
Barbara Ewell

1980
Jim Wayne Miller
Wilma Dykeman
Thomas Bontly
Dara Wier

1981
Fred Chappell
Robert Jackson Higgs (Jack)
Heather Ross Miller

1982
Cratis Williams
Jeff Daniel Marion
Loyal Jones
Max Apple

1983
Wilma Dykeman
Jeff Daniel Marion

1984
Marilou Awiakta
Gary Carden
Jean Shannon

1985
Gurney Norman
James Still

1986
George Ella Lyon
Ron Eller
Jo Carson

1987
Jim Wayne Miller
David Huddle
Anndrena Belcher
Jeff Daniel Marion

1988
Heather Ross Miller
Robert Jackson Higgs (Jack)
Anndrena Belcher
Denise Giardina

1989
Jim Wayne Miller
George Ella Lyon
Jo Carson
APPALKIDS

1990

Marilou Awiakta
Katie Letcher Lyle
Peter Stillman
Bill Brown
APPALKIDS

1991

Denise Giardina
Mike Seeger
David Huddle
APPALKIDS

1992

Wilma Dykeman
Rita Sims Quillen
Bill Brown
Les Dotson

1993

George Ella Lyon
Peter Catalanotto
Jeff Daniel Marion
Jo Carson

1994

Ruth White
Sue Ellen Bridgers
Nancy Ruth Patterson
Lou Kassem

1995

Jim Wayne Miller
Anndrena Belcher
Dorie Sanders

1996

Donald Secreast
Bill Brown
Elizabeth McCommon
Selu Sisters

1997

George Ella Lyon
Robert Jackson Higgs (Jack)

Peter Stillman
Denise Giardina

1998

Gurney Norman
Nikki Giovanni
Barbara Smith
Sharyn McCrumb

1999

Robert Morgan
Richard Hague
Betty Smith
Maggie Vaughn

2000

David Huddle
Ken Sullivan
Joyce Dyer
Kathryn Hankla

2001

Bill Brown
Chris Holbrook
Rita Quillen
Kevin Stewart

2002

Kathryn Stripling Byer (Kay)
Jeff Daniel and Stephen Marion
Robert Morgan
Wilma Dykeman

2003

Ron Rash
Robert Jackson Higgs (Jack)
Rita Sims Quillen
Mary Kegley

2004

Silas House
Sharyn McCrumb
Cathy Smith Bowers
Rick Mulkey

2005

David Huddle
Gretchen Moran Laskas

Diane Gilliam
Isabel Zuber

2006

Bill Brown
Ron Rash
Crystal Wilkinson
Jim Minick and Rita Riddle

2007

Marilou Awiakta
Sharyn McCrumb
Bill Brown
Jo Carson

2008

Darnell Arnoult
Frank X Walker
Dana Wildsmith
Rick Van Noy

2009

Crystal Wilkinson
Cathy Smith Bowers
Jim Minick
Donald Secreast

2010

Pamela Duncan
George Ella Lyon
Dot Jackson
Charles A. Swanson

2011

David Huddle
Diane Gilliam
Jeff Daniel Marion and Linda Parsons
Ralph Berrier, Jr.

2012

Karen Salyer McElmurray

Joseph Bathanti
Thorpe Moeckel
Anne Shelby

2013

George Ella Lyon
Diane Gilliam

2014

Jeff Mann

2015

Rita Sims Quillen
Robert Gipe

2016

Dana Wildsmith
April Asbury

2017

Jim Minick
Grace Toney Edwards

2018

Richard Hague
Mark Powell

2019

Crystal Wilkinson
Tim Poland

2020

No HSC, Cancelled because of Covid-19

2021

Diane Gilliam
Leatha Kendrick

About the Contributors

B. Chelsea **Adams** writes poems and stories in Riner, Virginia. Her MA is in creative writing from Hollins University. She taught at Radford University for over twenty years. Her publications include two poetry chapbooks, *At Last Light* and *Looking for a Landing*, a novel, *Organic Matter*, and work in *Floyd County Moonshine, Lucid Stone, BlackWater*, and *Connecticut River Review*. She attended many of the readings of the Highland Summer Conferences and a workshop.

Marilou **Awiakta** is a poet, storyteller and essayist who was born in Knoxville, Tennessee, in 1936. Her published works include *Abiding Appalachia: Where Mountain and Atom Meet, Rising Fawn and the Fire Mystery*, and *Selu: Seeking the Corn Mother's Wisdom*. Profiled in the *Oxford Companion to Women's Writing* in the U.S., she received the Award for Educational Services to Appalachia and Outstanding Contributions to Appalachian Literature. In 2020 she was selected for inclusion in *USA Today's* Women of the Century.

George **Brosi** in 1979, with his late wife, Connie Brosi, founded Appalachian Mountain Books, a retail business specializing in books about the Southern Appalachian Region. It brings a display of books for sale to events like the Highland Summer Conference and serves academic libraries. He has taught Appalachian studies for the University of Kentucky and Appalachian literature at Eastern Kentucky University. He was editor of *Appalachian Heritage* and is coeditor of *Appalachian Gateway: An Anthology of Contemporary Stories and Poetry*.

Bill **Brown** is the author of eleven poetry collections and a writing textbook. The National Foundation for Advancement in the Arts awarded him the Distinguished Teacher in the Arts. He is a two-time recipient of Fellowships in Poetry from the Tennessee Arts Commission. He has published hundreds of poems and articles in college journals, magazines and anthologies. The Tennessee Writers Alliance named him the 2011 Writer of the Year. In 2018, he published *The Cairns*.

Theresa L.**Burriss** has a BA in philosophy from Emory University, an MS in English from Radford University, and a Ph.D. in interdisciplinary studies and Appalachian studies/women's studies from the Union Institute and University. She serves as Radford University's Chair of Appalachian Studies and as Director of the Appalachian Regional & Rural Studies Center. She teaches graduate classes in Appalachian studies, Appalachian literature for the Department of English, and place-based education classes for the School of Teacher Education & Leadership.

Ricky **Cox,** recently retired, taught courses in English and Appalachian studies and coordinated the Farm at Selu for Radford University. He co-authored *The Water Powered Mills of Floyd County, Virginia: Illustrated Histories, 1770–2010* and co-edited *A Handbook to Appalachia: An Introduction to the Region.* He has published multiple essays and short stories in various journals and is popular as a storyteller and musician in the New River Valley of Virginia and beyond.

Ruth B. **Derrick** has an MA in English from Radford University along with a graduate certificate in Appalachian studies. For eleven years she taught in the Appalachian Studies Program and helped facilitate the Highland Summer Conference. The HSC quickly became her favorite time of the year with the rich writing environment and welcoming regional author-teachers. She credits the conference with the seeds of her published poetry chapbook, *Remnants.*

Pamela **Duncan** is the author of three novels: *Moon Women,* a Southeast Booksellers Association Award Finalist; *Plant Life,* winner of the 2003 Sir Walter Raleigh Award for Fiction; and *The Big Beautiful.* In 2007, she received the James Still Award for Writing about the Appalachian South, awarded by the Fellowship of Southern Writers. In 2017, the Mountain Heritage Literary Festival at Lincoln Memorial University awarded her with the Lee Smith Award. She teaches creative writing at Western Carolina University.

Grace Toney **Edwards** is a professor emerita of Appalachian studies and English at Radford University. She retired in 2010 as Chair of the Appalachian Studies Program and Director of the Appalachian Regional Studies Center at RU. She is coeditor of *A Handbook to Appalachia* and editor of *The Common Lot and Other Stories: The Published Short Fiction of Emma Bell Miles.* She has received the SCHEV Outstanding Faculty Award from the Commonwealth of Virginia and the Cratis Williams/James Brown Service Award from the Appalachian Studies Association.

Donia S. **Eley** completed an independent major in Appalachian studies at Mary Baldwin University in 2002, a Post-Baccalaureate Certificate in Appalachian studies from Radford University in 2008, and an MA in liberal studies with a concentration in Appalachian Studies from Hollins University in 2010. She has published two books, *Willard Gayheart: Appalachian Artist,* and *New Art by Willard Gayheart,* both released by McFarland as part of their Contributions to Southern Appalachian Studies series.

Bonnie Roberts **Erickson** retired from Radford University as a writer in the Office of University Relations after twenty-seven years of service. While at Radford, she enrolled in classes focusing on English, Appalachian studies and workplace communication. She formerly worked for the *Roanoke Times, News Messenger,* Commonwealth Press and Radford University Printing Services. She and her friend Neal Turner wrote the book *God Spoke, We Wrote.*

Diane **Gilliam** is the author of four collections of poetry: *Dreadful Wind & Rain, Kettle Bottom, One of Everything* and *Recipe for Blackberry Cake* (chapbook). She holds an MFA from Warren Wilson College and a Ph.D. in romance, languages and literatures from Ohio State University. She teaches as guest faculty at West Virginia Wesleyan College. She has received the Chaffin Award for Appalachian Writing, the

Ohioan Library Association Poetry Book of the Year Award, a Pushcart Prize, and the Gift of Freedom from A Room of Her Own Foundation.

Robert **Gipe** won the 2015 Weatherford Award for outstanding Appalachian novel for *Trampoline*. His second novel, *Weedeater*, was published in 2018, and his third, *Pop* in 2021. He directed the Southeast Kentucky Community & Technical College Appalachian Program in Harlan. He is a producer of the Higher Ground community performance series; coordinated the Great Mountain Mural Mega Fest; co-produces the Hurricane Gap Community Theater Institute; and advises on It's Good to Be Young in the Mountains, a youth-driven conference.

Richard **Hague** is the author of nineteen collections of poetry and prose, including *Earnest Occupations: Teaching, Writing, Gardening, & Other Local Work*, awarded a "Recommended" rating from *US Review of Books*, and the *Studied Days: Poems Early & Late in Appalachia*. He has been selected for the Weatherford Prize in Poetry and Poetry Book of the Year from the Appalachian Writers Association. His *Milltown Natural* was a National Book Award nominee. He is currently an artist-in-residence at Thomas More University in northern Kentucky.

Becky Dellinger **Hancock** was born in 1950 in Russell County. Her education began at age four, learning the alphabet on the giant Clinchfield Coal Company calendar in their home. As a student in Radford University's Master's program in English education, she discovered the Appalachian Studies Program. She developed and taught Appalachian studies classes in Pulaski County High School's English Department and in 1985 created The APPALKIDS, a student group that performed stories, songs, and original skits throughout the region.

Heidi **Hartwiger** is a freelance writer, a storyteller and a writing instructor for Christopher Newport University's Lifelong Learning Society. She wrote three nonfiction books, two novels, and a children's activity book. She has published over three hundred magazine and newspaper articles. Her *Natural Parent~Natural Child* series appears in *OVParent Magazine*. For sixteen summers she attended the Selu Writers' retreat at Radford University. Her writing is archived in the Appalachian Collection of the McConnell Library at Radford University.

David **Huddle** is the author of seven poetry collections, six short story collections, five novels, a novella, a book titled *A David Huddle Reader* and a collection of essays titled *The Writing Habit*. He won the 2012 Library of Virginia Award for Fiction for *Nothing Can Make Me Do This* and the 2013 Penned New England Award for Poetry for *Black Snake at the Family Reunion*. His poetry collection, *My Surly Heart*, and his novel, *Hazel,* were published in 2019.

Teresa Stutso **Jewell** was a non-traditional student graduating from Radford University's Master's program in May of 2010. At Southwest Virginia Community College she teaches developmental English, English composition, American literature, and Appalachian literature. She wrote and illustrated her first novel, *My Bucket's Got a Hole in It,* published in 2018, followed by a poetry collection, *My Appalachian Mountain Laurels*, in 2019.

Loyal **Jones** is an Appalachian scholar who founded the Appalachian Center (now named in his honor) at Berea College in 1970 and administered it for twenty-four years. He is the author of several books and numerous articles on the region and its people. His book *My Curious and Jocular Heroes: Tales and Tale-Spinners from Appalachia* was published in 2017 and features Cratis Williams, Bascom Lamar Lunsford, Josiah Combs, and Leonard Roberts.

Luther **Kirk** was born in the mountains of Southwest Virginia. After his military service he began a career in education as a teacher, principal and professor. His work has appeared in various publications, including two poetry chapbooks, *Appalachian Woman* in 2017 and *A Child of Appalachia* in 2018. His short stories, excerpted from his novel *Cry of the Nightjars,* have won awards from the Tennessee Mountain Writer's Conference and the Appalachian Heritage Literary Festival.

Parks **Lanier**, Jr., was a co-founder of the Highland Summer Conference in 1978. He continued to work with HSC throughout his teaching career at Radford University. He developed the videotaped series entitled "Conversations," interviews with each author who came to teach or to read at the Conference. He served as chair of the English Department in the 1990s, edited an essay collection called *The Poetics of Appalachian Space* and is the author of a collection of poetry entitled *Appalachian Georgics and Other Poems.*

Sam L. **Linkous** returned to college at the age of 40. He holds a BA in art and an MA in English with a concentration in Appalachian literature and folklore, all from Radford University. His writing has been published in *Appalachian Heritage* and *Appalachian Journal*, among others. Formerly employed at Hindman Settlement School in Kentucky and at the Augusta Heritage Center in West Virginia, he is retired from Virginia Tech's Department of Continuing and Professional Education.

George Ella **Lyon**, Kentucky Poet Laureate (2015–2016), has published in many genres, including poetry, picture books, novels, short stories and a memoir. Her poem, "Where I'm From," has gone around the world as a writing model. Recent collections include *She Let Herself Go* and *Many-Storied House.* Lyon makes her living as a freelance writer and teacher based in Lexington, Kentucky.

Jeff **Mann** has published five books of poetry, *Bones Washed with Wine, On the Tongue, Ash, A Romantic Mann* and *Rebels*; three collections of personal essays, *Edge, Binding the God,* and *Endangered Species*; a memoir, *Loving Mountains, Loving Men*; six novels, *Fog, Purgatory, Cub, Salvation, Country* and *Insatiable*; and three volumes of short fiction, *Desire and Devour, History of Barbed Wire*, and *Consent.* With Julia Watts, he co-edited *LGBTQ Fiction and Poetry from Appalachia.* The winner of two Lambda Literary Awards and four National Leather Association International literary awards, he teaches creative writing at Virginia Tech.

Jeff Daniel **Marion** has published nine poetry collections, four poetry chapbooks, and a children's book. His poems have appeared in *The Southern Review, Southern Poetry Review, Shenandoah, Atlanta Review, Tar River Poetry*, and many others. Marion received the first Literary Fellowship awarded by the Tennessee Arts Commission. *Ebbing & Flowing Springs: New and Selected Poems and Prose, 1976–2001* won the 2003 Independent Publisher Award in Poetry and was named Appalachian Book of the Year by the Appalachian Writers Association.

Elizabeth **McCommon** has been a song writer, professional actress, teacher, published writer, mother of five and former resident of Floyd County, Virginia. She now lives in Blacksburg, Virginia. Protection of clean water has been her life-long motivation and inspiration for her creative work.

Karen Salyer **McElmurray** has published a memoir, *Surrendered Child: A Birth Mother's Journey,* which was an AWP Award Winner for Creative Nonfiction and a National Book Circle Notable Book. Her novels are *The Motel of the Stars,* Editor's Pick by Oxford American, and *Strange Birds in the Tree of Heaven,* winner of the Chaffin Award for Appalachian Writing. With poet Adrian Blevins, she has co-edited a collection of essays, *Walk Till the Dogs Get Mean: Meditations on the Forbidden from Contemporary Appalachia.* Her novel *Wanting Radiance* was published in 2020.

Jim **Minick** is the author of five books, including the novel *Fire Is Your Water,* winner of the Appalachian Book of the Year Award. He has written a collection of essays, two books of poetry, and his honors include the Jean Ritchie Fellowship and the Fred Chappell Fellowship at UNC–Greensboro. His work has appeared in the *New York Times, Poets & Writers, Oxford American* and *Appalachian Journal.* He taught at Radford University, Augusta University, and is on the Core Faculty at Converse College's low-residency MFA program.

Robert **Morgan** was educated at the University of North Carolina at Chapel Hill (BA), and the University of North Carolina at Greensboro (MFA). He has spent his teaching and writing career at Cornell University. Morgan has produced more than a dozen volumes of poetry, six novels, four collections of short stories, two volumes of nonfiction, and a book of essays about poetry. His novel, *Gap Creek,* was selected as an Oprah Book Club choice. He has received the Thomas Wolfe Prize and the 2017 Southern Book Award for Historical Fiction.

Rick **Mulkey** is the author of six books and chapbooks including *Ravenous: New & Selected Poems, Toward Any Darkness, Bluefield Breakdown, Before the Age of Reason,* and *All These Hungers.* Individual poems and essays have appeared in *The Georgia Review, Poet Lore, Poetry East, Southeast Review, South Carolina Review,* and *American Poetry: The Next Generation.* His work has also been featured on *Poetry Daily Verse Daily* and the *Writer's Almanac.* He directs and teaches in the low-residency MFA program at Converse College in South Carolina.

Linda **Parsons** is a poet, playwright, editor, and the reviews editor at *Pine Mountain Sand & Gravel.* She has contributed to *The Georgia Review, Iowa Review, Prairie Schooner, Southern Poetry Review, The Chattahoochee Review, Baltimore Review, Shenandoah,* and Ted Kooser's syndicated column, *American Life in Poetry,* among many other journals and anthologies. Her fifth poetry collection, *Candescent,* was published in 2019. She is playwright-in-residence for the Hammer Ensemble, the social justice wing of Flying Anvil Theatre in Knoxville, Tennessee.

Matt **Prater** is a writer and visual artist from Saltville, Virginia. He is a Ph.D. student in comparative studies at Florida Atlantic University, and his work has appeared in *Poet Lore, The Moth, The Honest Ulsterman, Appalachian Heritage,* and *Still: The Journal,* among other publications.

Rita Sims **Quillen** published a novel, *Wayland*, a sequel to *Hiding Ezra*, in 2019, and a poetry collection, *Some Notes You Hold*, in 2020. Her poetry collection, *The Mad Farmer's Wife*, was published in 2016, and was a finalist for the Weatherford Award in Appalachian Literature from Berea College. Her novel *Hiding Ezra* was a finalist for the 2005 DANA Awards. One of six semi-finalists for the 2012–14 Poet Laureate of Virginia, she received three Pushcart nominations, and a Best of the Net nomination.

Ron **Rash** is a poet, short story writer and novelist who teaches at Western Carolina University, where he holds the Parris Distinguished Professorship in Appalachian Cultural Studies. In his list of accomplishments are four books of poetry, seven collections of short stories, and seven bestselling novels. Additionally, he has won multiple awards for his work and is acclaimed as a speaker and reader. He has a BA from Gardner Webb University and an MA from Clemson University.

Donald **Secreast** attended Appalachian State University, Johns Hopkins University, and the University of Iowa. For twenty-five years he taught in the English Department of Radford University and now lives in Bristol, Virginia. He has published two collections of short stories, *The Rat Becomes Light* and *White Trash, Red Velvet* and co-authored with Charles Frazier a Sierra Club Travel Guide, *Adventuring in the Andes*.

Kevin **Stewart** received his MFA from the University of Arkansas and is an associate professor of English at Carroll College. His 2007 book, *The Way Things Always Happen Here*, was a finalist for the Weatherford Award. His work has appeared in *Shenandoah, Now and Then, The Texas Review* and the 2017 anthology *Eyes Glowing at the Edge of the Woods*. Other works have appeared in *The Common, The Southeast Review* and *Fiction Southeast*. "Silenced" first appeared in *Appalachian Heritage* and received the 2007 Plattner Award for Fiction.

Charles A. **Swanson** taught English in a new academy for engineering and technology. His poetry and short fiction have appeared in such magazines as *Virginia Writing, Wildlife in North Carolina*, ALCA *Lines, Appalachian Heritage, Appalachian Journal, The English Journal,* and *Now & Then*. He has worked with writers such as Cathy Smith Bowers, Kathryn Stripling Byer, Robert J. Higgs, Jim Minick, Ron Rash, Donald Secreast, and Frank X Walker. He has two books of poems: *After the Garden* and *Farm Life and Legend*.

Tim **Thornton** has won national awards for column writing and environmental reporting, the Phillip D. Reed Memorial Award for Outstanding Writing on the Southern Environment and multiple state press association awards including the Virginia Press Association's D. Lathan Mims Award for "editorial leadership and service to the community." He teaches beginning guitar with the Junior Appalachian Musicians program and freshman composition and Appalachian literature at Virginia Western Community College.

Rick **Van Noy** is a professor of English at Radford University and the author of *Sudden Spring: Stories of Adaptation in a Climate-Changed South, A Natural Sense of Wonder: Connecting Kids with Nature Through the Seasons* and *Surveying the Interior: Literacy Cartographers and the Sense of Place*.

Frank X **Walker**, a professor in the Department of English and the African

American and Africana Studies Program at the University of Kentucky, holds degrees from the University of Kentucky and Spalding University, as well as honorary doctorates from UK, Spalding, and Transylvania University. He is a former Poet Laureate of Kentucky and is author of eight collections of poetry. Co-founder of the Affrilachian Poets, he is the recipient of multiple awards for his writing, teaching, and speaking in venues across the nation.

Dana **Wildsmith** published *The Poems of One Light*, set mostly on her family's acreage in north Georgia during the time of her mother's long dying from dementia. Her environmental memoir, *Back to Abnormal*, was Finalist for Georgia Author of the Year. Her novel *Jumping* explores the changing demographics of the U.S. southern border. She has worked as an artist-in-residence for Devils Tower National Monument and Everglades National Park. She is a Hambidge Fellow and a Fellow of the South Carolina Academy of Poets.

Index

Numbers in **bold italics** indicate pages with illustrations